For Jacob and Rob
and
Charlie

.

Contents

List of figures

List of tables

List of case studies

Preface to the second edition

When someone asks you to prepare a new edition of a book you have written, it means two things. First, the good news is that people are still buying the book and there is a perceived readership for it. The second reason is not so flattering: evidently the first edition is looking a little tired and dated.

Accordingly I have brought this new edition right up to date with revised material and a host of brand new cases. Each chapter contains at least one case study, which is intended to illustrate one of the key points in the chapter. I have taken the opportunity to weed out some of the old material, but some has firmly stood the test of time and stays in.

Before I started on this second edition I asked the users of this book how it could be improved. The resulting helpful comments from students, lecturers and new practitioners have informed the content of this edition. In particular I have added an entirely new section on lobbying. There are also words of advice on careers in and outside public relations, and the case histories of a number of successful public relations graduates.

The organisation of the book is, I hope, also improved. On the advice of the publishers I have provided a section at the beginning of each chapter explaining the aim of the chapter and the key points to be brought out. At the end there are summary points and questions for discussion.

Another new feature concluding each chapter is a section of recommended further reading, and a list of references. The complete list of references is also brought together at the end of the book so that the reader can find a source without having to remember which chapter it was in. References to web pages have been kept to a minimum: in the current evolving situation I was not willing to be blamed for the seemingly quixotic domain changes which occur daily. Perhaps if a third edition is commissioned this problem will have sorted itself out.

So much for the 'extras'. What about the real content? This continues to address the crucial questions for an introductory book on the subject: What is public relations all about? How, and why, does it work? Where did it come from and where is it going?

These are questions of interest not solely to those who are studying the subject but also to people considering entering the field, whether they be prospective practitioners or clients, and to those working in the related communications industries of marketing and journalism.

The increasing professionalisation of public relations means that there are more and more entrants to the business arriving with professional qualifications. I know, because I have the joy and occasional pain of teaching some of them. An understanding of public relations is increasingly demanded by managers in both private and public sectors, with short courses, professional updates and distance-learning packages being developed to service this market. I teach some of them, too.

We are beginning to see a good range of reading matter on the subject, from weighty tomes covering theory and principles to handy manuals on how to write a press release or produce a newsletter. The UK now supports two research-based academic journals on the subject to complement the body of knowledge being published in the USA, Europe, Australia and elsewhere. Some of the luminaries of the business have published entertaining books, packed with incident and anecdote, about their lives in public relations, and there is now a fair sprinkling of management guides which seek to explain and justify the role of public relations in strategic management thinking.

What is missing at the introductory level is the link from theory to practice: the approach which explains the theory and follows it up with examples of how it works in the real world. This book aims to fill that gap.

It will, I hope, be useful to students of public relations, communications studies, marketing, and business and management studies, whether they be undergraduates or working managers. It explains something of the theories of communication and the principles which underpin the successful practice of public relations. It explains not just how public relations works, but why. And it brings together the received wisdom on getting it right, as well as offering explanations as to how some public relations has gone spectacularly wrong.

But this is not simply an academic textbook. It is also for the public relations practitioner. When I left full-time practice to become an academic I received a certain amount of good-natured teasing about the irrelevance of study to the practice of public relations, but I also detected a wistful note. One colleague commented 'Of course, it would be very nice to have the luxury of thinking about it, but I'm too busy getting on with the job'. This book aims to cast some light on why, what you the practitioner do, works; to help you understand the theory behind what you do instinctively, from your experience and gut-feeling. If on reading it you exclaim 'Aha!', this book will have hit the spot.

I hope this book will also prove to be of value to anyone new to public relations, either through a change of career or because your job has changed to include new responsibilities – for community relations, staff communications, dealing with the media, or crisis planning. It is designed not to be read once and put away, but to be used as a reference aid while you are doing your job.

Shirley Harrison
April 2000

Acknowledgements

I would like to thank all those who have helped me with this book, either by contributing case studies, giving me the benefit of their advice, or granting permission for me to reproduce material. Special thanks are due to Emma Carle, one of my former students, who took time out from her hectic promotion of Furby, to provide the case study in Chapter 9, and to the graduates who contributed their biographies to Chapter 10. All copyright material in this book is reproduced by permission of the copyright holder. Full details of each publication are given in the bibliography.

My colleagues on the teaching team of the public relations group at Leeds Metropolitan University have been particularly helpful in suggesting and facilitating changes to this edition, and being supportive at a difficult time: to Liz, Ralph, Meriel, Melanie, Liz, Jo and Danny – thank you. Thanks are also due to the team and to Kyla for their flexibility and generosity which enabled me to take a semester away from teaching and to work in the rarefied atmosphere at Princeton. The staff at the Firestone Library, Princeton University, and the Princeton Public Library could not have been more helpful and I thank them for all the inter-library loans and other paraphernalia they organised for me.

My grateful thanks are also due to former clients and colleagues, working with whom has always been a valuable learning experience. Special thanks to Jackie Curthoys at International Thomson Business Press for her advice and for taking on some of the administrative work. And very special thanks to Jacob Harrison for his good humour and Rob Harrison for all his support, especially for rushing out in the middle of the night to buy a printer.

Acknowledgements

Public relations: what is it and why do we use it?

1

Key Issues

The aim of this chapter is to introduce you to public relations as both an activity and a subject for academic study. The key points covered are:

▶ definitions of public relations from a number of different standpoints;

▶ what public relations sets out to do and how that differs from other disciplines;

▶ a brief sketch of the state of the public relations industry in the UK today;

▶ an overview of the activities commonly undertaken by public relations practitioners.

Public relations means exactly what the words suggest – relations with the public. All living entities have relationships of one kind or another, whether by choice or not, and that includes companies and institutions as well as people. Relationships can be good, bad or indifferent and may change from time to time. Consider the relationships you have with friends, family members, colleagues, people you do business with, your dentist, teacher, boss, cleaner. Some of those relationships have to be worked at, and others simply exist. The distinctive thing about public relations is that it is deliberate. An individual or organisation which is aware of those with whom it comes into contact may want to make an effort to behave in a particular way so that it can get along with them better. This is the business of public relations.

Some definitions

Let us start by looking at some definitions of commonly used words and expressions which may help us to understand what public relations is about. The words are:

▶ public relations and publics

▶ marketing and some of its components: advertising, advertorials, sales promotion and publicity

▶ propaganda

Public relations

A typical class of 60 undergraduate students of business studies, when asked to come up with a definition of public relations, may put forward five or six versions. These range from the straightforward, such as 'what a company does to maintain good relations with the general public', to the downright cynical, such as 'putting a gloss on bad news'. Dictionaries tend to go for something like the former, but a dictionary definition does not always aid understanding, nor necessarily reflect the way in which a word or expression tends to be used now. As an example, look up the word 'prestigious' in your dictionary. If it is the *Shorter Oxford English Dictionary,* you will find the following: 'Practising legerdemain, deluding, deceptive' (SOED 1993).

The boards outside building sites which offer the opportunity to rent an office in 'this prestigious new development' are clearly not using the word in the sense of the dictionary definition.

One useful way of looking at the definition of a term may be to see what the experts who practise in the field usually mean when they use it. Let us look at the definitions which public relations practitioners themselves have thought up.

At its meeting in Mexico in 1978, the World Assembly of Public Relations Associations agreed that: 'Public relations is the art and social science of analysing trends, predicting their consequences, counselling organisation leaders and implementing planned programmes of action which will serve both the organisation's and the public interest'.

The Institute of Public Relations (IPR) is the professional body for public relations in the UK. The IPR framed a definition in 1987, which reads as follows: 'Public relations practice is the planned and sustained effort to establish and maintain goodwill and understanding between an organisation and its publics' (IPR 1991).

This has now been expanded to include the concept of 'reputation management' as follows:

> Public relations is about reputation – the result of what you do, what you say and what others say about you. Public relations practice is the discipline which looks after reputation – with the aim of earning understanding and support, and influencing opinion and behaviour. It is the planned and sustained effort to establish and maintain goodwill and mutual understanding between an organisation and its publics.
>
> (IPR 1999a: 1)

In1988 the Public Relations Society of America (PRSA) published a report on the terminology which had gained currency in recent years, including such terms as corporate communications and public affairs. The report concluded that there is no satisfactory alternative to the term public relations, definitions of which are given as follows:

> Public relations helps an organisation and its publics to adapt mutually to each other.

Public relations is an organisation's efforts to win the co-operation of groups of people.
Public relations helps organisations effectively interact and communicate with their key publics.

(White 1991: 3)

One of the reasons why terms other than public relations are being used is that the expression 'public relations' has come to have negative connotations. It has come to be used, with the addition of the word 'exercise', to denote falsity rather than truth, evasion rather than co-operation, and hindrance rather than help.

This stems partly from public relations' historical associations with hucksterism and press agentry. But the poor reputation of the profession probably has more to do with the ineptitude of some of the untrained people working within it and the dubious practices of a few of its most famous exponents today. It is unsurprising that the journalist who receives badly written, wrongly addressed, thinly disguised sales material headed 'Press Release' has a poor opinion of the public relations consultancy which sends it; or that the newspaper reader, unable to avoid stories about talentless nonentities who have become famous for being famous, derides the image-maker responsible for placing them. A contrary view is that public relations is disliked, not because its practitioners are bad at it, but because they are too good. The argument is that, when citizens and consumers notice that public relations is having an effect on institutions they believe should be left alone – such as government, national institutions, a free market and a free press – they do not like it. This idea, put forward by UK academic Kevin Moloney, holds that citizens do not want lobbyists to exert influence and thus reduce equality; that consumers do not want to be persuaded with misleading information provided by retailers and manufacturers; and that they resent 'being deceived by a servile, dishonest press beholden to government or to market suppliers (such as through the excessive, non-declared use of press releases)' (Moloney 1998).

Now we will turn to the definitions of public relations which have been considered by educators in the field.

Rex Harlow, an American professor, looked in 1976 at 472 definitions of public relations, from which he distilled his own, rather cumbersome version (Harlow 1976), explaining what public relations is and what public relations people do in broad terms. It brings in the idea of public relations as a function of management, in terms of communication with and responses to publics and the issues which concern them. It also refers to the concept of serving the public interest and behaving in an ethical fashion; both attributes of a mature and successful company.

A definition which finds favour both with practitioners and with academics teaching the subject can be found in Cutlip et al.: 'Public relations is the management function that identifies, establishes, and maintains mutually beneficial relationships between an organisation and the various publics on whom its success or failure depends' (Cutlip et al. 1985, 1994).

This definition makes clear that public relations covers a broad spectrum at a high level within organisations. It indicates the importance of sound public relations in securing the success or failure of the organisation. This notion of the viability of an organisation being dependent on public support echoes the views of the late Edward Bernays, the centenarian 'great-grandfather' of public relations in the USA, who said in one of his last interviews 'a public relations practitioner is an applied sociologist who advises clients or employers on the social attitudes and action to take to win the support of the public – upon whom the viability of the employer or the client depends'.

There are no universally accepted definitions of public relations. Any book on the subject will list a number and add to them. Some state very clearly that public relations is a persuasive activity, undertaken to change people's views or to get them to do something. Others concentrate on the idea of mutuality and two-way communication. A few bring in the idea of public relations as a socially responsible activity, pursued according to certain ethical standards and directed (at least in part) towards the public interest. All of them have been produced by academic writers or professional organisations, and although practitioners may be happy to agree with all or any of them, such definitions cannot give the flavour of what public relations is. Examples of public relations practice given throughout this book should help to rectify that.

Publics

The word in some of these definitions which often brings people up short is 'publics'. This is not a word we are used to seeing in its plural form. Its use in public relations equates with 'certain groups of people'. An organisation's publics are all those groups of people with which it is, ought to be, or wants to be, in communication. This may include its staff, its suppliers, its customers, its competitors, its neighbours and its investors. An individual may be a member of two or more 'publics': for example, an employee may live locally and own shares in the company, thus falling into the first, penultimate and last categories. Often the print and broadcast media are listed as publics of an organisation, and it is true that many public relations practitioners spend much of their time communicating with journalists. However, the media are usually a conduit, or intermediary, for reaching a public rather than a public in their own right. Exceptionally a journalist may be the final intended recipient, for example, when material is given 'for background' rather than 'for publication', to enable the journalist to understand the context of what he or she is passing on, while keeping the material itself confidential.

Every organisation will have its own set of publics, and some will be more important to it than others. Similarly, their relative importance will vary depending on what is happening in and to the organisation and its impact on the publics concerned. One of the jobs of an organisation's senior management team is to consider who its publics are and, with the help of its public relations adviser, to agree how they are to be reached, when and to what purpose.

The concept of publics is very important in public relations. In the 1970s James Grunig, an American professor of public relations, developed the situational theory of publics, to assist in developing and targeting messages to publics. He classified publics into those who are active on all issues, those who are apathetic, single issue publics (active only in their special areas of interest) and hot issue publics (interested in the newsworthy issues of the day). This more dynamic typology of publics will be considered further in Chapter 3.

Marketing

Public relations is sometimes listed in marketing textbooks as an activity in support of the marketing function. The Institute of Marketing says that marketing is the management process responsible for identifying, anticipating and satisfying consumer requirements profitably.

There is no doubt that public relations practice will indeed help a company to find out what its actual and potential customers might want, by exercising its abilities in two-way communication. But again, this is not what public relations is about, merely one of the uses to which its techniques can be put. With its emphasis on profitability of goods or services for sale, marketing is a narrower concept than public relations. A contrary view is put forward by Kitchen (1997).

Within marketing, a number of techniques are used which can become confused with public relations activities: advertising and its associated advertorials is one. Others are sales promotion and publicity.

Advertising

While advertising and public relations may both be used in a campaign to sell a product or service, they are very different activities. The Institute of Practitioners in Advertising defines advertising as the activity which presents the most persuasive possible selling message to the right prospects for the product or service at the lowest possible cost. There are three important words here to help us distinguish advertising from public relations: persuasive, selling and cost.

While one outcome of good public relations practice may be that someone is *persuaded* to do or believe something different, public relations' main aim is not usually to persuade but to enable the public to conclude for itself on the basis of the best possible information. A *selling* message is not generally the purpose of public relations communication, although information about a new product and a media relations campaign to excite the interest of identified journalists in such a product are legitimate public relations activities. Indeed, information leading to positive coverage in the press may help to make the potential customers for the product aware of its imminent existence, so that they already recognise the name when they actually see the advertising. This makes a public relations campaign-plus-advertising a much more cost-effective activity than advertising a new product or service 'cold'. Case Study 1.1 provides a novel example of how public relations was used in support of advertising. Finally, the *cost* element is somewhat different in public relations and advertising. The messages which advertising sends out in the form of advertisements, posters or commercials are paid for and appear in the location, form and style which has been ordered by whoever is paying. An advertisement for suntan lotion appearing in a newspaper can be booked for a specific position and an agreed date, whereas an article about the dangers of exposure to too much sun, in which the lotion is mentioned (favourably or otherwise), because the journalist has information about it as a result of a press release, can appear anywhere and at any time. In a joint public relations–advertising campaign, the advertising could be booked following the editorial coverage.

Because we all know that advertising is paid for, the messages on the advertising pages of newspapers carry less weight than those in the news pages.

Case Study 1.1	**Public relations and advertising** *Whiskas Singles: Ketchum Life* M & C Saatchi was the advertising agency responsible for coming up with an advertising idea for Whiskas Singles, single servings of cat food wrapped in individual foil packets. The agency made the first commercial ever to be targeted directly at cats themselves, rather than at their human owners, scheduling it to be shown at peak time on 27 January 1999. Ketchum Life ran a public relations campaign with the aim of getting the commercial massive media attention, thus adding value to the subsequent product trial. Having researched cat-loving journalists, the consultancy sent them engraved cat bowls, provided a cat behaviourist and cat-loving celebrities for comment, and offered cats for interview by the media. The story of the advertisement received widespread national print and television coverage, including an item on commercial television's rival BBC *Breakfast News*, and a phone-in line in the *Sun* for readers to call with information on their cats' response to the commercial. The editor of the advertising trade magazine *Campaign*, Stefano Hatfield, was quoted as saying of the success of the public relations campaign: 'They did a fantastic job in light of the fact that there was really only a tiny idea there. The ad itself was nothing special really. I'm somewhat astounded that so many newspapers lapped it up'. (*Source*: PR Week 1999a)

Advertorial

An advertorial or advertisement feature is a kind of public relations-advertising hybrid which can take one of a number of forms. The most common is usually to be found in a magazine or a local newspaper. A feature, possibly covering more than one page, is laid out and written in editorial style but gives solely favourable information about the products or services of the organisation which has paid for it. It is a kind of extended advertisement, but looks like the non-advertising pages of the publication.

In another version the advertorial links the advertiser's product or service to favourable editorial coverage by using a reader offer or competition, or by offering free samples of the product to those who write in. The publication has something to give away or sell cheaply to its readers, the product receives favourable endorsement on the editorial pages, and the advertiser gets a list of names and addresses of people interested in what it is selling.

There is a dilemma here. The strength of advertorials over advertisements is that their style and format give greater credibility to the products they are advertising, by explaining them in apparently objective terms through a third party, the journalist. But what does that do to the credibility of the journalist or the publication in which the advertorial appears? If there is no intention to mislead the reader into confusing the advertising message with a news or feature report, why not just use an advertisement? This is certainly a murky area for professional practice. The need for clarification was acknowledged by the IPR and the Incorporated Society of British Advertisers in their guidelines on advertorials, published in association with the Periodical Publishers Association, the British Society of Magazine Editors and the Public Relations Consultants Association (see Harrison 1994a).

In the USA there is an electronic variation of the advertorial: the infomercial. These are programme-length commercials, which have proliferated since the government deregulated commercial time limits. They are not supposed to look like ordinary television programmes, but the same dilemma arises as with advertorials – if the broadcast material simply looks like a long commercial, what is the point for the client of producing it? But if it looks like a normal television programme, how can the viewer distinguish it as advertising? In fact the Federal Trade Commission has had to prosecute a number of companies for 'false advertising' using infomercials disguised in one case as a news bulletin (Fahri 1992).

Sales promotions

These are distinguished by their short-term nature and often take the form of two for the price of one offers, give-aways or money-off coupons. Sainsbury's, a leading UK supermarket chain, ran for a long time a series of sales promotions on the ingredients for a dish which it advertised in television commercials. The sales promotion took the form of a free in-store recipe leaflet, and reduced prices for the principal ingredients, which were grouped together on one display with on-shelf arrows and signs, both to make an eye-catching display and to make it easier for the customer to find all the ingredients at once. Following a year of advertising and sales promotions, 12 of the recipes were grouped together to form the basis of a calendar, which was given away to purchasers of the Sainsbury's magazine. This approach, begun in 1994, has continued with variations for several years. The supermarket gets a lot of mileage out of the few recipes.

The public relations approach can also be used in sales promotion. For example, Debenhams, a UK chain of department stores, often display their goods on domestic-style tables carrying a notice which reads 'Please feel free to select from this table', in sharp contrast to the signs reading 'Do not touch' or 'All breakages must be paid for' in less enlightened shops. Debenhams' approach to sales promotion demonstrates the user-friendly attitude to communication with its customers which is the hallmark of good public relations.

Publicity

This is, very simply, what results from information being made known. Getting publicity for something or someone may be one of the objectives of a marketing or of a public relations campaign. For example, publicity may be used to make the name or function of a company better known to its target public. Simple publicity is sometimes used in support of public relations, as part of a public relations campaign, as well as in marketing.

Much has been written, and the debate continues, about whether marketing is a sub-set of public relations or the other way round. The way in which the functions are organised in a given company may help decide this in a particular case, for example, where the marketing manager reports to the director of public relations. However, in an introductory look at the subject, it is probably more helpful to suggest taking an informed view on which discipline is appropriate in a given set of circumstances.

Propaganda

Because public relations is sometimes seen as an instrument of persuasion, it is useful to distinguish it from propaganda. The word itself originated in the Roman Catholic Church of the seventeenth century, when the Congregation of the Propaganda was formed. This was a committee of cardinals in charge of foreign missions to seek out unbelievers and make converts.

Josef Goebbels, the prime propagandist of the Nazi movement in Germany in the 1930s, said:

> Propaganda is an instrument of politics, and a power for social control. The function of propaganda is not essentially to convert, rather its function is to attract followers and to keep them in line. The task of propaganda, given suitable avenues, is to blanket every area of human activity so that the environment of the individual is changed to absorb the movement's world views.

In effect, propaganda tries to 'spread the faith' and to persuade people to believe, perhaps through half-truths and distortion. When recognised as such, propaganda is generally treated with distrust or disbelief except by the very credulous. It is not considered to have a part in present-day public relations practice, although some of the early public relations practitioners were former government propagandists. We will see in Chapter 2 the role of propaganda in the formation of public relations practice today.

The public relations industry

How public relations developed and what the industry looks like in the early twenty-first century is covered more fully in the next chapter. For the moment, let us look briefly at the scale of the business.

Institute of Public Relations

The results of a survey undertaken for the IPR (IPR 1993a) indicated that there were about 48,000 people working in some way in public relations in the UK with about 6,000 of these eligible to join the IPR as full members. The IPR is currently trying to increase its membership and thus encourage the professionalisation of the business. There are four grades of membership: fellows (FIPR), members (MIPR), associates (AMIPR) and student members. The criteria for full membership are ten years' experience in public relations; or a minimum of four years' 'substantial experience at operating executive level in the practice of and an acceptable academic qualification in public relations' (see website www.ipr.org.uk). The growth of educational qualifications in public relations is detailed below. The IPR plans to attempt to attain chartered status in the near future, a move which it is believed would give the business and those who practise it greater kudos.

As public relations diplomas have only been available for 20 years and degrees for less than a decade, there are many practitioners in the industry who are highly respected, have lengthy experience and seniority but are not likely to take a professional qualification at this stage in their careers. The IPR recognises this by offering the alternative route to membership: members may be accepted if they have at least ten years' appropriate experience, although they may be required to attend an interview.

Associate membership of the IPR is available to those who do not fulfil the criteria for full membership, but who have at least three years' substantial experience or a recognised qualification in public relations. Those who are following a recognised, accredited public relations course in higher education can apply to join as student members. Fellowships are awarded for 'outstanding' work in the field of public relations although the criteria for selection of Fellows is not a public matter. For some time, members have been pressing for a clear set of criteria for Fellowship, as well as properly constituted arrangements for continuing professional development. In a recent membership survey it was found that 'members' main expectation of the Institute is that it should provide education, training and development opportunities' (IPR 1999b). One of the Institute's special interest groups, the long standing Local Government Group, took the initiative in 1994 and asked Leeds Metropolitan University to devise a Master's level programme of continuing professional development for practitioners.

Educational qualifications

When the founders of the IPR set out their aims, they included: 'to consider the institution of examinations or other suitable tests with the object of raising the status of those practising public relations to an agreed professional level' (Hess 1948 cited in L'Etang 1998a). Fifty years later the first students were enrolled on the IPR's Diploma course. However, there were a number of developments in between, which have led to the increasingly high education profile of IPR members.

A public relations version of the CAM (Communications, Advertising and Marketing) Diploma, consisting of a mixture of evening classes and distance learning, has been offered to practitioners since the 1970s and was for over a decade the only way to become professionally qualified in public relations. The first Masters (MSc) degree was made available at Stirling University in 1988, with a distance-learning option available from 1991. The first undergraduate (BA) degree was instituted at Bournemouth University. The IPR currently approves six bachelors and two masters degrees. In addition there are numerous undergraduate courses in public relations located in university business schools, media and cultural studies departments and journalism schools, together with eight further masters courses and postgraduate certificates or diplomas offered at Oxford University and Leeds Metropolitan University. While no reliable destination statistics are available, a reasonable estimate is that there are between 400 and 500 public relations graduates each year entering the industry. This is reflected in research which shows that the proportion of IPR members who have first or higher degrees has grown from 35.5 per cent in 1987 to 56.3 per cent in 1998 (IPR 1999b).

In 1998 the Institute's Diploma was launched. It is intended to provide a postgraduate level qualification to current practitioners, who attend one of the three centres (London, Leeds and Edinburgh) either in the evenings or on a day-release basis over a period of a year. The syllabus covers strategic public relations, public relations planning and the completion of two projects in a specialised field such as internal communication or public affairs.

Clearly the public relations industry in the UK is becoming better educated and qualified, and, as admissions officers will testify, there is no shortage of young people wanting to gain qualifications in the subject.

Why do we use it?

So what are all these thousands of public relations people doing and why? The IPR's most recent research indicates that they spend most of their time on 'communication production', with media relations at 37 per cent, brochure/video/print production at 14 per cent and event management at 10 per cent. However, 25 per cent of time is spent on 'advising management' and 9 per cent on research (IPR 1999b).

Media relations

As we have already seen, the media rarely constitute a public but are usually a conduit to the public or publics which an organisation wants to reach. Public relations practitioners spend so much of their time on media relations because it is essential for both parties that good contacts are made and kept. Sometimes media relations activities are intended to foster a long-term relationship so that the journalists and public relations people feel comfortable with each other and can trust each other.

For example, a computer company's public relations adviser will want to be on first-name terms with the appropriate journalists working on trade and special interest magazines such as *PC World*, and also will want to know the names and particular interests of the science or computer editors on the national newspapers, selected producers or researchers for television and radio programmes such as *Tomorrow's World*, *Horizon* and *Science Now* and the reporters who deal with community issues for the local and regional press, the local radio stations and regional television. With a good contacts list, the public relations officer will stand a better chance of interesting the appropriate media in a story on the launch of a new product, or deflecting problems which could arise for the company or the industry as a whole. When negative stories do appear, such as redundancies at the local factory or a possible safety problem, it is more likely that the public relations officer will be able to put the company's point of view, resulting in less damaging coverage. We will cover this area more thoroughly in Chapter 6.

If the reporter concerned knows that the public relations officer is trustworthy and can be relied on to give accurate and up-to-date information, it makes the job of reporting easier. The public relations officer can also help the reporter to get more information by smoothing the path to the chief executive or by acting as spokesperson for the organisation, so that a news story can carry appropriate quotes. Often the public relations office or press office keeps all the information on a company which is likely to be of value to a journalist, and which it is a bore for the journalist to have to find out – when the company was founded, how many employees it has, where it operates, what it makes or does, the names of key staff and so on. A well-run press office can complement the local paper's own resources, supplying relevant information and photographs to the media.

The Whiskas commercial described in Case Study 1.1 gives an example of how well researched a contact list can be, when it is able to pinpoint cat-loving journalists working in specific sectors of the media.

Sometimes media relations activity is designed to meet a short-term objective, for example, to raise awareness of a forthcoming event. An example is described in Case Study 1.2. This special event, a fiftieth anniversary re-enactment of the Normandy Landings on D-Day in 1944, took place over one weekend, but the organisers, the Virginia Beach Department of Convention and Visitor Development, hoped to increase the number of visitors to the resort overall.

Case Study 1.2

Media relations

The Commemoration of the 50th Anniversary of D-Day: Department of Convention and Visitor Development, Virginia Beach, VA, with Brickell and Associates Public Relations, Virginia Beach, VA

The Commemoration of the 50th Anniversary of D-Day, when allied forces landed in Normandy, signalling the beginning of the end of the Second World War, was a major event in a number of European countries, with the major focus on Britain and France. However, the largest 50th anniversary re-enactment in June 1994 took place not in France but in Virginia Beach, Virginia, in the USA. News releases were issued in March to 760 journalists, news kits sent out the following week and follow up phone calls made the week after that. Posters were also sent out to selected national media.

The event, which attracted 15,000 people, resulted in high bed occupancy in the resort, which normally saw a decline in weekend tourism after the Memorial Day weekend (end of May). It was covered by media teams from 125 different organisations from all over the USA and elsewhere, including television crews from Japan, France, Russia and Germany. The media relations programme cost less than $35,000 including production costs. The cost of the coverage, if it had been paid for at advertising rates, was estimated at $900,000.

(*Source*: Hendrix 1998: 97–112)

Public relations officers need journalists to help their organisations to communicate with their publics. So a typical public relations officer may send out regular press releases explaining what the organisation's plans are, how it is dealing with an issue of current public interest or what it is doing for the local community. The relationship between journalists and public relations practitioners is not always an easy one, nor would it be right for it to be too cosy. An illustration of this is given in the example of game theory as applied to media relations, shown in Chapter 3.

Other 'communication production'

While most public relations practitioners are heavily involved in media relations, the job of a press officer is specialised. It is discussed further in Chapter 9. The production of brochures, video and print are also a specialised area, and one which is not the concern of this book. The reading list at the end of this chapter suggests some of the more specialised books in the field of production.

This brings us to events management, which provides a useful way of looking at many of the other activities in which a public relations officer may be involved.

Events management

Public relations people are involved in the management of all kinds of events, from conferences to product launches and from banquets to open days. An open day held at a company's premises provides a snapshot of the activities which could be undertaken by the public relations team: the production of appropriate publicity material and a printed guide to the company's activities; organising signposting to and within the event; getting suggestions from staff and producing a special employee bulletin in advance of the big day; arranging for the local school brass band, sponsored by the company, to perform; arranging photography and catering; getting journalists there and giving them appropriate material; and ensuring that shareholders are aware of how and why the company has chosen to spend some of its profits on such an event. These jobs cover most of the activities which a public relations professional might ever be expected to master. This all seems like rather an expensive and complicated business. Organising a successful open day is indeed so. The reason why a company chooses to put the time and effort into doing so is likely to be that it values good public relations.

Advising management and research

It is generally agreed that public relations practitioners fall into two roles: the technician and the manager (Dozier 1981). Technicians provide the skills such as writing, editing, commissioning (and sometimes doing) design, photography, print and video production, organising events and so on. Managers plan and manage public relations programmes, according to policies agreed at the top level of the organisation. Increasingly the public relations 'manager' is a member of that top level as an executive director. Thus public relations is seen to be of strategic importance in organisations.

Public relations at this level also involves issues management. This means identifying issues which are on the horizon and which might affect the organisation, especially any trends in public opinion or expectations. Once identified and prioritised, these issues need to be considered by the organisation, which takes a position and forms a strategy to deal with the issues. This may require the planning of an internal communications programme or a lobbying campaign, the detail of which will be conducted by communication technicians.

Providing good management advice is impossible without research. We will look at the different types of research typically conducted in public relations practice in Chapter 4.

All of these public relations activities – communication production, events management, advising management and research – are conducted with the prime aim of building good relationships with publics. Being on good terms with your publics helps influence their behaviour towards you and makes them sympathetic to your aims. Generating and promoting mutual understanding gives an organisation the opportunity to anticipate trends, issues and events which might be disruptive to good relationships now or in the future. Goodwill and understanding are vital when the chips are down or at a time of crisis for the organisation. If your organisation is the target of food tampering, for example, the relationship of trust which you have built up with your customers will help you at least to survive and, possibly, prosper.

Summary points

✔ There are many definitions of public relations but none which is universally accepted. Most public relations practitioners would agree that public relations is about two-way communication and that it is a strategic management tool.

✔ Public relations is not the same as marketing or propaganda. Public relations is sometimes used in conjunction with marketing activities such as advertising and sales promotion, especially to raise awareness of a product or service.

✔ About 48,000 people are working in the public relations industry in the UK. There is a move towards greater professionalism in the industry, evidenced by more emphasis on qualifications and continuing professional development.

✔ Most time is spent by public relations practitioners on communication production, especially directed at the media. Increasingly public relations practitioners spend their time on research and on advising management.

✔ Building a relationship of trust through good public relations can help companies to survive and prosper, even at difficult times.

Questions for discussion

1 Why do you think Cutlip's definition of public relations finds favour with practitioners as well as academics? Can you improve on his definition?

2 Grunig and Hunt (1984 Chapters 3 and 4) argue that public relations serves as 'an ombudsman for the public' in an organisation. To what extent do you think that view reflects public relations practice in companies today?

3 Can public relations education and training produce practitioners who are both technicians and managers? Is the technician role a necessary stepping stone to becoming a public relations manager?

4 What differences can you find between public relations and marketing? Using an example of a product or service you know of, distinguish between public relations and marketing activity in support of it.

5 What similarities and what differences might there be between public relations practice in a commercial company, in a charity and in a government department?

Recommended further reading

For an overall view of public relations theory and practice in general, the basic American texts are usually recommended. In particular you should look at Cutlip et al. (1994), which is regularly updated with new editions every few years. Grunig and Hunt (1984) is a classic text, though rather out of date. Both of these titles appear throughout the sections of recommended further reading in this book, as do Baskin et al. (1997) Caywood (1997) and Newsom et al. (1993). These texts also have chapters on communication production.

Comprehensive introductory level books on public relations in Britain are harder to find. Kitchen's (1997) covers much of the ground and is probably the most useful. Probably because of its editor's background and interest, its focus is on public relations as a branch of marketing. Hart (1995) is a practitioner-led textbook into its second edition, and is in use on most public relations courses.

References

Baskin, O., Aronoff, C. and Lattimore, D. (1997) *Public Relations the Profession and the Practice*, 4th edn., Chicago, IL: Brown and Benchmark.

Caywood, C. (ed.) (1997) *The Handbook of Strategic Public Relations and Integrated Communications*, New York: McGraw-Hill.

Cutlip, S., Center, A. and Broom, G. (1985) *Effective Public Relations*, London: Prentice Hall.

Cutlip, S., Center, A. and Broom, G. (1994) *Effective Public Relations*, 7th edn., Englewood Cliffs, NJ: Prentice Hall.

Dozier, D. (1981) 'The Diffusion of Evaluation Methods Among Public Relations Practitioners', East Lansing, MI: Public Relations Division of the Association for Education in Journalism Annual Conference.

Fahri, P. (1992) 'Time Out from Our Commercial for a Word from Our Sponsor', *Washington Post national weekly edition*, March 2–8.

Grunig. J. and Hunt, T. (1984) *Managing Public Relations*, Orlando, FL: Holt, Rinehart and Winston.

Harlow, R. (1976) 'Building a Public Relations Definition', *Public Relations Review* 2 (Winter): 36.

Harrison, S. (1994a) 'Codes of practice and ethics in the UK communications industry', *Business Ethics: a European Review* 3 (2) 109–16.

Hart, N. (1995) *Strategic Public Relations*, Basingstoke: Macmillan.

Hendrix, J. (1998) *Public Relations Cases*, 4th edn., Belmont, CA: Wadsworth.

Hess, A. (1948) 'Our Aims and Objects', *Public Relations* 1 (1).

IPR (1991) *Public relations as a career*, London: Institute of Public Relations.

IPR (1993a) 'More research findings', *Public Relations: Journal of the IPR* 11 (3).

IPR (1999a) *Handbook*, London: Institute of Public Relations.

IPR (1999b) *1998 Membership Survey*, London: Institute of Public Relations.

Kitchen, P. (ed.) (1997) *Public Relations Principles and Practice*, London: International Thomson Business Press.

L'Etang, J. (1998a) 'The development of British Public Relations in the Twentieth Century', Glasgow: IAMCR Conference.

Moloney, K. (1998) '"It's a PR job": A question of reputation and its consequences for teaching, researching and doing PR' *Working Papers in Public Relations Research No. 2*, Bournemouth: School of Media Arts and Communication, Bournemouth University.

Newsom, D., Scott, A. and Turk, J. (1993) *This is PR: the Realities of Public Relations*, 5th edn., New York: Wadsworth.

PR Week (1999a) 'Campaigns', 19 February.

SOED (1993) *The New Shorter Oxford English Dictionary*, Oxford: OUP.

White, J. (1991) *How to Understand and Manage Public Relations*, London: Business Books.

2 Getting from there to here

Key Issues

The aim of this chapter is to provide a brief overview of the evolution of public relations practice up to the present day. The key points covered are:

▶ the history of public relations and its growth in the UK and the USA;

▶ differing views on the phases of public relations practice;

▶ the increasing professionalisation of public relations.

If public relations is all about promoting goodwill and understanding, it must have been going on for considerably longer than its professional roots would suggest. The foundation in 1948 of both the Institute of Public Relations in the UK and the Public Relations Society of America in the USA arguably marks the beginning of public relations as an organised profession, but activities which could be said to fall under the broad heading of public relations have been going on for centuries.

A brief historical overview

Authors of public relations and communications studies textbooks like to cite the carrying of colours into battle as the first attempts at corporate identity. The first trade associations, whose job was to protect the reputation of their members and to lobby for their interests, were the medieval guilds and their survivors, the Worshipful Companies. Unlike today's trade associations, however, the guilds created a mystique around the activities of their members in order to maintain exclusivity. This addiction to secrecy continued for centuries in some areas of operation and is still visible today in the attitude of a few companies.

The history of house journals goes back to the early days of industry. Charles Dickens refers to a magazine edited by cotton workers in New England in the 1840s; Lever Brothers and the Manchester Co-operative Society in England published employee journals over a hundred years ago.

The idea of a suggestion box and award scheme for staff, thought to be a relatively modern technique of good internal public relations, was first used by William Denny in 1880 in his shipbuilding company in Dumbarton.

Publicity-generating stunts, enacted in order to gain media coverage and influence public opinion, have been reported since newspapers were first published. The Boston Tea Party in 1773, when tons of tea were dumped into the harbour as a demonstration against the perceived unfair imposition of taxation by the colonial power, was one of the most famous and effective of these early publicity stunts. In 1881 the Scottish grocer Thomas Lipton arranged for 'the world's largest cheese', manufactured in the USA, to be delivered to his store in Glasgow in a blaze of publicity.

A press officer was used for the first time by government when the British Treasury appointed a spokesman in 1809. The Post Office, in its first annual report in 1854 declared the importance of explaining services to the public.

One of the earliest recorded speeches about the practice of public relations was made in 1842 by Hugh Smith to an audience of Columbia College alumni on the subject of the ethics of persuasion.

> Smith argued that efforts to influence opinion could be legitimate if they met three criteria: They had to avoid the employment of falsehood, avoid appeals to prejudices and passions, and avoid the 'proscription of those who will not fall in with particular opinions or practices'.
>
> (Olasky 1987: 12)

The term 'public relations' itself is thought to have been used for the first time in 1882 by Dorman Eaton, a lawyer, addressing the Yale Law School on 'The Public Relations and Duties of the Legal Profession'. He used the term 'public relations' to mean 'looking out for the welfare of the public'. In entitling its 1908 annual report 'Public Relations', the American Telephone and Telegraph Company used the same meaning. Its president, Theodore Vail, described public relations in these terms:

> Is the management honest and competent? What is the investment? Is the property maintained at a high standard? What percentage of return does it show? Is that a fair return? If these questions are answered satisfactorily, there can be no basis for conflict between the company and the public.
>
> (Bernays 1952: 70)

Grunig and Hunt give a helpful historical framework for the development of public relations in the USA (Grunig and Hunt 1984: 27–41), which falls into five distinct phases:

The public be fooled

'The public be damned!'

Public information

Propaganda and persuasion

Public understanding

The public be fooled

America in the 1830s was the land of the Western hero – Daniel Boone, Davy Crockett, Buffalo Bill and Calamity Jane. Their exploits, while based on fact, were often heavily embellished by press agents hired to promote the interests of landowners in Kentucky and other states which wanted to attract settlement by easterners. Stories about these popular heroes were created and placed by press agents to fill the pages of the penny press, so called because they cost only a cent, compared with six cents for most other newspapers. Among those contributing invented stories was Phineas T. Barnum, showman and press agent *par excellence,* and co-founder of Barnum and Bailey's Circus. Barnum promoted 'exhibits' such as Joice Heth, reputedly a former slave and nurse to George Washington over 100 years before. He wrote letters to newspapers in his own and pen names to keep her story going, pocketing a reputed $1,500 per week from New Yorkers eager to see this newsworthy phenomenon. His most famous remark, 'There's a sucker born every minute', was made in the context of restraint, however. Barnum believed that, because the public were gullible, they should be protected from hurtful exploitation such as that practised by lottery sharks or phoney auctioneers (Olasky 1987: 12). 'Contrary to popular belief, Barnum's great discovery was not how easy it is to deceive the public, but rather, how much the public enjoyed being deceived. Especially if they could see how it was being done' (Boorstin 1962: 210).

Barnum was the earliest and most famous in a long line of press agents who continue to work in a similar way today.

> The agents' methods were not quite so important to them as the results. All manner of stunts, such as fake jewel robberies, marital spats, and love affairs were reported; and a mine of misinformation about marriages, divorces, clothes (or lack of them), opinions upon any subject was constantly explored.
>
> (Marston 1979: 21)

The successors to these agents of 'the public be fooled' school survive today in the person of image-makers and celebrity press agents. Consultants such as Max Clifford take on clients with the express intention of making them famous, and successfully place stories and pictures of them in the pages of magazines such as *Chat* and *Hello.* The fact that serious newspapers such as the *Sunday Times* now devote several expensive colour pages each week to reporting the social lives and doings of minor pop stars and models indicates that there is still a thriving market for public-fooling press agentry and hucksterism of the Barnum variety.

'The public be damned!'

William Vanderbilt is credited, rightly or wrongly, with using the expression 'The public be damned!'. Far from courting public interest in the doings of his corporation, the New York Central Railroad, Vanderbilt claimed that he was working solely for his stockholders and did not care how useful or convenient the public found his company's services. The banker George F. Baker is supposed to have told a reporter 'It's none of the public's business what I do', while another banker, J.P. Morgan, is reputed to have said 'I owe the public nothing'. In general, the late nineteenth-century captains of industry had scant regard for public opinion: big business tended to believe that: 'the less the public knew of its operations, the more efficient and profitable . . . the operations would be' (Goldman 1948: 3).

Another railway magnate, George Washington Cass Jnr, made clear his opposition to public relations and lobbying when he wrote in these terms about a journalist:

> I agree with you that Gibson knows what he is writing about. There is only one way of keeping these fellows quiet if they are disposed to make a noise and that is to buy them up – and this I am not disposed to do.

and thus about a suggested government relations campaign: 'We have no emissary in Washington nor do we care to go into that kind of business. It is quite expensive and very seldom pays' (Olasky 1987: 17).

Cass may not have been prepared to pay off journalists in return for good media coverage, but many others were quite content to do so. Thus the practice of 'dead-heading' – granting free tickets or passes – became common. Criticism of this practice as a form of bribery was met with the response that journalists needed to be able to travel about freely on the railway system in order to be able to report on it.

The same argument is used today by travel editors, who accept free flights, accommodation and meals for their reporters, on the grounds that the newspaper could not otherwise afford to send its staff to interesting and exotic locations: if they want reports on anything other than a cheap package holiday, the travel writer's expenses will have to be met by someone other than the newspaper. This applies across the board in the UK, with the honourable exception of the *Independent*. In an interview with the *Guardian* newspaper, Simon Cunliffe, the deputy editor of the pages in which the travel section appears, said:

> From the first day we decided it wasn't acceptable to take a free meal and then write about the restaurant . . . However virtuous and objective any journalist is, a freebie means they must in some way be beholden to their host.
>
> (Diamond 1993)

Returning to the nineteenth century, straightforward bribery in the form of payment to newspapers for favourable coverage, was becoming so common that Olasky (op. cit.: 19) quotes this 'rate card' published by a Chicago journalist:

> For the setting forth of virtues (actual or alleged) of presidents, general managers, or directors, $2 per line. For complimentary notices of the wives and children of railroad officials, we demand $1.50 per line. Epic poems, containing descriptions of scenery, dining cars, etc., will be published at special rates.

Competition for customers had begun to make companies realise that they needed to promote themselves and their products, and there was a gradual growth in public relations and advertising. The Westinghouse electricity corporation set up the first corporate public relations department in 1889 to promote the Westinghouse alternating current in competition to the direct current supplied by the Edison company (Cutlip and Center 1978).

Sometimes the line between advertising and public relations became blurred as advertisers tried to get free space alongside the advertisements they had paid for. Press agents worked hard to get their clients' names into the papers, using every trick they could think of, and enjoying considerable success. The publicists of this era came to be known as 'flacks' because they adopted the approach of shooting all their weapons at the press in the hope that some of the material would hit home (Grunig and Hunt 1984).

Public information

Towards the end of the nineteenth century, a series of strikes took place, as workers protested about dangerous working conditions and exploitation. There was violence, and the newspapers were full of horror stories, provided by the strikers, about the numbers of workers – estimated at half a million – maimed and killed each year in America's factories and on its railways. The era of investigative reporting had begun.

In 1902 *McClure's Magazine* published a series of articles exposing corruption in high places: big business, municipal government and the New York City Police Department, whose commissioner was Theodore Roosevelt. Roosevelt coined the term 'muck-raking' for this type of journalism, for the perpetrators 'raked the muck wherever it may be'. At the same time there was a series of congressional hearings into the activities of big business which was, of course, fully reported. The climate of opinion was beginning to change, cooling towards the corporations, which were seen as either secretive or lying, and warming towards the press, which apparently told the people the truth.

Ivy Ledbetter Lee was a member of the press, writing for the business columns of newspapers and magazines in New York. He had worked his way through Princeton University by selling stories to the New York papers. Recognising that he was unlikely to have financial success as an investigative journalist, he developed a talent for putting across in a straightforward way complicated material about investments, banking and law. In 1902, having sold as a freelance several articles about business, he had a brain wave:

> the beginnings of muckraking sent an exciting idea through Lee's head. Was business' policy of secrecy really a wise one? If publicity was being used so effectively to smear business, could it not be used with equal effectiveness to explain and defend business?
>
> (Goldman 1948: 6)

In 1904, Lee opened a public relations agency, Parker & Lee, with a press agent called George Parker. Following a split four years later, Lee continued on his own until he opened the firm Lee, Harris & Lee in 1916. Lee's clients were drawn from the big business arena which he knew well; from the railroad companies, the anthracite operators, the mine owners and the oil companies. Soon after his appointment as public relations adviser to the coal companies in 1906, Lee formulated his Declaration of Principles, which accompanied all statements which he sent to the press (see Figure 2.1). It is worth studying, to show how far Lee had brought the practice of public relations from its murky recent past.

Lee convinced one of his clients, the Pennsylvania Railroad Company, to tell the truth about an accident instead of following the usual practice of trying to suppress details. He was permitted to bring reporters to the scene and helped them to cover the story, thus retaining some control over their activities. He felt that, if the public could see both sides of the story, they would be in a better position to make up their mind as to what had happened. By demonstrating to his clients that a policy of openness was more desirable, Lee prospered and the public became better informed. By 1921, Lee, Harris & Lee was issuing its bulletin, previously named *Notes and Clippings*, under the title *Public Relations*.

Propaganda and persuasion

As Lee's work was becoming better established and his style of operating was copied by others in the field of public relations, governments on both sides of the Atlantic were taking on staff to explain their practices and policies.

In Britain, Lloyd George as Chancellor of the Exchequer 'organised a team of lecturers to explain the first old age pension scheme' in 1912 (Jefkins 1992: 4). The government subsequently used public relations to ensure the public understood its health and housing schemes of the 1920s.

In the USA, the War Department became, in 1919, the first client of Edward Bernays' consultancy, formed with his wife, Doris Fleischman, after his wartime service with the US Information Service. Their job was to carry out a programme for the re-employment of ex-servicemen.

Ivy Lee's Declaration of Principles | **Figure 2.1**

Declaration of Principles

This is not a secret press bureau. All our work is done in the open.

We aim to supply news. This is not an advertising agency; if you think any of our matter ought properly to go to your business office, do not use it.

Our matter is accurate. Further details on any subject treated will be supplied promptly, and any editor will be assisted most cheerfully in verifying directly any statement of fact. Upon inquiry, full information will be given to any editor concerning those on whose behalf an article is sent out.

In brief, our plan is, frankly and openly, on behalf of the business concerns and public institutions, to supply the press and public of the United States prompt and accurate information concerning subjects which it is of value and interest to the public to know about.

Corporations and public institutions give out much information in which the news point is lost to view. Nevertheless, it is quite as important to the public to have this news as it is to the establishments themselves to give it currency.

I send out only matter every detail of which I am willing to assist any editor in verifying for himself. I am always at your service for the purpose of enabling you to obtain more complete information concerning any of the subjects brought forward in my copy.

Source: Ivy L. Lee Papers, Seeley G. Mudd Library. Used by permission of the Princeton University Library

During the First World War itself, propaganda had been used first in Britain and then in America, to convince the public of the necessity of military action on a scale never before experienced. When 60,000 casualties could be sustained by the British Army alone, on one day of battle on the Somme in 1916, it was imperative that cannon fodder be recruited on a massive scale. Small wonder that the famous image of Lord Kitchener's pointing finger, with the slogan 'Your country needs you', became such an enduring symbol of the times.

The USA remained neutral for the first three years of the First World War. Woodrow Wilson secured re-election as President in 1916 with the slogan 'He kept us out of war!'. But British propaganda and the threat of a second front on the US-Mexico border convinced the Americans to enter the war on the side of the Allies. Within a week President Wilson had appointed George Creel, a former news reporter, to head the Committee on Public Information. According to Bernays, who was a member of it, Creel's committee organised the biggest and most effective wartime propaganda machine ever:

> Intellectual and emotional bombardment aroused Americans to a pitch of enthusiasm. The bombardment came at people from all sides – advertisements, news, volunteer speakers, posters, schools, theaters; millions of homes displayed service flags. The war aims and ideals were continually projected to the eyes and ears of the populace.
>
> (Bernays 1952:74)

Edward Bernays' work in the 1920s and 1930s did much to explain public relations, and his writings provided a theoretical framework for his practice. A nephew of Sigmund Freud, Bernays possessed considerable intellectual ability and an interest in psychology. He believed that it was possible to persuade people, but only of what is in their best interests. His major theory, propounded in *Crystallising Public Opinion* which was published in 1923, held that the key to public relations success was to find out what the public likes, and then highlight that aspect of your business. He developed this in *The Engineering of Consent*, published in 1955 thus: first, determine the values and attitudes of the public you wish to persuade, and then describe the client in a way that conforms to those values and attitudes. In *Propaganda* he emphasised the social responsibility of the public relations practitioner.

> The conscious and intelligent manipulation of the organised habits and opinions of the masses is an important element in democratic society. Those who manipulate this unseen mechanism of society constitute an invisible government which is the true ruling power of our country.
>
> (Bernays 1928: 9)

In Britain at this time, the power of persuasion was being used in a number of ways, from gaining acceptance of conscription in the First World War to the promotion of fruit. Articles on the value of providing information to the public, a view driven largely by local government officials, started to appear in the 1920s. The Empire Marketing Board, set up in 1924, began to use public relations on a large scale to promote trade in Empire products. Its head, Sir Stephen Tallents, spent over a million pounds on campaigns involving posters, film and exhibitions. By 1930–31, 44 press or publicity officers were in place in 12 government departments, and in 1946, 32 public relations officers were appointed in local government, 16 of whom went on to found the Institute of Public Relations in 1948 under the presidency of Tallents (L'Etang 1998b).

The history of public relations in Britain, largely based on work done to explain government policies or promote government-backed bodies and services, reflects the public information, propaganda and persuasion phases. There was little public relations activity for commercial organisations in Britain before the 1950s. Although there was some in-house public relations – Frank Jefkins, the prolific author and lecturer, wrote his first press release for a London store in 1938 – consultancies did not really get off the ground until after the Second World War.

Throughout the 1940s Shell published motoring guides and made promotional films. The most enduring public relations footage of those years, however, was from the public sector: films produced by the Post Office Film Unit for the Royal Mail in the 1940s and 1950s, including the documentary *Night Mail* with a script by W.H. Auden, still regularly shown today. The film's director, John Grierson, was the founder of the Documentary Film Movement, underpinned by the ideal that film as a mass medium could lead to informed citizenship and break down social barriers.

Many former government information officers set up in the businesses of advertising and public relations after their wartime service, in both the UK and the USA. The British Ministry of Information became the Central Office of Information, which spawned the Government Information Service, subsequently re-named the Government Information and Communication Service (GICS) to encompass the idea of two-way communication. The GICS is the organisation responsible for recruiting information and press officers to work in government departments.

Propaganda and persuasion
The tobacco industry

Edward Bernays took on the job of persuading women to smoke during the late 1920s. The American Tobacco Company, makers of the brand leaders, Lucky Strike cigarettes, had already settled on the slogan 'Reach for a Lucky instead of a sweet', linking smoking with the new vogue for slimness. Bernays capitalised on this theme, enlisting expert opinion from as far afield as Britain to add weight to the cause. George Buchan, a former chief of the British Association of Medical Officers of Health, provided advice that

> the correct way to finish a meal is with fruit, coffee and a cigarette. The fruit hardens the gums and cleans the teeth; the coffee stimulates the flow of saliva in the mouth and acts as a mouth wash; while finally the cigarette disinfects the mouth and soothes the nerves.
>
> (Bernays papers, cited in Tye 1998)

Case Study 2.1

Following a widespread propaganda campaign to link cigarettes with good health ('reach for a cigarette instead of dessert'), Bernays was asked to make smoking in the street acceptable for women. He did this by hi-jacking the 1929 Easter Parade in New York, persuading ten fashionable young women to join the parade down Fifth Avenue smoking their 'Torches of Freedom', as a sign of their emancipation. This act was portrayed as a way of breaking down discrimination against women. Furthermore, it was seen (and reported) as an event dreamed up by the women themselves: Bernays ensured that no one knew that it had been organised by the public relations adviser to a cigarette manufacturer.

When in the 1950s research indicating the link between smoking and cancer became public, the tobacco industry again went to the public relations industry for advice. Hill and Knowlton helped the tobacco companies to set up The Tobacco Institute and were later sued by the State of Mississippi for their part in

> a co-ordinated, industry-wide strategy designed actively to mislead and confuse the public about the true dangers associated with smoking cigarettes. Rather than work for the good of public health the tobacco trade association refuted, undermined and neutralized information coming from the scientific and medical community.

According to the tobacco industry, the campaign was intended to promote cigarettes and to defend their product by 'creating doubt about the health charge without actually denying it, and advocating the public's right to smoke without actually urging them to take up the practice' (Stauber and Rampton 1995: 27–8).

(*Sources*: Tye 1998; Beder 1998; Stauber and Rampton 1995)

Public understanding

The final phase in the history of public relations is that of (some) current practice: developing and maintaining mutual understanding between an organisation and its publics. Bernays belongs, through sheer longevity, to this phase as well. He wrote the first public relations textbooks and set up the first courses in public relations at university level in 1922 at New York University. He also saw the importance of research and evaluation as part of the public relations process. Without measuring awareness of, or attitudes towards, the client at the start of a public relations campaign, and again at the end, how could the public relations practitioner expect the client to evaluate the success or failure of the campaign?

Following the Second World War, when governments had employed information and press officers in their thousands, there was a massive growth in public relations consultancies and in-house units, in the public as well as the private sector. As the British journal *Persuasion* pointed out in 1949, the war altered the relationship between local authorities and their citizens. When peace came, the climate for formalised public relations was good.

The post-war years also saw advances in the technology of communications and a corresponding increase in the methods and reach of different media, especially television. The advent of the microchip and the revolution in printing and publishing which it has brought about, has made it possible to publish high quality, timely, closely targeted public relations material cheaply and easily.

The public, and business' perception of their customers, have changed too. From the days of Nader's raiders in the 1960s, consumer power and the requirement of companies to listen to their customers if they want to succeed have become progressively more important. There are many organisations which have set themselves up to keep an eye (on the public's behalf) on government, business, and even on the public relations industry: Congress Watch and PR Watch are among them.

A heavier reliance on market and opinion research has made local and central government more concerned with obtaining the good opinion of the public. Customer service charters in both private and public sectors promise the public that the institutions subscribing to them will behave in a specific way, i.e. properly, and that they will be accountable to the public. Coupled with this is the concept of the public's right to know, which is held in great esteem, and includes everything from a company's policy on the use of hardwoods to information held about a customer on computer, from deliberations of council committees to ingredients in a packet of soup.

The present-day public relations practitioner's role may encompass many tasks which would not have been considered 50 years ago. Certainly in the UK it is a recent phenomenon to have a public relations adviser formulating strategy at senior management or board level, and acting as the public's representative in the boardroom. According to Harold Burson, one of the founders of the international group of public relations consultancies, Burson-Marsteller:

> The public relations executive helps formulate policies that will enable a corporation to adapt to [social] trends and communicates – both internally and externally – the reasons for those policies. One obvious objective is to make sure that business institutions perform as servants of the people.
>
> (Burson 1974: 224, 227)

The concept of the socially responsible organisation, with the public relations executive as company conscience and conduit, will be further discussed in Chapter 8.

Current public relations practice includes examples of all the previous types. There are still press agents, information officers and persuaders in the public relations business, and secretive corporations whose accounts public relations people would love to get, as Ivy Lee did. The mutual understanding model of public relations may, however, be operating more in theory than in practice.

Public relations as a profession

As we saw in Chapter 1, the increasing professionalism of public relations practitioners has not yet resulted in public relations being widely viewed as a professional calling, like medicine or the law. Sam Black, however, did see similarities between the professions of medicine and of public relations.

> There is an interesting analogy between medicine and public relations. A medical practitioner and a public relations practitioner must both first diagnose and then treat. It is common for both to be called in after the damage is done. Preventive public relations is just as important as preventive medicine and like the latter is equally rarely employed.
>
> (Black 1989: 11–12)

Suggesting that there are similarities in training and professional behaviour, Black went on to say:

> After completing lengthy and comprehensive studies, a doctor qualifies by the passing of professional examinations and is admitted to the medical register. Two common factors apply to all doctors: they all possess a minimum basic knowledge of medicine and surgery, and they subscribe to the Hippocratic oath.
>
> A parallel exists for those engaged in public relations. All public relations practitioners – whatever their particular field of work – need to possess a basic knowledge and experience of the methods and media of the art and should subscribe to an accepted code of professional conduct.
>
> (ibid.)

The differences, however, may be more telling than the similarities. A doctor cannot practice without registration and doctors who breach professional rules can be, and regularly are, struck off the register, disgraced, and unable to practice thenceforth. A public relations practitioner can set up in business or be employed as a member of staff without registration of any kind. Although professional bodies exist, membership is not mandatory. Even among those public relations people who do choose to join their professional body there is a view that such organisations have no real teeth – either because they do not withdraw registration for misdemeanours, or because a malefactor denied membership can in any case practise without registration or constraints of any kind other than the laws of the land.

Where Professor Black's analogy is useful, however, is in bringing together two of the elements which help to define a profession: a period of training at an advanced level and conformity to a set of norms or code of professional conduct. A further element may be that members of a profession should be driven by the desire to serve the public interest ahead of, but not excluding, the requirement to make profits. So, for example, a doctor should not perform unnecessary surgery for a private fee in preference to treating a casualty or, perhaps, in preference to undertaking research into a cure for AIDS.

The more commonly held view, however, is that a professional follows a vocation or calling which involves some branch of advanced learning, some practical experience, and adherence to a code of conduct or practice which guides members in the proper performance of their duties.

Codes of practice

There are a number of codes of practice or conduct governing the various branches of what may loosely be called the communications business: the media, advertising and public relations.

The media

Broadcasting on radio and television is subject to statutory controls such as the Broadcasting Act 1990. Regulation of broadcasting falls to such bodies as the Independent Television Commission (ITC), the Radio Authority, the Broadcasting Complaints Commission and the Broadcasting Standards Council. These bodies publish codes of practice and guidance going into great detail about what may or may not be broadcast, how and when. The ITC's Programme Code alone runs to 48 pages of closely printed text, covering guidance on everything from jokes about personal disability to interviews with politicians and prizes in children's programmes.

At the time of writing, the press is subject only to self-regulation, in the form of the Press Complaints Commission (PCC), with whose code of practice the newspaper industry is supposed to comply. From time to time there is a call for statutory control of the press in the UK, the most recent having been seen off in 1993. 'We say that standards have improved considerably and that fabricated interviews and intrusions into hospitals have become a thing of the past' (Culf 1993).

Nonetheless, there are still concerns about the behaviour of journalists and the way in which their stories are reported. There are problems in resolving this issue of the freedom of the press, the public's right to know and the privacy of the individual. Additionally, whenever a government makes an attempt to regulate the media, its motives come under scrutiny. Revelations of sleaze, corruption and other immoral behaviour by members of a government might lead the public to believe that any crackdown on 'investigative' methods of journalism was the result of a desire for retribution rather than to create higher standards in the press.

Advertising

Having been the subject of much opprobrium in the consumer rights heyday of the 1970s, advertising sought to clean up its act to prevent statutory control about twenty years ahead of the press. The industry was warned by the newly appointed Director General of Fair Trading and the Minister for Consumer Affairs to strengthen its unsatisfactory system of self-regulation or face legal control.

Now the advertising industry is regulated primarily through the Committee of Advertising Practice which publishes, updates and upholds the British Code of Advertising Practice (BCAP). The Advertising Standards Authority (ASA) investigates complaints about infringements of the BCAP and is also responsible for interpreting the code. Its provisions can be summed up in three statements.

All advertisements should be legal, decent, honest and truthful.

All advertisements should be prepared with a sense of responsibility to the consumer and to society.

All advertisements should conform to the principles of fair competition generally accepted in business.

Although there are similarities between the self regulatory bodies, the PCC and the ASA, there are marked differences in the way they operate in practice. While both bodies deal with complaints from aggrieved members of the public and organisations, the ASA is more active in preventing trouble, for example, by suggesting changes to advertising copy before it appears. Discussions between the ASA and the advertising agency responsible for an ad or commercial can sometimes result in a totally different creative treatment.

Public relations

While it may not be held in high public esteem, the public relations business has avoided the need to defend itself from legal controls. There has been no necessity to set up any kind of complaints machinery to cover the industry as a whole, although the professional bodies concerned will take and investigate complaints of and by their respective members. The only example of statutory regulation specific to public relations is that of the Local Government Acts of 1986 and 1988, which require local authorities to have regard to the Code of Recommended Practice on Local Authority Publicity.

The two main professional bodies which a public relations practitioner may be eligible to join are the IPR and the Public Relations Consultants' Association (PRCA). The former is open to all appropriately qualified applicants. Details of academic and work-experience qualifications currently in force can be found on the IPR's website at www.ipr.org.uk. The PRCA accepts into membership any consultancy which has been operating to a specified level of fee income over a specified period. In addition the British Association of Industrial Editors (BAIE) accepts members who are responsible for producing newsletters and journals for in-house and external audiences. Each body has its own code of practice, which is regularly reviewed and revised to take account of changing business practices and so on. The IPR and the PRCA have recently rewritten their codes so that they are virtually indistinguishable. There has been some talk of possible merger between the two bodies. The IPR's code appears on their website. The codes cover conduct towards the practice of public relations:

A member shall have a positive duty to observe the highest standards ... conform to good practice ... not conduct him or her self in any manner detrimental to the reputation of the Institute or the reputation and interests of the public relations profession.

Conduct towards the public, media and other professionals, such as: 'A member shall conduct his or her professional activities with proper regard to the public interest ... [shall] respect the truth ... honour confidences'.

Conduct towards employers and clients, such as: 'A member shall safeguard the confidences of both present and former employers or clients ... not misuse information [for gain] ... not guarantee the achievement of results'.

And conduct towards colleagues, such as: 'A member shall adhere to the highest standards ... giving credit for ideas and words borrowed from others' (IPR 1999a: 337–43).

Anyone taking membership of the IPR or the PRCA agrees to be bound by its code of practice.

The BAIE's Code of Professional Conduct is starkly practical, dealing in five sentences with integrity of information, confidentiality, injury to other members, reputation of the profession and conformity to legal requirements.

Further afield, the Public Relations Institute of Australia requires of its members that they fly the flag: 'All members shall maintain loyalty to Australia and devotion to high ideals in public and national life' (Potts 1976: 333). While the Public Relations Society of America declares, with echoes of the Constitution:

> Members base their professional principles on the fundamental value and dignity of the individual, holding that the free exercise of human rights, especially freedom of speech, freedom of assembly and freedom of the press, is essential to the practice of public relations.
>
> (Grunig and Hunt 1984: 74–5)

There has been criticism of the UK public relations industry's apparent inability to enforce its codes of conduct. In fact, both bodies do enforce their codes and discipline their members. The IPR's Professional Practices Committee investigates alleged breaches of the code, which may be referred to its Disciplinary Committee for action. However, despite attempts to tighten up the code in 1991 so as to deal more effectively with offenders, a consultancy which was caught apparently tempting freelancers with cash for placing articles in certain trade publications was not initially pursued by the IPR. The overhauled code of professional conduct endorsed at the institute's previous general meeting made it patently clear that such an action breached the industry's ethical code. But there was little attempt to establish whether an offence had taken place or not, despite a very public airing of the matter in *The Times*. Following the coverage, however, the IPR decided to look at the matter again.

In another case the following year the IPR found one of its Fellows, Philip Paul, guilty of conducting himself 'in a manner detrimental to the reputation and interests of the public relations profession' and reprimanded him for publishing an article entitled 'Where has all the PR gone? – a Lambeth mystery', which commented vigorously on his work for a previous employer. A footnote to their report indicates that the offence was not considered particularly grave within the IPR, however: 'The decision did not affect Philip's chairmanship of the IPR's Health and Medical Group' (IPR 1992).

The main enforcement problem for the public relations industry may not be to do with the severity of the punishment but with the lack of control over non-members. Forty per cent of those eligible for full membership of the IPR do not take it, and the figures are much worse for associate membership. The worst offenders are almost certain to be non-members and therefore no sanctions can be taken against them.

As an example, misgivings have been expressed about the reputation of public relations practice following revelations about the 'dirty tricks' tactics alleged to have been authorised or perpetrated by British Airways' public relations director, David Burnside, and public relations consultant, Brian Basham. But as the ex-president of the IPR, Roger Haywood, points out:

> it may be significant that neither David Burnside nor Brian Basham are members of the IPR. If they were, they would both be asked today to account for their behaviour before the professional practices committee of the IPR.
>
> (*PR Week* 1993b)

Although public relations is looking, through the IPR, to raise standards among its members by giving increasing attention to education, training and professional development, promoting its own code, looking to develop joint codes with others, and making its disciplinary procedure more credible, it still needs to address the problem of lack of members. In the eyes of many employers and potential clients, the letters IPR and PRCA may be meaningless. Clearly the industry needs to make a big effort to explain the benefits of membership – and the safeguards for a company of employing or retaining a member of the IPR or PRCA. If the IPR is serious in its attempts to go for chartered status it will in any case have to increase membership. One of the conditions which must be satisfied before application may be made to the Privy Council is that the body concerned must represent over 50 per cent of those practising in the field.

The general usefulness of codes and professional practice guides is in any case questioned by practitioners and academics in the field. Those who practise public relations at a high level, and who thus have control over much of public relations' output, are not usually to be found checking a code of practice before they make a decision.

Summary points

✔ Public relations practice as we know it began in the USA and the UK in the mid-nineteenth century. The early American experience was of press agents and showmen generating publicity. In Britain it was rooted in the concept of public information. In both countries war and peace-time propaganda were formative influences.

✔ Early public relations activities included bribery of journalists and a blurred line between advertising and public relations. Ivy Lee was the first public relations practitioner formally to declare the principles under which he operated on behalf of clients, and to distinguish between editorial coverage and advertising material.

✔ Persuasion, as practised by Bernays in America and Stephen Tallents in Britain, was the major development of the 1920s and 1930s. During the two world wars government departments ran information services, and many former government information officers and propagandists set up in business as public relations consultants in the aftermath of both wars.

✔ British businesses have been slower to embrace public relations than their American counterparts. However, organisations are increasingly seeing the importance of listening to their customers and being held in high esteem by the public. Public relations skills and activities are thus more in demand.

✔ The increasing professionalisation of public relations requires adherence to a code of practice. However, the profession has no disciplinary power over those who are not members of its governing bodies. Even those who are question the need for such a code.

Questions for discussion

1 What does the expression 'It's just a public relations exercise' mean to you? How do you think this expression came about?

2 Do you think former government propagandists would make good public relations consultants? What skills, if any, would you expect to be common to both?

3 'Public relations practice is in need of reform'. Do you agree? What reforms would you like to see implemented and why?

4 How, if at all, do professional codes of conduct affect the behaviour of journalists, advertisers and public relations officers?

Recommended further reading

There are many books and articles about the history and development of public relations, one of the more readable being Ewen (1996). Grunig and Hunt (1983), Cutlip et al. (1994) and Newsom et al. (1993) provide sections or chapters on the US development of public relations practice. Cutlip (1994) gives an account of twentieth-century public relations while Cutlip (1995) covers the period from the seventeenth century. Olasky (1987) gives a critical view of public relations as acting contrary to the public good by suppressing competition between corporations. Pearson (1992) contrasts different approaches to the history of public relations in America. Among the biographies of US public relations practitioners are Wallace (1959) on P.T. Barnum, Hiebert (1966) on Ivy Lee, Hill's (1963) autobiography and Tye (1998) on Bernays.

There is as yet no good history of public relations in the UK in book form but L'Etang (1998b) has written a fascinating journal article on its twentieth-century evolution. An overview of current public relations education in the UK can be found in Harrison and Yeomans (1999).

References

Beder, S. (1998) 'Manipulating Public Knowledge', *Metascience* 7 (1) 132–9.

Bernays, E. (1928) *Propaganda*, New York: Liveright.

Bernays, E. (1952) *Public Relations*, Norman: University of Oklahoma Press.

Bernays papers, Letter from Dr George F. Buchan, Box 85, Library of Congress, cited in Tye (1998).

Bierson, H. (1974) 'The Public Relations Function in the Socially Responsible Corporation' in M. Anshen (ed.) *Managing the Socially Responsible Corporation*, New York: Macmillan.

Black, S. (1989) *Introduction to Public Relations*, London: Modino.

Boorstin, D. (1962) *The Image, or What Happened to the American Dream*, New York: Atheneum.

Culf, A. (1993) 'Press toughens rules to avert statutory curbs', Guardian, 5 May.

Cutlip, S. (1994) *The Unseen Power: Public Relations, a History*, Hillside, NJ: Lawrence Erlbaum Associates.

Cutlip, S. (1995) *Public Relations History from the Seventeenth to the Twentieth Century*, Hillsdale, NJ: Lawrence Erlbaum Associates.

Cutlip, S. and Center, A. (1978) *Effective Public Relations*, 5th edn, Englewood Cliffs, NJ: Prentice Hall.

Diamond, J. (1993) 'Have pen, will travel . . . and get paid for it', *Guardian*, 7 June.

Ewen, S. (1996) *PR! A Social History of Spin*, New York: Basic Books.

Goldman, E. (1948) *Two-way Street: the Emergence of the Public Relations Counsel*, Boston, MA: Bellman.

Grunig, J. and Hunt, T. (1984) *Managing Public Relations*, Orlando, FL: Holt, Rinehart and Winston.

Harrison, S. and Yeomans, L. (1999) 'Public Relations Education in the UK: A Review of Its Relevance to Public Relations Practice' presented to PRSA Educators Academy Research Conference (18–12 June): University of Maryland.

Hiebert, R. (1966) *Courtier to the Crowd: The Story of Ivy L. Lee and the Development of Public Relations*, Ames: Iowa State University Press.

Hill, J. (1963) *The Making of a Public Relations Man*, New York: David McKay.

IPR (1992) 'News Item', *Public Relations: Journal of the IPR*, London, May.

IPR (1999a) *Handbook*, London: Institute of Public Relations.

Jefkins, F. (1992) *Public Relations*, 4th edn, London: Pitman.

L'Etang, J. (1998b) 'State propaganda and bureaucratic intelligence: the creation of public relations in twentieth century Britain', *Public Relations Review* 24 (4) 413–441.

Marston, J. (1979) *Modern Public Relations*, New York: McGraw-Hill.

Olasky, M. (1987) *Corporate Public Relations: A New Historical Perspective*, Hillsdale, NJ: Lawrence Erlbaum Associates.

Pearson, R. (1992) 'Perspectives on Public Relations History', in Toth, E. and Heath, R., *Rhetorical and Critical Approaches to Public Relations*, Hillsdale, NJ: Lawrence Erlbaum Associates.

Potts, J. (1976) *Public Relations Practice in Australia*, Sydney: McGraw Hill.

PR Week (1993b) 'Letters from the Grass Roots', 13 May.

Stauber, J. and Rampton, S. (1995) *Toxic Sludge is Good For You! Lies, Damn Lies and the Public Relations Industry*, Monroe, ME: Common Courage Press.

Tye, L. (1998) *The Father of Spin*, New York: Crown Publishers.

Wallace, I. (1959) *The Fabulous Showman: The Life and Times of P.T. Barnum*, New York: Alfred Knopf.

The theoretical framework

3

Key Issues

The aim of this chapter is to introduce you to the theoretical framework within which public relations is practised. The key points covered are:

▶ communication theory, and an exploration of some of the barriers to communication;

▶ theories which help us understand how people adopt new ideas, such as diffusion theory and the 'hierarchy of effects' model;

▶ game theory, showing its application to media relations;

▶ uses and gratifications theory, which explains how and why people choose the media they use;

▶ Grunig's situational theory of publics and the four models of public relations practice;

▶ Bernstein's Wheel and its use to plan public relations activities.

In addition to requiring entry qualifications of its members, a profession needs to be grounded in a body of theory. Developing theories and testing them to see how they work in practice enables practitioners working in the field to make the best decisions about how they conduct their business. Providing models to show how public relations works in theory can both validate practical public relations programmes and obviate the need to think up a brand new way of tackling each project.

Perhaps because public relations is a relatively recent entrant into the academic world in Britain, most of the theoretical framework comes from the USA. Even in America, where the subject has been on the university syllabus for 70 years, there is a dearth of published theoretical material which is purely related to public relations. Much of what has been written takes models from the social sciences and even from engineering and adapts them to the theory of public relations.

In this chapter we will look at communication theory, borrowed from electrical engineering; game theory, borrowed from the social sciences; uses and gratification theories, from the study of mass communication; and marketing theories, all of which can help in planning a public relations campaign. We will also look at Grunig and Hunt's four models of public relations in practice, and at Grunig's situational theory of publics.

While an increasing number of practitioners know something about such theories, there are many who do not and who have no use for theoretical considerations. When asked why they are doing what they are doing they tend to say that they do things in a particular way because they have an instinct or gut-feeling about it. The practitioner who says 'I do it this way because I've tried it before and it works' is, though, using a model which has previously been constructed, whether or not the person would call it such.

Communication theory

Communication is defined in Webster's Dictionary both as 'the art of expressing ideas' and 'the science of transmitting information'. But this views communication as a one-way process and ignores the recipient's role. The *Shorter Oxford English Dictionary* does better with 'imparting, conveying or exchange of ideas, knowledge etc. by speech, writing or signs', bringing in with 'exchange' the concept of two-way traffic; and with 'signs' the notion that communication can take place without words. Signs and symbols can be very powerful in transmitting information to the recipient, whether or not the message is intended. The company logo, or a status symbol worn ostentatiously on the wrist, communicate a message about the owner; and where would Sherlock Holmes have been without the visual and olfactory clues which he took such pains to observe? Perhaps a better definition of communication is 'the transmission of information and understanding through the use of common symbols' (Gibson et al. 1985: 532).

The classic model of communication was developed by Shannon and Weaver (1948) and Schramm (1953: 3–26), based on five questions: who ... says what ... in what way ... to whom ... with what effect? (Lasswell 1948: 37–51). The basic elements in the process are shown in Figure 3.1.

Taking as an example a telephone call to a university in late August, we can look at these elements in turn to see how communication can fail. The caller is interested in attending a one-day course, run by the Institute of

| **Figure 3.1** | *A model of communication* |

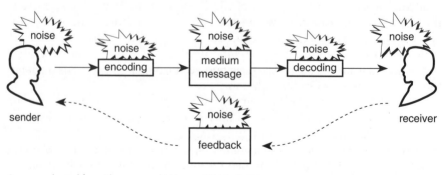

Source: adapted from Shannon and Weaver 1948: 3–26

Public Relations, and to be held at the university in September, before the academic year starts. There are vacancies on the course. The switchboard is inundated with inquiries about degree courses starting in October and in any case has not been told anything about the one-day course.

Sender: the person with information to communicate: the caller.

Encoding: the way in which the information is expressed: spoken English.

Medium: the form in which the message is carried: the telephone.

Message: the information itself as encoded by the sender: 'I'm looking for a place on the Public Relations course'.

Decoding: interpretation – the receiver's thought processes on getting the message: this is a prospective student for the new intake in October; that course is full.

Receiver: the person who receives the information: switchboard operator.

Feedback: the element of the receiver's response which the receiver communicates to the sender: 'That course is full'.

Noise: any kind of interference which results in distortion, so that the receiver gets a different message from the one that was sent: incomplete information.

In this case, the description of a one-day course as 'the Public Relations course' leads to misunderstanding, and the feedback compounds the difficulty: the sender and receiver are talking about two different courses. Clearly, then, to be effective there should be a commonalty of understanding between sender and receiver, that is, they should both be talking about the same thing. 'The course' is precise enough for the sender, who is only interested in one course; the receiver has to cope with inquiries about hundreds of courses and must guess at which course is meant if insufficient clues are given.

Barriers to effective communication

Although the communication model is straightforward, the process of communicating is, as we have seen in the example above, fraught with hazard, and there are many obstacles to the successful communication of a simple message. Receivers may not get the intended message for a number of reasons. Kotler (1984: 605) lists three:

> *selective attention*, in that they will not notice everything around them
> *selective distortion*, in that they will twist the message to hear what they want to hear
> *selective recall*, in that they will retain only a small fraction of the messages that reach them.

He goes on to quote Schramm's view that the likelihood of attention is a function of reward, punishment and expenditure of effort. In essence, if your message is easy to understand and offers high rewards to the receiver, you are more likely to get the receiver's attention.

Noise can appear anywhere in the system and distort the process. David Bernstein suggests that there are three types of noise: channel, psychological and language.

Channel noise

This is physical interference, such as a radio next door or not enough light. Bernstein gives an example in an anecdote about a television commercial for a disinfectant, which pictured a toddler on a kitchen floor.

> The voice-over spoke of the danger areas where germs lurk. Each of the areas was numbered. To emphasise these we had numbers painted on large kiddies' building bricks. Viewers contacted the television station to ask where they could buy – not the disinfectant – the numbered bricks. That's channel noise.
>
> (Bernstein 1986: 29)

Psychological noise

This occurs as a result of the relationship between the sender and receiver, causing the receiver to read something else into the sender's message. Body language may create noise if the posture or gesture give contradictory messages from that spoken by the sender. Bernstein suggests 'Judge the effect of saying "I thought it was a great idea" whilst holding your nose'.

Language noise

This arises from a mismatch of code between sender and receiver. If the message is encoded in a language or set of symbols which are meaningless to the receiver, the receiver cannot successfully decode it. See the hapless parent trying to decode the message of the wailing infant: Are you hungry? Waaaah! Are you tired? Waaaah! Do you hurt somewhere? Waaaah! Each party is urgently trying to communicate in a language which the other does not understand.

More diverting are examples of misunderstanding resulting from language noise. The famous wartime headline is one: EIGHTH ARMY PUSH BOTTLES UP GERMANS. Bernstein also quotes the Canadian motorist who thought the sign FINE FOR PARKING was encouragement rather than a warning.

Figure 3.2 shows eight barriers to effective communication. These are as follows.

Fields of experience

Sender and receiver can only communicate effectively within the area covered by their common fields of experience: the greater the commonalty of experience, the more effective the communication is likely to be. Although the sender and receiver may be using a common language, the encoding/ decoding process is affected by their respective experiences, and the message will thus be set in a different frame of reference for each party. Different fields

Some barriers to communication   **Figure 3.2**

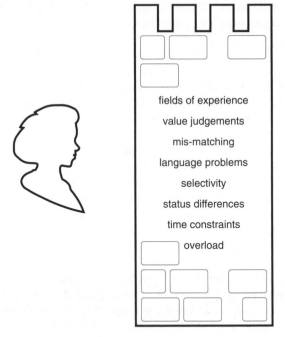

fields of experience

value judgements

mis-matching

language problems

selectivity

status differences

time constraints

overload

of experience explain why the bosses and the workers may have different perceptions of the same message; similarly parents and teenagers, men and women, even consultant and client. If the sender takes care to establish the receiver's field of experience, encoding the message in a way which will enable the receiver to decode it accurately, this barrier can be overcome.

Value judgements

The message may be perceived to be worthless if the receiver has no respect for the source, or if the medium has no credibility. In each case the receiver is making a value judgement which distorts the sender's message. In my household, for example, any envelope coming through the letterbox addressed to 'The Occupier' is deemed to be junk mail and tends to pause only briefly before going into the re-cycling box. The sender's message may have been to offer me a wonderful deal on car insurance, but the message I received was 'junk'. The sender can only counteract the effect of value judgements if research has been done to find out what the receiver's opinion is of the sender and the sender's previous messages. The most important factors in source credibility are expertise, trustworthiness and likeability.

Mis-matching

Where there is a significant mis-match between the medium chosen and the message it relates to, or an inappropriate medium is used by the sender, the message will be distorted. One of the rules of business is that if you vacate premises, take your name off the building. Otherwise your message, your company name, may become associated with decline: broken windows, fly-posted activities of dubious legality, or simply bankruptcy.

Language problems

Even when both sender and receiver are native speakers of the same language, misunderstandings can occur. Simple words such as 'big', 'cheap' and 'old' can mean different things to sender and receiver. The word 'soon' may mean 'now' to the child and 'not now' to the parent who says it. Language problems are made worse by the use of technical terms and jargon. While it is right to use the correct term, it is also vital in transmitting understanding for the sender to check that the receiver understands the meaning of the words used. Sometimes it is better to have a non-expert write an instruction manual intended for non-experts, and then run it past the expert for checking.

Selectivity

As we have already seen, Kotler identifies selectivity in attention, distortion and recall. It is characteristic for people to block out what they do not want to hear, and only to retain messages that reinforce what they already believe. This is why it is hard to persuade people to do something different: for example, to wear seat-belts in cars – so hard, in fact, that a law had to be passed to make it compulsory. A company with a poor reputation has an uphill struggle to convince its customers that it is doing a good job, even when it is. Ask any rail commuter how often their train is late and it will almost certainly be more often than the rail operator indicates in its performance reports.

Status differences

Differences in class, wealth or position in the hierarchy can all affect communication. At its most extreme, sender and receiver may never meet, never know anything about each other, and yet need to communicate. In organisations status differences are sometimes institutionalised, such as the factory which has eight different grades of canteen for its workforce. Some managers are so protected from their subordinates by their secretaries that there is no hope of communication between them. While this may help the manager's time-management, it acts as a barrier to communication and helps create a negative value judgement. Where status differences cannot be reduced, a solution may be to pass the message via a sender who is closer in status to the receiver.

Time constraints

It may not always be possible to communicate effectively because of time constraints. For example, your leaflet may need colour pictures to show the product at its best, but you may not have time to get colour printing done: if you use black and white you may distort the message. Lack of time is often the reason given for failing to research the audience for a message, but lack of knowledge of the receiver's language, status, values and experience are all barriers to communication. The answer lies in planning. A timetable for a communications programme should work backwards from what you want to do, to include the time taken to do it properly. Even in a crisis situation, forward planning helps the sender to deliver the message effectively.

Overload

The growth and increasing sophistication of information technology, with the advent of affordable desk-top publishing systems and accurate databases, means that there are many more messages aimed at the receiver than he or she can take in. Consequently the receiver screens some out, on the basis of their provenance, perhaps, or because they arrive at a busy time. These messages do not even get decoded, so there is no hope of effective communication. Close targeting can reduce the quantity of messages from any one sender, but the sender has no control over the amount landing on the doorstep of the receiver.

These, then, are some of the barriers to effective communication. We will now go on to look at some social science theories which have relevance to public relations and the communication process.

Diffusion theory and the hierarchy of effects

How do people process information and adopt new ideas? Without venturing too deeply into psychology at this stage, we can look at what diffusion theory has to say. According to diffusion theory (Lionberger 1960: 32, cited in Baskin et al. 1997: 60), an individual will adopt an idea only after going through five distinct stages. These are:

1 *awareness*: becoming aware of the idea;

2 *interest*: the individual's interest has to be aroused;

3 *evaluation*: consideration of how useful the idea is;

4 *trial*: trying out the idea on others;

5 *adoption*: final acceptance of the idea.

Creating awareness is often the objective of a mass-communication programme, for example, using the media.

Kotler (1984: 611–3) brings together a number of marketing models to demonstrate what he terms the 'response hierarchy'. Each seeks to elicit a response from the prospective customer or public to which they are directed. The response may be:

cognitive: trying to put something into the mind of the respondent;

affective: attempting to affect or change the respondent's attitude;

behavioural: getting the respondent to do something.

Although these models are drawn from marketing and are aimed at buyer response, they can be adapted to be useful for public relations. A cognitive response in public relations terms may be to make a specified public aware of the name of an issue or a new product; the affective response may be to have the public think kindly of the matter, and the behavioural response may be for them to join your campaign, make a donation to your cause or simply go out and look for your product.

Kotler uses the hierarchy of effects model, but the communications model is probably more appropriate for us. Using as an example the National Children's Home for Runaways, winner of the Grand Prix in the 1992 *PR Week* Awards, we can see both in the Case Study and in Table 3.1 how the target public passed through the three 'buyer readiness' stages.

Case Study 3.1

'Buyer readiness'

National Children's Home for Runaways

Cognitive stage

There were plenty of stories about young runaways leaving the north for a life of crime in London, but the National Children's Home (NCH) set out to find out the reality of the situation. They published a report based on the findings of research into 17,000 cases of missing children. Five thousand copies of a summary were sent to MPs, peers and senior policy-makers in the police and local authorities. Following a press launch with the actress Jane Asher and a number of former runaways at Victoria station, extensive media coverage ensured that the issue was firmly in the minds of the target public – those who could do something about it.

Affective stage

The attitude of the target audience began to change. One thousand five hundred copies of the full report, priced at £10, were requested by and sold to police and social services departments. A national conference on runaways attracted over 150 influential policy-makers. Clearly the issue of runaways was in the news, and something had better be done. During the media campaign and immediately after it, the NCH lobbied MPs and peers and in July the House of Lords debated the report's findings. The government subsequently announced its intention to act.

Behavioural stage

The government agreed to establish a Missing Persons Bureau and to hold the first ever inter-departmental meeting on runaways.

(Source: author)

| | | Table 3.1 |

'Buyer awareness' communication model in action

Stages	Response	NCH case
Cognitive	Exposure–reception–cognitive response	▶ Research and report received by target publics ▶ Media coverage ▶ Message received and understood
Affective	Attitude–intention	▶ Concern shown by target publics; purchase of report ▶ Attitude changes demonstrated at conference ▶ Government intentions announced
Behavioural	Behaviour	▶ Agreement to establish Missing Persons Bureau ▶ Meeting on runaways

Source: adapted from Kotler (1984: 612). Reprinted by permission of Prentice Hall

These models illustrate the importance of knowing in advance the kind of response sought from a target public so that the most appropriate route can be chosen to achieve the result.

Game theory

Developed in the 1950s, game theory has been applied to sociology, anthropology, psychology, economics and even to the study of evolution. Dealing as it does with situations of conflict and co-operation, it could prove useful in modelling the public relations process. Game theory looks at the essential elements present in a competitive situation and studies them in order to find the best probable outcomes for each or all of the players.

The 'players' in the public relations 'game' could be a public relations practitioner and a public, such as the readers of the financial press. Let us look at an example.

> To take an example of a simple public relations 'game', a company may need to decide exactly when to distribute a news release about its quarterly earnings. In order to get maximum publicity, the company wants to publish earnings before its chief competitor does; otherwise, it may receive less attention in shared coverage. In game theory terms, this is a classic 'duel' situation in which the opponent's strategy is not known. Most practitioners would solve this game by instinct and historical experience. But game theoretical guidelines can suggest which strategy will lead to the best outcome for this dilemma.
>
> (Murphy 1989: 176)

Different types of game are identified within game theory.

Zero-sum games are games in which, if one player does well, the other must do badly, that is, if player A scores ten points, player B must lose ten points. The sum of their gains and losses will always equal zero. In public relations terms:

> a reporter may obtain some information that would considerably damage a company's reputation if revealed – but publishing it would enhance the reporter's reputation equivalently. Company A's loss is Reporter B's gain. In specific terms, the *New York Times'* publication of the Pentagon Papers might be construed as a zero-sum game.
>
> (ibid.)

This is very much an adversarial game, pitting one player against the other, and not likely to be much encountered in the world of public relations.

Non-zero-sum games, however, give all players the opportunity to gain some points, and have more to do with the mutuality of good public relations. Co-operation between players is valued above straight winning and losing, as the point of the game is for all players to get a pay-off of some kind. Olasky, who sees a conspiracy between corporations and government to present an untrue picture of corporate America, would probably see theirs as a non-zero-sum game, played without the general public getting a seat at the table.

Games of timing hinge on the importance of making your play at the right moment. In public relations terms, is it better to release information at one time than another? A good press officer will know by heart the times when local newspapers go to press, when local news is featured on radio and television, and deadlines for weekly or monthly publications, and will almost certainly be castigated by one of the media for giving unfair advantage to another through timing of an announcement.

Bargaining games require the players to negotiate with one another in order to achieve the best possible outcome for all concerned. In August 1993 the British government launched Operation Irma to bring a little girl out of Sarajevo to a British hospital for treatment. There immediately followed calls for further evacuations of sick and wounded Serbs. Over the following few days there were reports of bargaining going on between the medical staff in Sarajevo, the United Nations representatives and the British to ensure that appropriate patients were evacuated. Critics said that Britain only wanted photogenic children so that they could gain a public relations victory for a deeply unpopular government. The medical authorities in Sarajevo wanted to be given the resources to be able to treat patients themselves. The UN's assessment committee wanted to keep responsibility for making decisions on medical grounds. In the event, a mixture of patients was airlifted out, but the press on the whole were cynical about the motives of the 'players' in this bargaining game. Although Irma's story left the front pages long ago, this example is typical of the way in which bargaining games continue to be played, especially when different parties are looking to position themselves in a way which gives them greater advantage.

Murphy (op. cit.) gives a lengthy example of a bargaining game, in which Smith, the public relations director of XYZ company, has to decide how to deal with expected media coverage of the firm's decision to make 250 employees redundant. Meanwhile Jones, an ambitious reporter on the local paper, has had a call from an XYZ employee who is distraught at the rumours that XYZ is to lay off 500 staff. The paper is due to go to press in an hour. Table 3.2 shows how a table might be constructed to enable Smith and Jones to deal with the story with the best possible outcomes for both.

The numerical values given to the pay-offs do not denote a real value. They are simply shown to indicate the relative merits to each participant of each action. Nor is it for a moment suggested that Smith and Jones would go through the laborious process of producing such a table before making decisions on what to do. However, they would probably both be doing something akin to mental arithmetic – each considering the pay-offs and disadvantages attaching to all the possibilities, before deciding how to proceed.

While public relations practitioners may find this somewhat sterile and technical, the approach does have some merits, not least that of imposing an orderly and logical procedure on to an unstable situation. In addition, the use of game theory as a predictor of outcomes can be valuable in assessing the likely effect of a public relations programme on its publics. In crisis planning and issues management, game theory can be used to work through what-if? scenarios to determine the likely best courses of action.

Uses and gratifications

Uses and gratification theory is a way of classifying how people select and use the media available to them. People use the news, and especially the broadcast, media for the following:

as entertainment
to scan the environment for items important to them personally
as a diversion (for example, when the television is on and no one is in the room)
as a substitute for personal relationships
as a check on personal identity and values

(Baskin et al. 1997: 62–3)

This underlines the difference between output and outcome in public relations. *Output* is simply what is put out, in the form of news features, articles, items on television or messages in an employee's pay packet. If the intended recipient is not interested in the output or is in some way (by noise, for example) prevented from receiving it clearly, then he or she will simply choose not to take it in. The desired *outcome*, a change in awareness, opinion or behaviour, will not be achieved.

Grunig and Hunt's theories

A situational theory of publics

It is essential to be able to identify publics, to estimate how best to reach them and to watch out for the barriers that exist in communicating with

Table 3.2	*Game theory in public relations planning: sample pay-offs for XYZ Company story outcomes*

Main outcome	Contingent effects	Smith* pay-off	Jones† pay-off
	OUTCOME 1		
NO STORY		+10	0
S & J discuss potential lay-offs. J decides material not timely enough	Relieved XYZ President/Disappointed news ed.	+8	−5
	S pleased/J disappointed	−2	+8
	TOTAL	**+16**	**+3**
	OUTCOME 2		
NO STORY		+10	−8
S stonewalls. J can't get material soon enough to print	Relieved XYZ President/News ed. angry at J	+10	−10
	S gloats/J feels cheated	−10	−2
	TOTAL	**+10**	**−20**
	OUTCOME 3		
POSITIVE STORY		+8	+2
S uses lay-offs to promote XYZ's progressive outplacement programme	XYZ President pleased/News ed. wonders about a con	+10	−3
	S pleased by J's compliance/J wonders about a con	−3	+8
	TOTAL	**+15**	**+7**
	OUTCOME 4		
NEUTRAL STORY		−2	+8
S and J go over facts. Story seen as newsworthy but not a major economic blow	Uneasy XYZ President/mildly pleased news ed.	−3	+2
	S feels treatment was fair/J feels S was honest	+8	+3
	TOTAL	**+3**	**+13**
	OUTCOME 5		
NEUTRAL–NEGATIVE STORY		−8	−5
S levels with J. J's story compares this event with previous lay-offs	XYZ President displeased/news ed. pleased	−8	+8
	S feels betrayed/J feels S deserved story	−8	−10
	TOTAL	**−24**	**−7**
	OUTCOME 6		
SENSATIONAL STORY		−10	−10
S explains facts of lay-offs. J reports 'major economic setback'	Angry XYZ President/pleased news ed.	−10	−5
	S is furious/J feels S deserved story	−8	−10
	TOTAL	**−28**	**−15**
	OUTCOME 7		
SENSATIONAL STORY		−10	−10
S stonewalls. J retaliates by printing exaggerated rumoured numbers	Angry XYZ President/news ed. feels vindicated	−10	+5
	S is furious/J feels vindicated	−10	−10
	TOTAL	**−30**	**−15**

*Smith is PR director for XYZ Company. His pay-offs based on impact of story on: public opinion of the company; probable opinion of his boss about his actions; Jones' probable opinion of his co-operativeness.

†Jones is a reporter on local newspaper. Her pay-offs based on: degree to which the story reflected reality; opinion of her boss about her actions; Smith's probable opinion of the resulting coverage.

Source: adapted from Murphy in H. Botan and V. Hazleton (eds) (1989) *Public Relations Theory*. Reproduced with permission from Lawrence Erlbaum Associates, Inc.

them. James Grunig has added a further refinement by introducing the situational theory of identifying publics. He proposes a set of independent variables to find out whether or not communications with publics will be effective: these are problem recognition, constraint recognition and level of involvement. If a public does not *recognise the problem* then they will not be in a position to communicate or receive communication about it. Even if they recognise it, they may be too overwhelmed by the *constraints* they perceive as getting in the way of a solution to concern themselves with the problem. They may recognise the problem and feel able to cope with the constraints, but if they do not see a connection between themselves and the problem they will not become *involved*.

Grunig uses his theory to identify different types of publics ranging from the apathetic or uninvolved through latent publics to the aware and active publics. He groups them into activist, apathetic, all-issue and single-issue publics. Having placed publics into the appropriate category, the public relations practitioner can make more informed decisions on the best ways of reaching them (Grunig and Hunt 1984: 147–61).

Four models of public relations

Looking at the evolution of the public relations business, Grunig and Hunt (1984: 22) described four types of public relations as models in theory and in practice. Their characteristics are shown in Table 3.3.

The *press agentry/publicity* model's purpose is propaganda, and communication is one-way, from sender to receiver. This model allows for economy

Characteristics of four models of public relations				**Table 3.3**
	Model			
Characteristic	Press agentry/publicity	Public information	Two-way asymmetric	Two-way symmetric
Purpose	Propaganda	Dissemination of information	Scientific persuasion	Mutual understanding
Nature of communication	one-way; truth not essential	one-way; truth important	two-way; imbalanced effects	two-way; balanced effects
Communication model	Source–receiver	Source–receiver	Source–receiver–source (feedback)	Group–group
Nature of research	Little; 'counting the house'	Little; readability, readership	Formative; evaluates attitudes	Formative; evaluates understanding
Leading figures	P.T. Barnum	Ivy Lee	Edward L. Bernays	Bernays, educators, professional leaders
Where practised now	Sports, theatre, product promotion	Government, non-profit organisations, business	Competitive business, agencies	Regulated business, agencies
Organisations practising now (estimated)	15 per cent	50 per cent	20 per cent	15 per cent

Source: adapted from Grunig and Hunt (1984: 22)

with the truth. There is little concern for research: 'counting the house' – bottoms on seats at the event – is enough. The most famous exponent is Phineas Barnum. This model is still widely practised in sports, theatre and product promotion and accounts for about 15 per cent of public relations activity nowadays. Those using it have something to promote or sell.

The *public information* model is used to disseminate information to one or more publics. It is one-way, from sender to receiver, but truth is important. Research may be undertaken to establish that the information to be transmitted is understandable by the target public, and data may be collected to determine who and how many of the public received the information. The leading historical figure for this model is Ivy Lee. It is estimated that this model is the most widely used today, by perhaps 50 per cent of organisations, primarily government (local and national), non-commercial organisations of all kinds, and business in general. They use press releases, leaflets, reports, guides, fact-packs, videos and exhibitions to tell their publics about their existence or functions.

The *two-way asymmetric* model uses scientific persuasion, as propounded by Edward Bernays. Communication is two-way, from sender to receiver and with feedback from the receiver, but the power lies with the sender, whose intention is to persuade the receiver to accept and support the sender organisation. The organisation is not changed by the process, but intends that the attitudes of the receiver shall be. Research is undertaken to establish what attitudes the public have so that the campaign can be formed (hence the term formative research) to be most effective. About 20 per cent of organisations use this model. The purpose of the feedback they receive is solely to help organisations target their messages in a way acceptable to the publics. An example is the way in which cosmetics manufacturers and retailers have discerned the changed attitudes of their customers to animal testing and environmental concerns. Such companies now make much of their commitment to no (or less) animal testing, less or re-usable packaging and banning aerosols which use CFCs.

The *two-way symmetric* model is based on the ideal of mutual understanding. It is truly two-way, taking the form of a kind of dialogue between the organisation and the public; both parties are capable of being persuaded to modify their attitudes or behaviour as a result of the public relations activity. Edward Bernays was a leading proponent of this model, as are the academics and professional bodies of today. Research attempts to evaluate understanding. It is estimated that about 15 per cent of organisations, largely those who are regulated and thus must be seen to be socially responsible, use this model. Typical activities include the use of focus groups to discuss an issue of common concern. For example, the police may organise meetings between their representatives and the local community to discuss the problem of car thefts in the area and to try and achieve an improvement in behaviour or conviction rates. At the end of the process, the police should have a better idea about the concerns of the community, how it operates and what it wants; the community should understand what the police can and cannot do to solve the problem.

Models present abstractions of the real world, and no one would seriously suggest that public relations practitioners operate according to only one of the four models all the time. It can be helpful to refer to them, though, when considering what action to recommend to solve a communication problem using public relations.

Bernstein's wheel

The final model for consideration in this chapter is that drawn up by David Bernstein (1984: 117–24). Although this model is an abstraction, it differs from those we have already considered in that it can be used as a tool or a checklist to plan public relations activities.

A version of the wheel is shown in Figure 3.3. It differs from the original in replacing 'public relations' with 'media relations', as the other channels can all be viewed as public relations activities. Let us look at the wheel in detail and see how it works.

The communication wheel | **Figure 3.3**

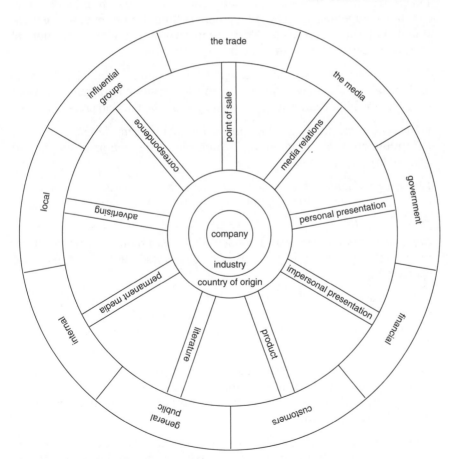

Source: adapted from Bernstein 1986: 124

The organisation planning to communicate is at the centre or hub of the wheel. It is set in the context of its sector and country of origin, so that, for example Peugeot is a French company in the motor-manufacturing sector. Thus when Peugeot communicates with its publics, the receivers filter the company's message through their perceptions of the motor industry as a whole and through their view of France and French goods.

The spokes of the wheel are the channels of communication which the organisation could use to reach its desired publics: there are nine channels. The rim of the wheel is made up of those publics, and there are nine of these. Some spokes seem more suited to some publics, the clearest example being media relations and the media. However, a wheel was chosen as the model because it rotates. Imagine that you could turn the spokes within the wheel. Any one channel could line up with any one public, giving 81 combinations of medium and audience.

The channels of corporate communication are:

Product or service: what is it? how does it perform? how is it branded and packaged? The product or service and how it is delivered to the public passes a message from the organisation to the receiver.

Literature: annual reports, leaflets and brochures, handbooks and manuals, bulletins, employee newsletters and house-journals, educational material for schools. The design, wording and presentation of literature convey messages in addition to the words.

Media relations: news releases, press conferences, launches and facility visits for journalists. This may mean getting the organisation known to the media or trying to shift negative attitudes by attracting favourable press coverage.

Permanent media: these are the signs, vehicles, uniforms, letterheads, even the architecture of the buildings, which reflect the company's style and personality.

Personal presentation: person-to-person or group presentations are a way of communicating with a small target public. This channel is regularly used in internal communication.

Impersonal presentation: includes video, slides, exhibitions (although these may include personal presentation elements), notice-boards, and sponsorship.

Correspondence: the style and use of letters, faxes, telex and memos often reveal more about an organisation than it would like. Carefully targeted direct-mail to a public, internal or external, can, however, be effective if used appropriately.

Advertising: corporate (as opposed to brand or product) advertising seeks to give a message about the organisation as a whole along the lines of 'here's who we are, here's what we can do for you and here's what we think' (Worcester 1983).

Point of sale: generally used for displays, special offers and competitions, all of which are communicated to the receiver at the time of purchase.

They are purely promotional tools and not much used in corporate communication.

Any one or more of these channels can be used to convey messages to the target audiences.

The audiences or publics for corporate communication are:

Internal: the staff employed by the organisation as individuals, and those representing the staff, for example union representatives and works committees.

Local: the local community, including members of other publics such as the staff, the local media and local government.

Influential groups: activist and pressure groups may or may not be influential; voluntary groups such as residents associations or the local history society, chambers of commerce and trade and political groups may all have, or seek to exert, influence on the organisation and/or public opinion of its activities.

The trade: includes all suppliers of services and distributors used by the organisation, together with other organisations in the same sector; they may all be identified with the organisation itself when good or bad publicity ensues.

Government: local and national; possibly supra-national, in the sense that those who have passed laws to regulate commercial or industrial behaviour will take an interest in the behaviour of any organisation operating in that sphere.

The media: the local, regional, national and international press, television and radio, the trade and technical press, and specialist magazines and journals operating in your field.

Financial: banks or other institutional investors, shareholders and opinion leaders in the financial community such as influential City journalists.

Customers: those who receive the organisation's goods or services, whether they pay for them directly or through taxation, for example. Customers may be internal (within the organisation) or external and may or may not be customers by choice.

General public: everyone with an interest in the organisation, including potential and past employees and customers of the organisation, and anyone who could influence decisions or opinions about the organisation.

Bernstein's wheel, or one's own customised version of it, can help a public relations officer or consultant to think through the process of communicating the organisation's message. The wheel acts as a prompt: who do I want to reach? It reminds the user of the available methods: how shall I reach them? By using the company sector and country of origin, it sets the organisation in context and reminds the user of the corporate nature of the communication process. This should stimulate fresh ideas and a well-co-ordinated public relations plan.

Summary points

✔ Communication is the transmission of information and understanding through the use of common symbols. The basic elements of the process are the source; the receiver; the message, which is encoded by the source and decoded by the receiver; and feedback.

✔ Noise can get into the communication process at any stage and distort the message. Receivers may not get the intended message because of their selective attention, selective distortion or selective recall. Channel noise, psychological noise and language noise can all interfere with the message.

✔ There are many barriers to effective communication. Equally there are ways of reducing and eliminating these. Game theory can be applied to public relations to help the practitioner judge what would be the best strategy to adopt to accomplish the most favourable outcome. It provides a useful mechanism for use in what-if? scenarios. The hierarchy of effects model used in marketing theory can be adapted for public relations practice. The cognitive stage may be to generate awareness, the affective stage to gain interest and acceptance, and the behavioural stage to produce the desired action.

✔ Grunig and Hunt's four models of public relations practice cover press agentry/publicity, public information, two-way asymmetric and two-way symmetric models. The public information model is thought to be the most widely practised.

✔ Bernstein's wheel, which shows the organisation in its industry and geographical context, can be used to match channels of communication to appropriate publics.

Questions for discussion

The Jacobs Engineering Group has decided to sell off one of its smaller companies, Alexander plc. The directors of Alexander are attempting a management buy-out. The company's public relations manager needs to consider how she will construct and transmit messages to Alexander's publics, who are generally unsure as to what is happening.

1 What are the likely barriers to communication between the management of Alexander and the following publics: staff; shareholders; customers? How might they be overcome?

2 Demonstrate how game theory could be used to determine Alexander's public relations strategy for dealing with Jacobs; the media; potential investors.

3 How could the public relations manager make use of the buyer awareness model of communication to achieve her objectives?

4 Show how the public relations manager could use Bernstein's wheel to plan her public relations campaign.

Recommended further reading

In addition to the appropriate sections of Cutlip et al. (1994) (Chapters 7 and 8), Newsom et al. (1993) (chapter 7), Grunig and Hunt (1984) (much of parts I and II), and Fischer in Baskin et al. (1997), there are a number of texts which concentrate solely on theory and are recommended at an introductory level. McQuail (1994) is generally considered to be an excellent introduction to mass-communication theory and is now in its third edition. At a more advanced level, Windahl et al. (1992) is particularly helpful on the uses of communication theory, while Van Riel (1995) concentrates on corporate identity and corporate image and provides a number of models. Botan and Hazelton (1994) is a useful American text.

References

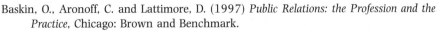

Baskin, O., Aronoff, C. and Lattimore, D. (1997) *Public Relations: the Profession and the Practice*, Chicago: Brown and Benchmark.

Bernstein, D. (1986) *Company Image and Reality*, London: Cassell.

Botan, C. and Hazelton, V. (1994) *Public Relations Theory*, Hillsdale, NJ: Lawrence Erlbaum Associates.

Fischer, R. (1997) 'A Theoretical Basis for Public Relations', in Baskin et al., op. cit.

Gibson, J., Ivancevich, J. and Donnelly, J. (1985) *Organizations*, Plano, TX: Business Publications.

Kotler, P. (1984) *Marketing Management*, Englewood Cliffs, NJ: Prentice Hall.

Lasswell, H. (1948) *Power and Personality*, New York: Norton.

Lionberger, H. (1960) *Adoption of New Ideas and Practices*, Ames: Iowa State University Press.

McQuail, D. (1994) *Mass Communication Theory*, London: Sage.

Murphy, R. (1989) 'Game Theory as a Paradigm for the Public Relations Process', in Botan and Hazelton, 1994, op. cit.

Schramm, W. (1953) 'How Communication Works', in W. Schramm (ed.), *The Process and Effects of Mass Communication*, Urbana, IL: University of Illinois Press.

Shannon, C. and Weaver, W. (1948) *The Mathematical Theory of Communications*, Urbana, IL: University of Illinois Press.

Van Riel, C. (1995) *Principles of Corporate Communication*, London: Prentice Hall.

Windahl, S., Signitzer, B. and Olson, J. (1992) *Using Communication Theory*, London: Sage.

Worcester, R. (1983) 'Measuring the Impact of Corporate Advertising', *Admap* September.

4

Planning for results

Key Issues

The aim of this chapter is to help you understand the public relations planning process. The key points covered are:

▶ the factors which lead to effective planning of public relations programmes, including the importance of monitoring and control;

▶ the increasing focus of the industry on evaluation;

▶ the role of research in public relations planning and evaluation;

▶ the different types of public relations provision and the advantages of in-house, consultancy and hybrid forms of public relations practice.

Whether the public relations practitioner draws up a game plan or spins Bernstein's wheel, some form of planning is underway. It is natural to assume that planning always precedes action, but that is not always the case, in the world of public relations or anywhere else for that matter. Planning is often replaced by responding to requests. Instead of planning an advertising campaign, a food manufacturer may say to an advertising agency 'I want a 48-sheet poster with a picture of my soup on it'.

In the same way, a timber merchant, worried about imminent changes in regulations on the sale of timber, may say to a public relations consultancy 'Can you do me a leaflet explaining why we're changing from imperial to metric measurement?'. The consultant's reaction to this may be 'Yes, of course'. It takes a little courage to reply by asking the client what the company is trying to achieve, and to offer a different solution from the ubiquitous A4 gatefold.

In Chapter 3 we looked at a model of communication which could be summed up as 'Who says what to whom and with what effect?'. A model of planning for communication could take a similar form: 'Why do we want to say what to whom; how shall we do it and how measure its effectiveness?'. This is shown as a simple model in Figure 4.1.

Why: aims and objectives

Planning starts with analysis. It may mean going back to basics and analysing what the organisation is for, what its business is and where it is

A model of communication planning | **Figure 4.1**

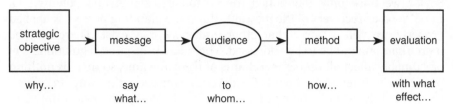

Source: Author

trying to position itself. Certainly no public relations planning should begin until the organisation is sure of the answers to these strategic questions. Let us assume for the purposes of this chapter, however, that the organisation has done its strategic groundwork and now plans to undertake some public relations activity.

Staying with our example of the timber merchant, whom we will call GoodWood, the company's overall public relations aims may be to increase its customer numbers and maintain its reputation for customer service. The objective of this particular public relations activity may be to forewarn customers of the change to metric measurement, so that they are not inconvenienced unnecessarily.

Generally, an aim is an indication of the broad direction in which you want to go. An objective is more specific: something which you want to achieve. So the objective of keeping the customer happy by producing a leaflet on measurements would fall into the general aim of maintaining a reputation for customer service. If the leaflet were particularly helpful, or GoodWood the only company to have thought of producing something like it, the leaflet might also help meet the aim of increasing GoodWood's customers: new customers might be attracted by the tone and content of the leaflet, in contrast to the lack of information provided by their usual supplier.

What: the message

While the message may seem straightforward, it pays to look again at what you want to say, and make sure you have got it right. GoodWood may think that the message is 'From 1 October all our products will be sold in metric measurements instead of feet and inches'. When prompted to think again, the client may add to the message, 'and we apologise for any inconvenience to our customers'.

The public relations consultant's view of the message could be different: 'The European Union insists we use metric measurement; we understand that this will inconvenience you; but we will help you adapt and do your job better'. The message may not be in that form, but the gist will be to deflect criticism from the company and to reinforce its reputation for caring for the customer.

Who: the receiver

So far we have only mentioned the customers, actual and potential, of GoodWood as receivers of the message. But if the planning process is applied properly, we will discover that other audiences may exist. There may be more than one public to be addressed. The new EU-inspired regulations will presumably affect all timber merchants at the same time, so there is nothing particularly interesting about GoodWood. However, the way in which GoodWood deals with the change may offer the company opportunities to work towards its aims by reaching other audiences.

GoodWood's reputation for customer service could be enhanced if the trade journal for the timber business ran an article on the company's efforts. A newsworthy event connected with the change might interest the local and national press and consumer programmes. Even within the public which we have called 'customers', there may be more than one audience to address. Customers may range from the occasional do-it-yourselfer, who knows very little about the products and how to use them, through the enthusiast, or the joiner running a small business, to a large firm of building contractors. Treating all the audiences as if they are the same may be counter-productive, and could result in alienating one or more of the publics being addressed.

How: the programme of activity

The 'how' of public relations planning includes when, where and how much: a timetabled and costed programme of activity. There will be some clear constraints, such as the completion date, which in our example needs to be before 1 October – but how long before? The amount of money which GoodWood is willing to pay for the activity will also be a constraint.

Once the resource constraints are agreed, this is the time for the public relations consultancy to give vent to its creativity and imagination. We know what the message is and to whom it is to be communicated, but how shall we do it? We could hold an open day at GoodWood's premises and produce give-away ready-reckoners. We could send out press releases or contact a few key individuals in the media and brief them. We could recommend taking a public announcement-style advertisement in the press. We could lobby the Department of Trade and Industry to do the advertising instead. We could write a personal letter to all our account customers. Or should we simply do what the client first asked us to do: produce an A4 gatefold leaflet for customers to pick up when they come to buy?

We are now beginning to see that there are many possible ways of tackling this issue, and that responding to the client's initial request is only one of a range of solutions.

How effective: evaluation

The first thing to remember about evaluation is that it only applies to something which can be measured against a standard. If you do not know what people think of you before you undertake a public relations programme, there is little point in asking them what they think of you when the programme is complete, for you will not be able to draw any sensible conclusions about effectiveness.

A surprising amount of rubbish is written about evaluation, both by those who believe it is a chimera in public relations practice, and those who have devised (and will sell you at a hefty price) complicated pseudo-scientific systems for measuring success. However, evaluation is a vital element of public relations planning and practice and is increasingly seen by practitioners and their clients (who, after all, have to pay for it in the end) as worth doing. The industry is making attempts to standardise evaluation systems and *PR Week* has included in its annual awards a new category – the Proof Award. The 1998 winner's evaluation system is outlined in Case Study 4.1.

GoodWood may evaluate the effectiveness of this particular programme of activity by simply calculating market-share before and after the change, or by counting the customers on a typical day before and after the event. They may commission a small survey which asks customers questions about how they found the change-over and gives them the chance, prompted or not, to say what they thought was good or bad about GoodWood's attempts to help them. The public relations consultancy may collect favourable press clippings about GoodWood which have resulted from their efforts, and

---

Evaluation

Case Study 4.1

BATV: British Airways

BATV is the internal communications television system provided by British Airways. The project itself has a £3.5 million budget, £100,000 of which has been spent on research and evaluation. In the summer of 1997 focus groups, consisting of a cross section of BA employees, provided information on what employees thought about the company and BATV, helping determine future BATV formats and editorial positioning.

There are ongoing types of research and measurement. Diagnostic and development work captures audience reaction to style and content; comments about viewing locations and installations are picked up in discussion at different UK sites each week, international locations being less frequently visited but covered by telephone research; performance against strategic objectives is tested by external researchers according to agreed criteria; and operational research is conducted to provide information on viewing figures, habits and barriers to viewing. BA also conducts research to evaluate the performance of its contractors.

BATV won the 1998 *PR Week* Proof Award. The judging panel commented on the consistent use of research, not only for evaluation purposes, but also to shape the future development of BATV.

(*Source: PR Week* Public Relations Awards 1998)

| **Figure 4.2** | *Contunuing model of evaluation* |

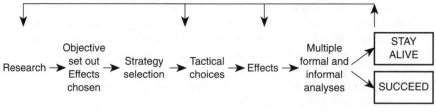

Source: Watson (1997)

may bind these in an impressive folder, with tables showing how much it would have cost GoodWood to get such coverage if they had had to pay for advertising.

Whenever a public relations campaign is evaluated, valuable lessons are learned by the public relations practitioner and the client. The results of the activity help the client to see how the company is doing, so that the company's public relations strategy overall can be revisited and, if necessary, revised. Figure 4.2 shows this dynamic model in action.

In-house or consultancy

In the example of GoodWood, the company retained a public relations consultancy to help formulate public relations strategy and to undertake public relations activity on its behalf. Many companies and other organisations, however, employ their own staff to do this work. Such in-house units can range from a single press officer to a staff of fifty or more, while consultants can operate from their sitting room or from a multi-storey office block. Companies such as British Airways, whose evaluation activities are described in Case Study 4.1, use a combination of an in-house public relations department with specialist companies contracted to provide certain services. There are a number of advantages of both the in-house and the consultancy approach (see Table 4.1), and there is a variety of 'mixtures'.

In-house

The major advantages which in-house provision has over consultancies are listed below.

Full-time

The in-house public relations staff work full time for the organisation, and are available to the organisation at any time they are needed. They are never working on another account, and when in-house staff are on holiday, off sick or otherwise absent, there is usually someone else looking after their work.

In-house	Consultancy
Full-time	Independent
One client	Collective experience
Up to date on client's business	Up to date on media
Good communication and access to client	Access to suppliers
Continuity	Specialist expertise
On the spot	Additional locations
Response to media inquiries	Close to media centres
Staff loyalty, ownership	Short-term, renewable contracts
Trust	Costs

In-house or consultancy: the advantages **Table 4.1**

One client

In-house staff usually only have one client: their employer. Thus there can be no conflict of interest between one account and another, and the chance of the same person working on a specific area of business for the whole time is increased. In consultancies the account is sometimes passed on to someone junior if the volume of work declines.

Good communication

Because the channels of communication are shorter and more direct, it is likely that in-house public relations staff will be able to communicate better with their client than an external consultancy could. Also the public relations staff are likely to 'speak the same language' as their parent organisation, which could be an important consideration.

Continuity

Staff tend to stay longer in in-house units than in consultancies. Lower turnover means better continuity.

Specialist knowledge

Although a consultancy may have specialist knowledge of your field of business, staff who work in the same organisation are pretty well certain to be better informed about the sector in which you operate and the company itself.

On the spot

An in-house unit is there at the heart of the organisation, possibly only a few yards from the chief executive's door. An instant response is therefore likely.

Access

Linked to good geographical proximity is good access to information – from elsewhere in the organisation, from its branches, from the personnel department, from the public relations unit's own library – and access to the decision-makers of the organisation. This can be valuable for getting authorisation when needed.

Response to the media

An in-house press office can usually respond instantly to media inquiries and will be able to act as organisation spokesperson, which is less common for external people.

Staff loyalty

The staff of an in-house public relations unit are the staff of the organisation which employs them and thus have a personal stake in their employer's success. They may also be thought more able to be trusted with sensitive information about the organisation which would not usually be available to outsiders.

In-house staff sometimes lack some of the attractions of consultants: they do not take their clients out to lunch, they are sometimes casual about accounting for the time and money spent on specific public relations activities, and they are not seen to have the 'clout' of experts from outside the organisation. But some of the most successful public relations is practised by in-house staff who work, in effect, as consultants to their own organisation. Case Study 4.2, which comes from a large local authority in England, provides an example of how this can be accomplished.

Case study 4.2	**An in-house consultancy**

In 1986 the council (local authority) had an old-style publicity department, employing 40 staff grouped loosely into nine units: a design studio, three photographers, a number of publicity assistants who worked on events and 'stunts', a campaign unit which was formed to resist central government's attempts to limit local councils' income (rate-capping) in the early 1980s and had never been disbanded, the Lord Mayor's secretariat who looked after all ceremonial affairs, an international section responsible for town-twinning links, a tourism section which ran the tourist information centre and tried to attract visitors to the city, an advertising section which ran an in-house advertising agency and oversaw outdoor advertising contracts, and a press section consisting of two people to deal with an organisation of over 30,000 employees and a budget in the tens of millions. There was a great deal of expertise, but it was not always effectively deployed and its quality was certainly not appreciated. When public expenditure cuts began to bite, the publicity department was seen as a soft target and was threatened with closure.

By re-organising the staff, clarifying their roles, auditing their expertise, and instituting a system of costing and charging fees for work which had previously been done for nothing, a new public relations department, looking very much like a public relations consultancy and training establishment, came into being. Following formulation of a public relations strategy, the public relations department was formally constituted to put the strategy into effect. Figure 4.3 shows an extract from the report which sanctioned the new approach.

The council now had a corporate press office to deal pro-actively with the media, to set guidelines for all departments in handling the press, and to offer training in dealing with the media; an in-house consultancy service to deal with communication issues for individual departments of the council; a strategic role within the council overall; and a range of technical services on hand for producing or commissioning material. In effect, the council had its own public relations consultancy, but a consultancy which was on the spot, knew its client's business intimately and had a vested interest in its client's (employer's) success. It also had a much better bargain financially. By 1993 the public relations department required a contribution to overheads from central funds of less than a quarter of its 1990 budget, the additional resources coming from advertising revenue, fees and charges to clients.

The PR Unit has continued to experience spending cuts every year since 1993, and its staff in 1999 had reduced to 17. It has therefore concentrated on its core functions of media relations, print design, advertising and photography (although only one in-house photo-grapher now remains). A reorganisation of the City Council's departments to form five Directorates in 1997 resulted in the attachment of one press officer to each Directorate. This enabled each press officer to build up an area of expertise, which is vital in a large, multi-functioned local authority. Each press officer does, however, devote part of his or her time to corporate matters, thereby retaining an overview of the council's affairs while specialising in one area.

(*Source*: author)

Consultancy

The main advantages of consultancies are as follows.

Independent

Precisely because the consultancy has no personal stake in the organisation it represents, its staff can look dispassionately at the organisation and offer an independent view.

Figure 4.3	*Extracts from a report of the chief executive to the Policy Committee, 30 April 1991*

4.3

Identification of issues of policy or service delivery which do or will affect the Council's relation with its publics, whether for good or ill, presupposes awareness and understanding of public relations. Some success could be achieved by professional public relations practitioners taking on the job themselves, but it is desirable for the PR consciousness of officers and members generally to be raised and then supported and sustained by the professionals. The key requirement in public relations is to keep the initiative. This may involve rethinking a plan; undertaking a public consultation exercise; talking to the media; writing, designing, printing and distributing a leaflet; making and showing a video; preparing and mounting an exhibition; or a number of these. 'Damage limitation' responses are very much a second best.

4.4

Many skills necessary to achieve this objective are available to the Council in the present Publicity Department. It is proposed that these skills be brought together in a way which will enable Public Relations to deliver a range of services, set out in the following paragraphs.

4.4.1 *Corporate public relations* on major issues affecting the Council as a whole or across a number of individual services; and running a corporate press office.

4.4.2 *Contribution to and advice on public relations strategies* within departments, and working with departments' own officers to improve their understanding of public relations and develop their skills.

4.4.3 *Training* for members and officers in a range of subjects from media awareness to desk top publishing.

4.4.4 *Consultancy* in a number of areas . . .

4.4.5 *Technical services* including copywriting and editing, design, photography, printing and distribution, to be provided direct by Public Relations or subcontracted through its specialists, to take advantage of the Council's purchasing power, to ensure consistency of standards and high quality, and to safeguard the Council's corporate identity.

Source: Sheffield Council 1991

Collective experience

In a large consultancy, the organisation can expect to be able to draw upon the experience of a number of the staff, who may have a wider variety of previous working experience than in-house staff.

Up-to-date on media

Because consultants often deal with a wide range of clients, they sometimes have a wider and more up-to-date knowledge of what is going on in the media than their in-house counterparts, who may be in touch with the same media contacts all the time.

Access to suppliers

An in-house unit may have to order supplies through an intermediary, or may have to buy print, for example, from elsewhere within its own organisation. A consultancy can usually pick and choose to get the price and quality required.

Costs

In-house staff have to be paid all year round, whereas the consultancy only bills the client for time spent on the account: costs should relate directly to work done. Although clients will pay some of the consultancy's overhead costs, these may not be as great as they are for an in-house unit.

Short-term, renewable contracts

Contracts with consultancies can be short term, and renewable only if the client is satisfied with the work done. With permanent staff, this is not so straightforward.

Location

For a company outside London, a London consultancy can provide a metropolitan presence, and especially can be closer to Westminster, Fleet Street and other important audiences. Similarly a consultancy with a network of regional offices can provide a regional presence for a London-based organisation.

Case study 4.3

Outsourcing

In contrast to the metropolitan district council's experience, a London borough council put its public relations activity out to tender and reduced its in-house provision to one person who commissioned work from a consultancy. That one person, the council's head of communications, had this to say about the contracting-out process:

> The vast majority of agencies which applied for the tender were either too expensive or seeking to do public relations on the cheap. Few could compete with the old in-house department and yet we had some of the best agencies in the UK to choose from because we are based in central London.
>
> *(PR Week* 1993)

The consultancy which won the account ran a 24-hour press office, was responsible for marketing council initiatives, provided daily media monitoring and briefings for senior council members and officers, and provided strategic advice. It was run almost as an in-house unit, with its eight staff occupying an office in City Hall, as the in-house unit used to do. This closeness to the client did not, however, prevent embarrassing incidents. One such occurred in November 1992 when the consultancy sent out a press release announcing the appointment of a private company to handle the council's £42 million street cleaning contract before council members had voted to accept the tender. While in-house units make mistakes as well, it is inconceivable that local government public relations professionals, steeped in committee procedures and the provisions of the Local Government

(Access to Information) Act 1985, would have made a blunder such as that.

In this case, consultancy provision may not have been more effective than the in-house version, but it did satisfy ideological considerations.

(*Source*: author)

Other provision of public relations services

In-house plus consultancy

The combination of an in-house unit and use of external consultants is common in large organisations. *PR Week*'s annual in-house surveys show that up to two-thirds of the top UK organisations surveyed use external consultants to complement their in-house provision. In general, in-house units have tended to be responsible for press relations, internal communications, corporate affairs, events management, sponsorship, design and lobbying, while the specialists might have been hired for strategic advice, financial relations, crisis management, literature production and the provision of technical or specialist services such as research, video production or photography. However, there is a trend in the larger organisations, both public and private sector, to make public relations appointments at board level, thus bringing the provision of strategic advice into the organisation's own ambit.

In-house teams look for creativity above all when hiring a consultancy, followed by sector knowledge and speed of response. Common complaints about working with consultancies are that the consultancy does not know enough about the client's business, overruns its budget, does not adequately evaluate its work or fails to deliver. Another significant complaint is that junior staff are put to work on the account. Often the pitch for business is made by the most senior members of the consultancy but the actual work is done by someone much cheaper.

Advertising and multi-service agencies

Advertising agencies sometimes offer public relations as an extra service. In recent years a number of multi-service agencies have been set up offering advertising, design, public relations and marketing advice. Another trend is for groups of freelance consultants, designers, photographers, copywriters and printers to set up shop close together, sharing secretarial services, computing and other electronic gadgetry, maintaining their individual independence, but occasionally working together and sometimes passing clients on to their colleagues.

Multi-service agencies may seem cheap or free, but you usually get what you pay for. If the public relations activity is tacked on to the end of the advertising budget 'free of charge', the client is probably paying too much for the advertising. Advantages are that the client only has one port of call, and, in theory at least, marketing, advertising and public relations strategies can all be integrated by the consultant.

Do-it-yourself

Many organisations operate this form of public relations. Whoever answers the phone speaks to the media, or no one speaks to the media.

Non-experts working for the organisation may do some public relations jobs. For example, the personnel officer could be responsible for internal communications and may put together a staff newsletter; the managing director's secretary may order the food and look after the visitors when an exhibition is held. If the company is small it may not see any need, or not be able to afford, professional public relations. If it is the kind of company which has grown with its charismatic founder-managing director, it may not feel public relations advisers are needed: the boss can always be relied on for a quote or a stunt. But this can be a dangerous strategy. For every Richard Branson, high-profile founder and head of the global Virgin empire (who, for all his do-it-yourself style, employs some of the most highly regarded public relations professionals in the business), there is at least one Gerald Ratner, former head of Ratner's, a chain of cut-price jewellery shops, whose off-the-cuff remarks to a journalist about the 'crap' quality of his jewellery sent his company to perdition.

Planning versus doing

We started off this chapter looking at a model of planning for communication, and we have just seen the different ways in which public relations can be supplied. Just as many practitioners are too busy doing to do much planning, we have spent our time so far planning, not doing. In the following chapters you will see how public relations people 'do' public relations. Let us see for the moment how the planning relates to the doing, using as always a real-world example. You will see that this is a long-term public relations plan, covering ten years, so the importance of planning is even more obvious.

Case Study 4.4

Long-term public relations planning

Rhône-Poulenc: BRAHM PR Leeds

Client

Rhône-Poulenc Agriculture Ltd, manufacturers and suppliers of agrochemicals such as pesticides, herbicides, fungicides and seed treatments.

Statement of problem/opportunity

The industry has come under increasing pressure from legislators in the UK and Europe, from pressure groups and from individuals, concerned about the application and use of agrochemicals, and about their effects on the environment. The over-supply of grain in Europe has led to the set-aside policy and a growing call from the public for organic type farm systems, in the belief that they will result in less damage to wildlife and the environment.

Brief from client

Rhône-Poulenc (RP) manages a farm at Boarded Barns, next to the company headquarters in Ongar, Essex. Historically the 57-hectare site has been farmed commercially but RP felt it could be used to support the company in a more effective way. After consultation and brainstorming with its public relations consultancy, the company decided to go ahead with a management and environmental study at the farm, as an integrated part of a broader public relations campaign entitled Operation Country Practice. In November 1994 RP announced an extension to the project by introducing an Integrated Crop Management study on farmland at Bundish Hall Farm, adjacent to Boarded Barns Farm. Results will be compared with those of the conventional and organic studies referred to in the original brief.

Aim

To promote RP as an innovative and research-based enterprise.

Objectives

1 to undertake a major research project directly comparing organic and conventional arable farming systems on the same site;

2 to increase RP's understanding of organic farming methods;

3 to build closer relationships with key publics involved in arable farming and with conservation organisations.

Public relations plan

1 Publics

RP employees; farmers (end users); UK and EU government departments of Agriculture and the Environment; RP agrochemical distributors (customers); farm analysts and consultants; organic farming organisations; educational establishments; public utilities (e.g. water companies); trade and conservation organisations (National Farmers Union, British Agrochemicals Association, British Trust for Ornithology, etc.); journalists (agriculture and environmental correspondents from the nationals, tv and radio), farming, environmental and food trade media; the general public.

2 Timetable

Launch in autumn 1989. The programme runs for at least ten years with annual reports publishing all research findings.

3 Methods used to reach audiences

Press and VIP guest launch in autumn 1989; regular press visits to the farm since then; all visitors put on mailing list; production and direct mailing to key targets of data sheets, information leaflets and annual reports; continuous programme of visits from universities, schools, distributors, farmers, conservationists, media; exhibition display panels used at major agricultural exhibitions; regular news bulletins and newsletters.

4 Resources

Approximately £15,000–£25,000 per annum for the public relations element (farm project costs and income not included). Staff involved: 1 public relations consultant, 5 RP staff.

Annual programme of activity

Regular issue of news releases on progress of on-site research activities including:

► farm management accounts (direct comparison between conventional/organic inputs and income);

► research into field and marginal flora;

► research into farmland arthropods;

► bird survey (see Figure 4.4);

► butterfly and dragonfly study;

► soil and water analysis;

► small mammals and soil invertebrates study;

► studies of quality of flour and bread, wheat diseases and aphids population.

Ongoing programme of farm visits from media and other targeted publics.
Publication and mailing to targets of Annual Report.
Specific features written and targeted to media, e.g. food magazines.
Review and updating of general information literature.
Presence at appropriate agricultural exhibitions.
Regular co-operators meeting with educational and government bodies involved with the specific research projects on the site.

Evaluation

Annual review of all on-farm projects with findings published in Annual Report.
    Number and type of visitors to farm; interest expressed by farming and conservation organisations.

| **Figure 4.4** | *Farmland common birds census* |

Farmland Common Birds Census:

*estimates of breeding numbers from
territory mapping, March - July*

British Trust for Ornithology

Name	County:	O ESSEX
J.G. & G. COURT		N ESSEX

Code	Year	Area	Region	Altitude	Easting	Northing	
1411	92	65.8	EE	50.0	55	20	

Code				Code				Code			
005	2	LG	Little Grebe	304	l	CK	Cuckoo	472	3	WW	Willow Warbler
035		CA	Cormorant	307		BO	Barn Owl	482	✓	GC	Goldcrest
039	✓	H	Grey Heron	313		LO	Little Owl	484	2	SF	Spotted Flycatcher
057		MS	Mute Swan	314		TO	Tawny Owl	486		PF	Pied Flycatcher
059		GJ	Greylag Goose	327	✓	SI	Swift	388	3	LT	Long-tailed Tit
068	l	CG	Canada Goose	332		KF	Kingfisher	386		MT	Marsh Tit
071		SU	Shelduck	338		G	Green Woodpecker	387	✓	WT	Willow Tit
075		T	Teal	341	l	GS	Gt Sp Woodpecker	382	✓	CT	Coal Tit
072	3	MA	Mallard	345	l	LS	Lr Sp Woodpecker	380	20	BT	Blue Tit
087	✓	TU	Tufted Duck	357	4	S	Skylark	379	10	GT	Great Tit
105		GD	Goosander	365		SM	Sand Martin	391		NH	Nuthatch
113	l	SH	Sparrowhawk	361	2	SL	Swallow	394	l	TC	Treecreeper
115		BZ	Buzzard	364	l	HM	House Martin	375	l	J	Jay
148	l	K	Kestrel	497		TP	Tree Pipit	372	2	MG	Magpie
143	l	HY	Hobby	493		MP	Meadow Pipit	371	✓	JD	Jackdaw
157	4	RL	Red-legged Partridge	506	✓	YW	Yellow Wagtail	370	✓	RO	Rook
160		P	Grey Partridge	505		GL	Grey Wagtail	368	2	C	Carrion Crow
162	5	PH	Pheasant	503	l	PW	Pied Wagtail	367		RN	Raven
173	7	MH	Moorhen	397		DI	Dipper	518	6	SG	Starling
177	2	CO	Coot	398	15	WR	Wren	525	10	HS	House Sparrow
182		OC	Oystercatcher	490	9	D	Dunnock	528	l	TS	Tree Sparrow
191		RP	Ringed Plover	400	18	R	Robin	555	15	CH	Chaffinch
185	✓	L	Lapwing	402		N	Nightingale	533	9	GR	Greenfinch
221		SN	Snipe	407		RT	Redstart	535	3	GO	Goldfinch
223		WK	Woodcock	409		WC	Whinchat	536	✓	SK	Siskin
202		CU	Curlew	412		W	Wheatear	537	6	LI	Linnet
206		RK	Redshank	424	25	B	Blackbird	539		LR	Redpoll
214		CS	Common Sandpiper	431	6	ST	Song Thrush	548	2	BF	Bullfinch
263		BH	Black-headed Gull	432	3	M	Mistle Thrush	558	10	Y	Yellowhammer
255		CM	Common Gull	439		GH	Grasshopper Warbler	574	3	RB	Reed Bunting
257	✓	LB	Lesser Black-back	450	✓	SW	Sedge Warbler	557		CB	Corn Bunting
256		HG	Herring Gull	446		RW	Reed Warbler	.....	✓		Gadwall
275		CN	Common Tern	462	2	LW	Lesser Whitethroat	.....			....
297	✓	FP	Feral Pigeon	461	10	WH	Whitethroat	.....			....
298	✓	SD	Stock Dove	460	l	GW	Garden Warbler	.....			....
299	n.c.	WP	Woodpigeon	457	8	BC	Blackcap	.....			....
302	5	CD	Collared Dove	475		WO	Wood Warbler	.....			....
300	3	TD	Turtle Dove	473	3	CC	Chiffchaff	.....			....

tick/'P = present, no clusters; nc/X = not counted; N = nest count; blank = absent during census; * = count not comparable with previous year's

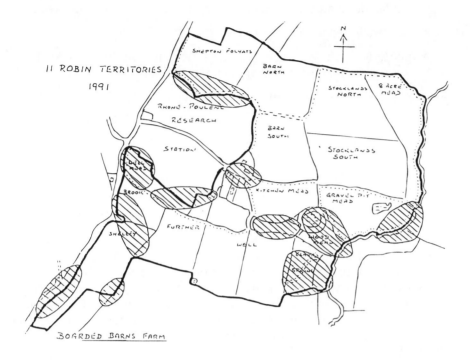

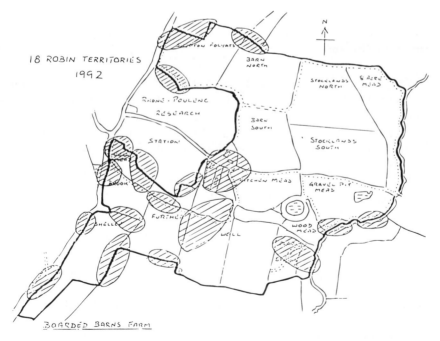

Source: Brahm PR/Rhône–Poulenc

Public relations element of programme reviewed quarterly and through media monitoring; coverage includes:

▶ regular news and features in farming trade and local Essex press;

▶ three major editorials in *Financial Times*;

▶ quarterly farm visit and regular interviews on BBC Radio 4's *Farming Week* and *Farming Today* programmes;

▶ major editorial feature in *Accounting* magazine;

▶ major editorial feature in *European Food and Drink* Review;

▶ *ad hoc* coverage in national and regional media.

(*Source*: BRAHM PR, Leeds. Thanks to Malcolm Cowing at BRAHM PR and Bob Joice of Rhône-Poulenc Agriculture Limited.)

Clearly, a public relations campaign with long-term objectives requires meticulous planning. A project manager has been appointed by RP, and he oversees the research programmes, although these are carried out by independent bodies such as the universities of Southampton and Reading and the Soil Survey and Land Research Centre. It is vital for the credibility of the programme that scientific research work is undertaken by bodies external to RP.

Keeping control

However careful the planning, and regardless of whether the public relations programme is devised and undertaken by consultants or in-house staff, monitoring and control are essential. Both the client and the public relations staff working on the programme need to check that progress is being made according to plan, deadlines are being met, and the budget is not being overspent.

Monitoring can take a number of forms, for example, a weekly or monthly meeting, involving the public relations consultant and the client; the consultant's completing a monitoring or progress sheet and sending it to the client periodically, or by a quarterly report. Project report forms, showing progress made against agreed targets, time spent on specified public relations activity and costs incurred, are a helpful tool for keeping control.

One successful method of keeping track is to create a 'job-bag' system. The 'bag' can be a box-file, a computer file or just allocated space on a shelf or rack. Into it goes everything to do with the client's job: client contact details; job name or number; brief; agreed programme and timetable of activity; notes of meetings; agreed budget; expenditure to date (actual and committed); delivery dates; estimates, invoices and receipts; time-sheets; copyright permissions; draft and agreed copy, photographs and illustrations;

| Example of a job-bag front sheet for an event. This was for a press reception | **Figure 4.5** |

Job No	Client/Ac exec	Description
	Progress	**Ordered/sent/confirmed**
Location		
Parking/transport		
Room layout		
Equipment, mics		
Invitations		
Catering		
Press kits		
Photographer		
Other		
Other		
Evaluation report		
Invoiced		
Satisfaction report		
	Signed off	Ac Exec/date

Source: Author

notes of telephone calls with the client and with suppliers; and the finished job – leaflet, video cassette or photographs of an exhibition stand – with a copy of the final bill.

Someone – the account executive working on the job or a member of the team known as the progress chaser – will be responsible for ensuring that deadlines are met and the job is completed to time and to budget. Progress chasers usually have some kind of check-list attached to the front of the job-bag which serves as a reminder of the jobs that need doing and the information that needs to be kept. It has a secondary use: if the progress chaser falls under a bus, someone else can easily pick up the job and see what has been done and what needs doing next. If the client suddenly wants to know about what is happening to the job, how the budget is being spent and when to expect delivery of the finished article, a quick glance at the check-list should provide the answers.

The importance of research

Before we leave the subject of planning, we need to look at another essential: research. As we saw in Chapter 3 (Table 3.3), some kind of research is a feature of all kinds of public relations activity, whether it is as crude as counting bottoms on seats at an event, or a sophisticated opinion research survey. There are a number of uses of research in public relations and we will look at each one in some detail.

Attitudes and perceptions

The perception which your target public has of your organisation affects that public's attitude towards you. The only way to find out how your public perceives you is to conduct research into the public's attitudes. Such research may begin by establishing what kind of person is a member of that public and describing them in terms of their age, sex, occupation, family size, what kind of house they live in and whether they own it or not, their purchasing habits, use of credit, readership and TV watching habits, how often and where they go for holidays, what their voting intentions are and many more factors which may be of importance to you. Once you know who they are, you can start to find out what they think about you. Depending on how the information is collected, you can begin to see how different types of people in your target public view your organisation. You will find out all kinds of interesting things about the differences – and similarities – between men and women, young and old, rich and poor.

When you have analysed the research you should have a clearer idea of how you need to plan your public relations strategy. Do you need to change attitudes, or reinforce them? Do you have an educational role to play, or should you be lobbying? Is your target audience so different from your perception of them that you need to think again about who you are trying to reach and why?

Defining and measuring target groups

Market research companies can measure almost any kind of target group or public which you care to define. Some of the most common forms of analysis are

demographic: classifying groups by age, sex and similar factors;

geographic: by area or region, by postcode, by electoral ward, or using the ACORN classification of residential neighbourhoods, which analyses according to family size, affluence and similar factors;

consumer: those who buy your product or your competitor's product, or intend to do so. *Consumer readers* are consumers classified according to the newspaper they read;

psychographic: by attitude;

psychometric: by personality type and how it affects their attitudes and behaviour;

multi-variate: uses a number of variables to define respondents such as 'shopper types', for example as high or low mobility.

Testing

Researchers can do pre-testing, tracking and post-testing.

Pre-testing allows you to try out draft materials, to pilot a campaign and to get feedback from a representative sample of your public before you go on to run your campaign. Pre-testing can prevent expensive disasters. For example, a holiday company pre-tested its brochure which featured deserted beaches. Their target audience said they would not go there, because clearly nobody else did. The final brochure appeared with people on the beaches.

During a campaign a company may undertake *tracking studies.* This type of research is ongoing throughout the campaign and enables the company to track the effect the campaign is having over time, or in different regions, or among different target publics. Adjustments can then be made while the campaign is progressing.

Post-testing enables you to see how your public relations effort achieved its objectives, and can help you to evaluate its cost effectiveness. If the objective was to increase awareness of the name of a brand, it is relatively straightforward to check the results of research measuring awareness before and after the public relations campaign.

Creating stories

Reports of research carried out form the basis of many news stories. Sometimes the sole reason for carrying out the research in the first place is to create a newsworthy story, and sometimes the results of research are interesting enough to merit a news release as a by-product.

Any issue of current public interest can be researched and form the basis of an interesting news story, but those which are controversial, amusing or have a human interest angle are likely to receive most coverage by the media. A financial services company based in Scotland commissioned research to find out how the Scots and the English make provision for their old age. Whatever the outcome of the survey, the results were bound to be newsworthy, on both sides of the border. The survey showed that the Scots were more canny than the English in preparing for their retirement, and the company's research received good coverage in the national press in England and Scotland.

However, because the provider of the research cannot control how the story is subsequently written, use of research for this purpose can provide opportunities for bad publicity as well as good. Case Study 4.5 provides an example.

Case Study 4.5

Use of research
Colman's mustard: Beer Davies Publicity

As sponsors of their local soccer team, Norwich City, Colman's wanted to capitalise on this link and to associate themselves with good food, via coverage in the media. Beer Davies Publicity proposed conducting a research project into food at football grounds, which was published as a 132-page book, *Colman's Football Food Guide.* The media found the story an interesting one, not least because soccer grounds are notorious for the poor quality of the food available to fans. The guide was mentioned by name in all the major media: 13 items on national television, 23 on national radio and 35 in the national press.

However, the publicity generated by the research did not result in universally positive coverage. Arguably the most memorable story, which appeared in a number of media, followed from Leyton Orient fans' (Orient's catering was rated worst in the survey) chant to the tune of 'He's got the whole world in his hand'. They sang, with evident accuracy, 'We've got the worst pies in the land', not a message which associates Colman's with good food.

(*Source*: *PR Week* Public Relations Awards 1998)

A research-based news release will be more interesting to a newspaper if it has something to say about that paper's readers. A readership question asked as part of the survey helps to target audiences with future messages, but it also enables the public relations officer to tell editors 'Here is what your readers had to say about this issue', so making it more likely to be used.

We have now covered the essentials of theory and planning. The following chapters of this book give a flavour of some of the most important areas of public relations practice.

Summary points

✔ Public relations planning starts with analysis, considering the aims and objectives of a public relations activity within the context of the organisation's business plan. The aims give the broad direction while the objectives of a public relations campaign are more specific, stating what the campaign is supposed to achieve.

✔ A model of communication could take the form of this question: Why do we want to say what to whom, how shall we do it and how shall we measure its effectiveness? The final stage, evaluation, teaches valuable lessons on how to do it next time.

✔ Public relations planning and activity may be undertaken by public relations consultants, by an organisation's in-house staff, or by a combination of the two; by advertising or multi-service agencies, or as a do-it-yourself activity. Each has its own advantages and disadvantages which need to be considered along with the organisation's size, structure and requirements.

✔ Monitoring and control are essentials in public relations practice. Progress made, costs incurred and time spent must all be logged and kept within the resources and deadlines agreed. Paperwork should be straightforward and easy to understand so that any member of the team can provide the client with progress details, whether or not the account executive is there.

✔ Research is a feature of all kinds of public relations activity. It can be used to find out what perceptions a target audience has of the organisation and what their attitudes and behaviours are. Researchers can pilot campaigns to ensure that expensive mistakes are not made; can track the effect of a campaign as it proceeds; and can help evaluate its effectiveness by measuring perceptions at the end of a campaign. The results of research can often provide interesting stories which may be covered by the media in their own right.

Questions for discussion

Borsetshire Cable is shortly to begin digging up the pavements and streets throughout the entire county of Borsetshire in order to lay cables for television, telephone and computer use. They are expecting a public outcry on three fronts: the disruption which will be caused to traffic; the dirt and mess generated on residential streets by digging and re-surfacing; and noise from drills and other equipment. Imagine you represent a firm of public relations consultants, considering how you might bid for Borsetshire Cable's account.

1 How would you formulate a public relations plan of campaign? What might it look like? Who are your target publics?

2 Consider why you are recommending the methods you have chosen for communicating with the target publics.

3 How would the timetable for your recommended public relations activity fit in with the physical work being undertaken by the client?

4 What use would you make of research? What methods would you use and when would you undertake research? On what basis would you decide whether to commission research from an external supplier or to undertake it yourself?

5 What criteria would you set for monitoring and evaluating the public relations programme?

Recommended further reading

Cutlip et al. (1994) discuss planning as an integral part of the public relations process, with specific reference to measurement and evaluation in Chapters 9 and 12.

Grunig and Hunt (1984) Chapters 5 to 9 in Part II, Principles of Management, cover the steps which make up public relations planning, including budgeting and evaluation.

Gronstedt (1997) in Caywood is a comprehensive chapter on research and evaluation as an essential part of the public relations planning process.

Hendrix (1998) outlines in Part 1 the ROPE (Research, Objectives, Programming, Evaluation) process, while the remainder of the book provides examples of public relations programmes in the form of detailed case studies.

Van Riel (1995) Chapter 5 deals with the provision and the planning of public relations programmes, and discusses the factors critical to their success.

In addition the other major texts listed in full in the references and referred to below necessarily cover the planning and management of public relations programmes. Note that the dates and edition numbers are the most recent at the time of writing.

Baskin et al. (1997) 4th edition.

Caywood (1997).

McElreath (1997) 2nd edition.

Newsom et al. (1993) 5th edition.

Seitel (1995) 6th edition.

References

Baskin, O., Aronoff, C. and Lattimore, D. (1997) *Public Relations: the Profession and the Practice*, 4th edn, Chicago, IL: Brown and Benchmark.

Caywood, C. (1997) *The Handbook of Strategic Public Relations and Integrated Communications*, New York: McGraw-Hill.

Cutlip, S., Center, A. and Broom, G. (1994) *Effective Public Relations*, 7th edn., Englewood Cliffs, NJ: Prentice Hall.

Gronstedt, A. (1997) 'The Role of Research in Public Relations Strategy and Planning', in Caywood, C., op. cit.

Grunig. J. and Hunt, T. (1984) *Managing Public Relations*, Orlando, FL: Holt, Rinehart and Winston.

Hendrix, J. (1998) *Public Relations Cases*, 4th edn, Belmont, CA: Wadsworth.

McElreath, M. (1997) *Managing Systematic and Ethical Public Relations Campaigns*, Chicago, IL: Brown and Benchmark.

Newsom, D., Scott, A. and Turk, J. (1993) *This is PR: the Realities of Public Relations*, 5th edn., New York: Wadsworth.

PR Week (1993) 'The Westminster Experiment', *PR Week* 13 May.

PR Week (1998) '*PR Week* Public Relations Awards'.

Seitel, F. (1995) *The Practice of Public Relations*, 6th edn, Englewood Cliffs, NJ: Prentice Hall.

Van Riel, C. (1995) *Principles of Corporate Communication*, London: Prentice Hall.

Watson, T. (1997) 'Measuring the Success Rate' in Kitchen, P. (ed.), *Public Relations Principles and Practice*, London: International Thomson Business Press.

Corporate public relations

5

Key Issues

The aim of this chapter is to distinguish the concept of corporate public relations from other areas of public relations practice. The key points considered are:

▶ definitions of terms used in corporate public relations;

▶ the elements of the corporate public relations process;

▶ how an organisation's corporate image is constructed;

▶ implementing corporate identity programmes;

▶ the use of corporate advertising.

In Chapter 1 we looked at definitions of public relations, and at some of the terminology which has recently come into use. Some of these terms, such as 'corporate communications' and 'public affairs' are often used as a synonym for 'public relations' on the grounds that they sound better and do not suffer from the negative connotations of 'public relations'. However, there is a discrete area of public relations which deals with the corporate face of organisations, and this is the practice of corporate public relations.

Some more definitions

Corporate strategy

'Corporate' comes from the Latin for 'body' and a corporation is a group of individuals acting as one body. The senior management of an organisation typically hammers out its corporate strategy as a result of making decisions about the scope of its activities, what it wants to achieve in the long term and how it will prioritise and allocate resources to achieving its corporate, strategic goals.

Corporate communications

This term encompasses all the communications activities which an organisation undertakes as a corporate entity: everything, in effect, which comes from head office, is aimed at all staff, or which reflects the organisation as a whole. It excludes, therefore, such communications as departmental newsletters and public relations activities on behalf of brands or subsidiaries. It includes the company's website, annual reports, corporate identity programmes, corporate advertising and most investor relations activity.

Public affairs

This term is a little more ambiguous. One definition says that public affairs is 'concerned with those relationships which are involved in the development of public policy, legislation and regulation, which may affect organisations, their interests and operations' (White 1991: 20).

In simple terms, a public affairs specialist will usually be on the look-out for issues which are likely to affect the organisation in the future, such as possible new regulations, or consumer trends; and will tend to be involved in lobbying. The ambiguity arises when the term is used interchangeably with public relations. An organisation whose public relations activities are largely bound up with public policy issues may refer to these activities as 'public affairs' rather than 'public relations': there is an obvious link with 'affairs of state'. The Metropolitan Police, for example, calls its public relations department the Directorate of Public Affairs.

Corporate identity and corporate image

These terms mean different things, but they are sometimes used interchangeably. Most theorists and practitioners would agree that an organisation's corporate identity lies in its physical manifestation: its logo, company colours, house style of dress, decor and so on. Corporate image, however, is the impression that people have about the organisation as a whole. The two are linked, just as the verbs 'to imply' and 'to infer' are, but they describe different concepts. We will look at these later in this chapter.

Corporate advertising

Organisations place corporate advertisements in order to: 'establish, develop, enhance and/or change the corporate image of an organisation' (Worcester 1983).

Corporate reputation

An organisation's corporate reputation is based on the way all those who come into contact with it perceive its behaviour, or experience its products or services. An organisation's values and its culture affect its reputation. Corporate advertising is often undertaken in order to project an organisation's personality, culture and values to the outside world.

The corporate public relations process

While all strategic decisions are the responsibility of the board of a company, those decisions are taken following the advice of the functional experts. Thus the corporate public relations process starts with consideration by the senior management of the communications strategy required to fulfil its corporate strategic objectives. For example, a company wants to position itself within the retailing sector as environmentally friendly: it adopts the 'greening' of the company as a corporate objective. How it communicates this and puts it into action will be the job of its corporate public relations advisers, whether they are in-house or external consultants.

The corporate public relations process typically comprises the following four stages:

1 finding out where you are;

2 formulating your corporate communications strategy;

3 implementing a programme of corporate public relations;

4 monitoring and reviewing.

This ties in with the planning model in Chapter 4: why do we want to say what to whom, how shall we do it and how measure its effectiveness?

Starting from where you are: the communications audit

How do you find out where you are? Simply, you look around you, ask some questions and draw your conclusions. A communications audit is a formalised way of doing this. It is simply a review of the organisation's communications activities: what they are, how they work, what they cost and what they accomplish. In the process any differences of opinion about the organisation between its publics can be noted, and action can be taken by the organisation to remedy these.

Undertaking a communications audit is a major task, and it may not always be necessary or desirable. Because it involves research and analysis, and because its results must be seen to be objective, an audit is usually carried out by external consultants and the costs can be very high. Students following the Public Relations degree course at Leeds Metropolitan University undertake a communications audit during their final year, their clients usually coming from the charitable and voluntary sectors – organisations who would not otherwise be able to afford the cost of conducting an audit. An extract from one such audit report can be found in Chapter 7 as Figure 7.3.

The audit needs to be undertaken to a clear brief. This may cover internal or external communications, or both. It will often involve questionnaires, interviews, discussions with staff or other important publics, and content analysis of material currently in use. Auditors will typically investigate the environment in which the organisation operates; flag up any opportunities or threats which may be on the horizon; investigate the scope and cost of current communications activity; evaluate its effectiveness; and, probably, recommend policy changes.

Formulating your corporate communications strategy

Once the analysis has been undertaken, whether or not a communications audit takes place, the organisation must formulate its strategy by identifying what decisions it needs to make to bring about the changes it requires. Those strategic public relations decisions must be endorsed by the senior management of the organisation.

Elements of a corporate public relations programme

The elements of a corporate public relations programme will vary depending on the aim and objectives which your analysis has thrown up. Typically, however, the following will need to be considered.

Corporate identity

If the organisation's corporate identity is confused or non-existent, the public relations programme may start with an overhaul and implementation of a new identity.

Corporate advertising

Although advertising is usually seen as part of the marketing function in an organisation, corporate advertising is more closely allied to public information than it is to sales. So corporate advertising tends to be in the province of public relations and the director of corporate communications is more likely to have responsibility for corporate advertising than the marketing director.

Issues management

Although an issue of concern to the organisation may arise anywhere, perhaps seeming only to impinge upon one particular area of the organisation's business, issues management is a function of corporate public relations. Issues need to be tracked and managed from the corporate perspective. If this is not effectively done, it may lead to the following.

Crisis management

Although localised damage limitation may be the responsibility only of the sector of the organisation affected, crisis management is also an essential function of corporate public relations. Issue and crisis management are discussed more fully in Chapter 6.

Investor relations

All organisations need to maintain good relations with those who provide the resources to keep them in business – shareholders, financial institutions, the government or donors, depending on the kind of organisation. This specialised branch of corporate public relations is dealt with in more detail in Chapter 9.

Staff communications

Whatever the programme of activity, staff understanding of and commitment to the corporate policy is vital. There is more on this in Chapter 7.

Community relations

Corporate public relations is often aimed at the community in which the organisation operates – its neighbours, and those from whom its workforce is drawn.

Sponsorship

A company's sponsorship strategy should be formulated within the context of its corporate public relations policy. What it sponsors and how, will be part of its corporate public relations programme. There is more on community relations and sponsorship in Chapter 8.

Monitoring and reviewing

As we saw in Chapter 4, monitoring the progress of a public relations campaign and reviewing its effectiveness teaches an organisation valuable lessons. Each element of the programme may require its own system, with an evaluation of the overall programme which depends on the success of the strands.

Corporate connections

We have looked at how an organisation might think through its corporate public relations strategy and the steps it needs to take to turn that into a programme. Let us now turn to the publics at which this programme is aimed and see how they are likely to receive what is transmitted to them.

Corporate public relations is aimed at one or more of the following:

▶ the general public;

▶ investors and financial analysts;

▶ opinion leaders;

▶ the organisation's own sector, including its competitors and suppliers;

▶ powerful bodies: regulators, legislators, pressure groups.

How such publics perceive the organisation is not, though, entirely dependent upon the organisation's well thought-out corporate public relations programme. An organisation's corporate image arises from four elements which are inter-connected. They are shown in Figure 5.1 in the form of the corporate image jigsaw.

Personality

An organisation's personality is the sum total of its characteristics as perceived by the outside world. One technique which is used to gauge a person's view of an organisation's personality is to ask: if this company were a celebrity – an actor, or a politician, or an entertainer – who would it be? Marilyn Monroe, Kate Winslet or Judi Dench? Tony Blair, Ronald Reagan or Nelson Mandela? Companies do certainly have personalities as any discussion will show. Here are some examples of the descriptions which have been given of company personalities:

Virgin: lively, dynamic, fun;

Body Shop: concerned, caring, kind;

Cadbury: paternalistic, benevolent;

Marks and Spencer: efficient, safe, dull.

Reputation

An organisation's reputation is what people believe about it, based on their own or others' experience of its products or services. So an organisation may have a reputation for fast service, good quality, and consumer care with its customers; for fair dealing with its suppliers; and for solid achievement with its shareholders. Companies may have a good reputation, a bad reputation, or no reputation at all, because they are not well enough known.

Figure 5.1	*The corporate image jigsaw*

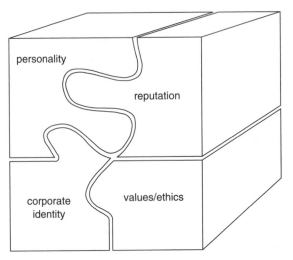

What qualities contribute to a good, positive reputation?	**Figure 5.2**

Qualities of corporate heroes

✔ quality of management

✔ financial soundness

✔ quality of products and services

✔ value as long-term investment

✔ capacity to innovate

✔ quality of marketing

✔ community and environmental responsibility

✔ ability to attract, develop and retain top talent

A good reputation has to be earned. In a survey carried out by Loughborough University for the *Economist* in 1991, 1800 British business people were asked what qualities contributed to a good, positive reputation. They came up with the list shown in Figure 5.2. The long established retailer Marks and Spencer was the company which was felt to have the best reputation. M&S was especially admired for the way in which it had transferred its good name, earned in quality clothes and food, to financial services, because it is trusted as a company by its customers.

The list in Figure 5.2 is almost identical to that used by the American magazine *Fortune* in its annual survey of directors, executives and analysts. Since 1984, *Fortune* has published the results of its survey of 6000 to 8000 respondents. In seven out of the ten years from 1986 to 1995 the pharmaceutical company Merck has taken the top slot, with Rubbermaid winning twice and IBM, the undisputed winner of the early 1980s, winning only once. However, looking at the 'top ten' companies during those years it is interesting to see that there has been a high turnover: clearly reputation is a dynamic concept.

Values

An organisation's values contribute to the reputation it has. Corporate values, what the organisation's standards are, form the corporate culture of an organisation. This affects, and is affected by, the people who work for the organisation. Increasingly companies are thrashing out and publishing statements about their values, sometimes in the form of mission statements. Considering and formally stating what those values are makes it easier for staff, customers, suppliers and so on to know what to expect from the company.

Sometimes organisations formalise their values into a company code of conduct or ethics, which gives guidelines to staff on how to behave so that they do not jeopardise the company's reputation. Here is an extract from one such code, which makes clear how values translate into reputation.

Our company's reputation means a lot to us. It's an asset money can't buy. It opens doors for us when we call on customers, when we look for business partnerships, when we deal with governments, and when we work to improve the communities in which we operate. By all measures, HP enjoys one of the best reputations any company has – in any business – anywhere in the world.

This hasn't happened by accident. Over the years employees at every level have endeavoured to build HP's reputation by fair and honest dealing in every business transaction and relationship.

These Standards of Business Conduct are intended to inform all employees of their legal and ethical obligations to HP, its customers, competitors and suppliers. Simply stated, every HP employee must comply with these standards.

The day-to-day performance of each of us adds to – or subtracts from – HP's reputation as a company. Uncompromising integrity is part of the HP Way and part of every HP job; it always has been; it always will be.

(Copyright © 1993 Hewlett-Packard Company.
Reproduced with permission)

Corporate identity

The fourth piece of the jigsaw is corporate identity: the physical manifestation of the organisation, or, according to corporate identity consultant Wally Olins, 'making business strategy visible through design. Identity is expressed in the names, symbols, logos, colours and rites of passage which the organisation uses to distinguish itself, its brands and its constituent companies' (Olins 1989).

An organisation can use its corporate identity to reflect its personality, to express its values, or simply to show how it is structured. Some organisations have such clear corporate identities that their names and logos or colours are synonymous: Shell is an example of this use of a symbol. Coca Cola is thought to 'own' the bright red it uses in its logo and advertising, and IBM has been so closely linked with blue that the company's nickname was for many years 'the Big Blue'.

Sometimes elements of an organisation's identity threaten to overwhelm the corporate identity itself. The Walt Disney Company has made the image of Mickey Mouse so famous and widespread that elements of it – the gloved hand, the ears and the silhouette – are instantly recognisable. This can work to the disadvantage of a company, as Disney found out in 1994 when the company failed in its attempt to site a new theme park in Virginia, against the wishes of local people. Advertisements, mailshots and posters all featured elements of Mickey Mouse, and an article in *The Washingtonian* (1995: 59–63, 114–27) was headlined 'Hit the Road, Mick' (Hendrix 1998).

These four elements – personality, reputation, values and corporate identity – contribute to the corporate image which its publics have of an organisation. An organisation's image is determined by its performance: no one can sustain a false image for very long. The closer the image is to the reality of the organisation, the more likely it is that the organisation will be seen as trustworthy and honest.

Implementing corporate public relations programmes

As we have seen, a corporate public relations programme may include the use of internal (staff) communications, issues and crisis management, investor relations, sponsorship and community relations, all of which are discussed later in this book. Corporate identity and corporate advertising are the other elements. We will look at these in turn from the practical point of view.

Corporate identity

There are plenty of reasons why an organisation may think it needs a new corporate identity. Here are a few.

It is changing its name: the Victorian charity for destitute children, Dr. Barnardo's, became simply Barnardos, with a new identity programme as part of its re-launch. The old name was thought to ground the charity too much in its past, and to perpetuate an image of the homeless orphan, a far cry from the type of client which the charity was now in business to help. The charity did not want to distance itself entirely from its founder and his principles, hence they kept his surname.

The old identity looks tired or dated: the Public Relations Consultants' Association in the UK changed its logo in 1994 after 25 years with the same design. The Shell oil company has regularly updated its identity since its founding a century ago, although it continues to use some version of a sea shell as its logo. The BP oil company's corporate identity re-vamp in the early 1990s was widely criticised for being a very expensive operation which simply resulted in a slight slanting of the letters 'BP'. Nonetheless, the 'new' BP logo did look more modern than the old version.

There is a need to put across a different message about the company: Robinson's, the health products manufacturer, ditched its 'Robinson's of Chesterfield' style, complete with picture of the small town's parish church, in favour of a new logo 'Rob1nson', denoting its aspiration to be number one in its field. British Airways wanted to be seen as a global carrier and not simply as a national airline, and became the first airline to abandon the use of a corporate logo on the tail of its fleet. It replaced the corporate logo, with its hint of the British Union Jack, with a number of different 'artworks' created by artists from countries as far afield as Japan, Scotland and South Africa.

It needs to bring sectors of its business together under one banner: Prudential, formerly an insurance company, launched a new corporate identity in

1986 expressly for this purpose. The company wanted a new identity to
encompass all the financial services it now offered. On a larger scale,
when company A takes over company B it may want to keep company B's
name in the short term, perhaps because of the value of the brand, or so
as not to create too many ripples at once. But in the longer term it could
give company B a new identity with a closer relationship to company A,
or drop B's name altogether, as happened when the Hong Kong and
Shanghai Banking Corporation took over the Midland Bank. Of the
Midland's name and famous logo, a golden griffin surrounded by gold
coins, there is now no sign. The HSBC's double red triangle logo now
appears over the branch banks from Manchester to Manhattan.

The organisation has a new leader: As organisations become distinct entities
in their own right, they often lose their connection with their founder or
leading manager. But the arrival of a new person at the top of an
organisation can sometimes be a spur to looking again at the
organisation's corporate identity. When Aston University appointed Sir
Frederick Crawford as its new Vice Chancellor his immediate plan was to
improve the university's performance, and thus its image: this had to be
translated into visual terms in the form of a new corporate identity.

The impetus for change of corporate identity will often emerge from the
corporate public relations process described earlier in this chapter, and
might be one of the recommendations following a communications audit. A
corporate identity programme usually goes through the following five stages.

Development

A new corporate identity is developed following extensive research and
consultation. This work is often done by an external corporate identity
consultant, who may have a management, public relations or design
background. The consultant usually works with a group or working party
from within the client organisation. There will often be a fair amount of
discussion and disagreement when it comes to making recommendations for
a new corporate identity. Objectivity flies out of the window when people
start discussing real designs, and the fact that they hate purple or love
abstract art becomes much more important. However, once all the members
of the working party have thrashed out their disagreements and come to a
decision, they then need to present it.

Approval

The final corporate identity package, or a short-list of three or four, will then
be presented to the board of senior management of the organisation. There
is likely to be heated debate at this stage as well. How the presentation is
made is crucial. It must be clear that the final choice has been reached
following research, that the consultant and working party have stuck to
their brief, and that what has emerged is presented for sound reasons. It will
also be helpful to demonstrate to management how the designs will be

implemented: what the logo will look like in its different forms, how the identity will translate across different media and possibly across geographical frontiers.

Launch

The style of launch will depend on the organisation's size, culture, and the reasons why the new identity was required in the first place. The launch of the Prudential's new identity, which was largely targeted at staff, was a massive affair. A third of its total staff were brought to presentations in London, addressed by the Chief Executive and the Public Affairs Manager, and sent away, in the latter's words, 'two feet taller than when they went in'. The press and, unusually, competitors, were invited to the launch presentations and a vast amount of positive media coverage ensued.

Whether the launch is a low-key affair or takes the form of a big party, one thing is vital: it must demonstrate that the senior management of the organisation is fully committed to the new identity and that everyone in the organisation is required to implement it as instructed. 'As instructed' may take the form of a letter to staff from the Chief Executive Officer, a video, a package of material including, say, the new company tie, or a series of meetings at which implementation can be discussed face to face. The prior consultation process should have ensured that staff are aware of, and comfortable with, their individual roles in the process.

Implementation

During the development stage the working party will have given considerable thought to how the new identity is to be implemented. They should have talked to staff who generate written material, especially those who are responsible for correspondence, to get their views. Simple things, such as printing letterhead details at the bottom of the page, or placing a design so that it interferes with the use of window envelopes, can cause secretarial staff immense irritation if they have not previously been consulted.

At or immediately before the launch, staff will have been given a timetable for implementation. This may say that none of the old material is to be used after a specified date, or it may give a list of dates for gradual implementation, or it may take the approach that the new material is to replace the old only when stocks of the old material run out. The details will vary from organisation to organisation, and may be more to do with budgetary considerations than anything else. If old material is to be ditched, it is helpful to ensure staff know it will be re-cycled – most people cannot bear to waste what they see as perfectly good resources, and will be reluctant to throw clean stationery into the bin.

The organisation will have a style guide, put together to show how the new identity will look in the different media to which it is applied. There may be two versions of the guide: one, for general use, which will show how material should look in broad terms and which may give staff using it guidance on straightforward matters such as word-processing, ordering and photocopying. The other guide will be much more detailed and will provide comprehensive instructions which designers, typesetters and printers can use: Pantone colours, precise sizes, instructions on layout, whether or not various techniques such as reversing-out are allowed and how the corporate identity is to be used in different circumstances, and in conjunction with departmental or brand identities. An extract from a style guide is shown in Figure 5.3.

A comprehensive style guide may run to 100 pages and can cover:

all printed material for correspondence, business cards, forms, documents, reports and other publications, catering disposables such as sugar wrappers and napkins;

promotional material including print, but also advertising material, banners, sponsorship material, give-aways such as carrier bags, company gifts;

packaging including boxes, wrappings, instructions, labels;

signs on buildings, directional signs inside and outside, notices and notice-board applications;

livery uniforms or badges, hard hats, lab-coats and other safety wear, vehicle livery;

design of premises including decor, furniture, use of plants or flowers.

Maintenance

All the hard work and hard cash which have gone into a new corporate identity can be wasted if it is not properly maintained. Sometimes the identity consultant takes on the job of maintenance, sometimes it is the responsibility of a small group of staff who were involved in the working group, but more often it is the responsibility of the public relations department. If the department has its own designers, who can offer an advisory service to the organisation as a whole, so much the better.

Maintaining the identity can be difficult. There is a tendency for rigid instructions to be ignored either because staff think it does not matter, or because someone wants to be 'creative' and adapt the identity. If the groundwork has not been done before the launch stage, there may be ill-feeling in parts of the organisation, resulting in deliberate flouting of the style guide. Strong leadership at board level is important here. In any case, a senior manager must take overall responsibility for maintenance. This person should be able to tread the fine line between acting as corporate police officer and allowing too much leeway to departments.

Mechanisms for maintenance include:

meetings of design group: involving appropriate staff from across the organisation;

checking: material from across the organisation can be checked, randomly or according to a pre-determined plan, to ensure consistency of application;

Layout / guidelines

Reverse Out

When reversing out of a solid background use the single colour artwork. Only reverse out of fairly solid colours, do not use light or weak background colours.

Minimum size

The Corporate mark must not be reproduced smaller than this.

Digitised

It must not be digitised on a computer and the print-outs used as artwork for printing.

Distortion

It must not be distorted or the spatial proportions altered in any way.

Positioning

It must not be used at an angle or in any other unusual position.

Adding Titles

Do not add any other lines of type which appear to be part of the symbol.

Shapes

Do not contain the symbol within enclosed shapes

Symbol / 3 line variant

Important

The examples of the variant symbol illustrated below are for specific uses. They should only be used where it is impossible to use the standard symbol due to space restrictions

or structural restrictions. It's main uses are for external signage and classified advertising. Apply main symbol guidelines as to productions from master artwork and use of colours etc.

If you require any further advice please contact Communications and External Relations or Media Services.

2 Colour

Single Colour

Reverse out

Labels

Minimum size

Masthead or Banner

Source: 'Corporate identity guidelines for use of the main symbol', Leeds Metropolitan University, 1993

ordering: all orders for materials bearing the corporate identity can be routed through the corporate identity experts either at departmental level or within the central purchasing department;

staff involvement: new staff on induction into the organisation, and current employees, need to be reminded of everyone's role in maintaining corporate identity.

Corporate advertising

There are so many definitions of corporate advertising that it is perhaps easier to say what it is not, than what it is. Simply, corporate advertising does not seek to promote a brand or sell a product or service. Its purpose is to put across the organisation's name in one or more of the following contexts.

name awareness: companies whose corporate name is not well known may take out corporate advertising so that the public gets to know their name;

issues: an organisation may want to announce its stance on a specific issue which is being debated, such as shop opening hours;

positive news: winning a major award or prize, publishing excellent financial results or completing a successful take-over may provide the reason for some self-congratulatory corporate advertising;

recruitment: most recruitment advertising is corporate, but sometimes organisations facing particular skill shortages may want to place advertisements extolling the benefits of working for the organisation in general, rather than in specific jobs;

information: much corporate advertising is in the form of information or announcements about the organisation, covering share issues, changes in company policy, and availability of further information or advisory services provided by the organisation.

Case Study 5.1

Corporate public relations
Shell International: Fishburn Hedges/J Walter Thomson/Shell in-house team

Following a review of its public relations and advertising strategies, Shell launched its first global corporate communications campaign in 1999. The company's objective was to re-position itself as a caring, open and environmentally responsible organisation. The campaign used public relations to make its case in communicating with its stakeholders: consumers, employees, environmental groups and opinion formers.

Corporate advertising was used in support of the public relations effort. The advertisements offered two different perspectives, one positive and one negative, on a series of issues of current concern, with headlines such as 'Cloud the issue or clear the air?' on pollution, and

'Exploit or explore?' on rainforest destruction. The advertising copy stresses Shell's commitment to the positive resolution of these problems but concludes without a strap-line. Their public relations consultant says this is because 'there's no single thought we want to leave the audience with. The response to the campaign must come from the audience – that's definitely a PR-led idea – whereas strap-lines tell audiences what to think'.

Shell's in-house team was responsible for a media relations campaign as a component of the corporate public relations programme, including the launch of Shell's second annual 'social' report. They are also heavily involved in the internal communications strand of the campaign, designed to ensure that the company's 100,000 employees in 132 countries take on board Shell's social and ethical business principles in their day-to-day working. Compliance with these principles is also a condition of acceptance for any contractor company that wants to work with Shell.

The new corporate public relations campaign included an improved website design with access to a discussion forum.

(*Source*: *PR Week* 1999b)

David Bernstein (1986: Chapter 27) quotes two surveys on corporate advertising. The first gives a list of ten possible objectives:

1 Build awareness of a corporation's identity.

2 Improve understanding of a company's area of business.

3 Overcome poor attitudes to a company.

4 Explain corporate philosophy and policies.

5 Illustrate achievement.

6 Enhance a company's image as an investment.

7 Advocate social change useful to a corporation.

8 Secure support of useful legislation.

9 Provide a unified view of a corporation to its employees.

10 Aid in recruitment.

(Garbett 1981, cited in Bernstein 1986: 181)

The second, conducted in 1982 by Research Services Ltd and the *Financial Times*, asked companies to give the primary and secondary objectives of their corporate advertising. Combining responses from the first 32 companies, Table 5.1 shows that the most important factors were to improve awareness of the nature of their business, to improve their reputation as a company to do business with, to provide marketing support, to demonstrate the company's contribution to the British economy, and to improve the company's standing in the financial community.

| Table 5.1 | *Objectives of corporate advertising* |

This objective is . . .	primary (%)	secondary (%)
To improve awareness of the nature of your business	34	50
To provide unified marketing support for the company's present and future products, services and capabilities	25	34
To inform your target groups about issues of importance to the public and to the company, its industry or business in general	6	31
To communicate the company's concern and record of achievement on social or environmental issues	—	19
To demonstrate the company's contribution to the British economy	9	38
To improve the company's standing in the financial community	13	34
To motivate private shareholders	3	13
To improve your reputation as an employer	—	22
To improve your reputation as a company to do business with	19	41
To overcome some bad publicity or correct bad image	—	13
To withstand or to launch a take-over/merger	—	6

Source: Financial Times/RSL survey adapted from Bernstein (1986: 182)

Tench and Yeomans (1997) reported that the purpose of corporate advertising had changed from 'goodwill' in the 1960s, to issue and advocacy advertising in the 1970s, 'umbrella' advertising in support of a range of products or brands in the decade of mergers and privatisations, the 1980s, and a focus on the organisation's strategic aims and objectives in the 1990s. They found that while newspapers remain the favoured medium for placing corporate advertising, the Internet is increasingly being used.

A corporate advertising campaign is usually costly. Advertisements have to look good and be placed in the right surroundings. The message needs to be appropriate and memorable. But much corporate advertising is rather soft-focus: a nice picture of the globe, say, or a new born baby, and copy along the lines of 'We're great, we care, we're here when you need us', with a strap-line claiming something either innocuous or meaningless. Companies such as Union Carbide ('Advancing environmental excellence') and Bayer ('Expertise with responsibility') could probably swap lines, with no one noticing. The TI Group, with 'World leadership in specialised engineering' is a little more specific, but could probably be claimed by half a dozen companies without stretching belief.

The important point to remember about corporate advertising, as with the other elements of the corporate public relations process, is that it should have an objective and the results should be evaluated. While it is rather a long shot to claim that a series of advertisements has changed people's attitudes towards one's company, recall of advertisements in specific media can be checked, share prices can be tracked and positive (or absence of negative) comment and articles can be noted. BP certainly felt their expenditure on corporate advertising over two decades was worthwhile, and believed that measures such as advertisement recall were important (Tench and Yeomans 1997: 203–6).

Summary points

✔ Corporate public relations encompasses all the communications activities which an organisation undertakes as a corporate entity. It excludes departmental or branch activities, or public relations undertaken on behalf of a product, service or brand.

✔ The corporate public relations process falls into four stages: finding out where you are, formulating a corporate public relations strategy, implementing the programme which follows from it and monitoring and reviewing the results.

✔ A communications audit is a useful tool to help organisations find out where they are. The elements of a corporate public relations programme may include overhauling the organisation's corporate identity; a corporate advertising campaign; an investor relations programme; ensuring staff understand corporate policy; a programme of community liaison; and sponsorship.

✔ An organisation's corporate image is the way in which it is perceived by others. It is made up of perceptions about the organisation's personality, its reputation, its corporate identity and an understanding of its values.

✔ A change of corporate identity may arise for a number of different reasons: change of name; dated look; the need to transmit a different message about the company; change in company activities; change in direction.

✔ The five stages of a corporate identity programme are development, approval, launch, implementation and maintenance.

✔ The purpose of corporate advertising may be: to generate or improve name awareness; to proclaim the organisation's views on an issue of the day; to publicise positive news; as an aid to recruitment; or simply to give information about the organisation. Much corporate advertising is unmemorable and the messages given by firms are often interchangeable.

Questions for discussion

1 'Solid profits and a strong balance sheet help make a great company. But they may not be enough to make it admired. Admiration counts' (*Economist* survey, 1991). Which companies do you admire, and why? Are there specific qualities which admirable companies have and if so, what are they? How are they projected?

2 Suppose you were asked to contribute the proceeds of a fund-raising event for famine relief to one of the following charities: War on Want, Oxfam,

Christian Aid, an appeal launched by the United Nations. What image do you have of these different organisations? How would the image you have of them affect your decision?

3 Look at the recruitment advertising in one of the quality newspapers and compare the logos of organisations advertising there. Consider how the design relates to the organisation. How does it look on the page? What messages does it convey to you? Do some logos work better than others? Why?

Recommended further reading

Van Riel (1995) is probably the most useful single text on the subject of corporate communication. David Bernstein's (1986) very readable book provides a good range of examples of corporate communication in action, as well as thoughtful insights into the purpose and function of corporate public relations. Caywood (1997) views public relations as integrated communication and most of his contributors are exponents of corporate communication in one sector or another.

The value of corporate image in relation to the organisation's reputation is the subject of Fombrun (1995), who provides good analyses of the dynamic nature of reputation. Haywood (1994), is worth reading for a UK perspective on the subject of reputation management. Tench and Yeomans (1997) have written a fascinating (and rare) chapter on corporate advertising in the UK. Design consultant Wally Olins' (1989) attractive book gives examples illustrating different approaches to the implementation of corporate identity.

Booth (1988) and Hamilton (1987) give practical advice on conducting a communications audit.

References

Bernstein, D. (1986) *Company Image and Reality: a Critique of Corporate Communications*, London: Cassell.

Booth, A. (1988) *The Communications Audit: a Guide for Managers*, Aldershot: Gower.

Caywood, C. (1997) *The Handbook of Strategic Public Relations and Integrated Communications*, New York: McGraw-Hill.

Fombrun, C. (1995) *Reputation: Realising Value from the Corporate Image*, Boston, MA: Harvard Business School.

Garbett, T. (1981) *Corporate Advertising: the What, the Why and the How*, New York: McGraw-Hill.

Hamilton, S. (1987) *A Communication Audit Handbook: Helping Organisations to Communicate*, Harlow: Longman.

Haywood, R. (1994) *Managing Your Reputation: How to Plan and Run Communications Programmes that Win Friends and Build Business*, London: McGraw-Hill.

Hendrix, J. (1998) *Public Relations Cases*, London: Wadsworth.

Hewlett Packard (1993) *Standards of Business Conduct*, Palo Alto, CA: Hewlett Packard Company.

Olins, W. (1989) *Corporate Identity*, London: Thames and Hudson.

PR Week (1999b) 'Analysis' 19 March.

Tench, R. and Yeomans, L. (1997) 'Corporate Advertising: the Generic Image', in Kitchen, P. (ed.), *Public Relations: Principles and Practice*, London: International Thomson Business Press.

Van Riel, C. (1995) *Principles of Corporate Communication*, London: Prentice Hall.

Washingtonian, The (1995) 'Hit the Road, Mick', January.

White, J. (1991) *How to Understand and Manage Public Relations*, London: Business Books.

Worcester. R. (1983) 'Measuring the impact of corporate advertising' *Admap* September.

6

Crisis public relations

Key Issues

The aim of this chapter is to show how public relations is used in crisis management. The key points considered are:

▶ recognition of issues and crises;

▶ the principles of crisis management: planning and preparation, managing the provision of accurate, authoritative and timely information, sensitivity and learning from experience;

▶ the importance of training and rehearsal;

▶ the effects of crisis public relations on those involved.

No public relations textbook would be complete without a chapter on crisis management. Crises, disasters, scandals and emergencies are certainly big news stories, but crisis public relations is not only about dealing with the media. Planning for the unexpected, thinking the unthinkable, knowing the unknowns: these are different ways of expressing the idea that forward planning for a crisis is important.

This chapter looks at the general principles of crisis management which have been outlined by public relations practitioners and examines why they should work, and how they did work in some well-publicised cases.

Avoiding a crisis: issues management

The idea of issues management as a discrete and vital function originated in the 1970s (Ewing 1997: 173) when companies began to wake up to the idea that public policy and public opinion (in the form of special interest groups) could have a major impact on their profitable operation. If an issue is identified by the organisation at an early enough stage, something can be done about it: the organisation can change its plans, re-direct its communications effort or lobby government on its own behalf. But if an issue is ignored and taken up by the media or other opinion leaders it can easily turn into a crisis for the company concerned.

A good example of the escalation of an issue, initially of very little interest to anyone, into something which attracted the attention of the media and the public, is McVitie's, the UK biscuit manufacturer. The issue – the use of fish oil in biscuits – was brought to public attention by the environmental pressure group Greenpeace. The process involved in sourcing the fish oil which McVitie's used was endangering the food supplies of the puffin, a very cute looking sea bird which every child could recognise by its striped bill. Greenpeace brought this to the attention of McVitie's. When the company took no notice, Greenpeace protesters, dressed up as puffins, undertook a demonstration outside the firm's factory, ensuring that it would be well covered by the media. The story, accompanied by full colour photographs of the 'puffins' outside the factory, made a splash in the national press and caused McVitie's to announce a change to its ingredient sourcing policy on the spot. The issue had become a crisis, and the only way to deal with it was to change company policy.

What is a crisis?

A crisis can be defined as a dramatic change, usually for the worse. It may be a disaster: an event which involves loss of life or extensive damage to property; or it may be a situation when an organisation finds itself under unwelcome scrutiny because of its behaviour or that of its staff. A crisis may occur as a result of an accident or act of God; it may arise because of the negligence or criminal behaviour of an individual or organisation; or it may happen to a company as a result of product tampering or other sabotage. It may happen suddenly or there may be a slow build-up as a local difficulty escalates into a full-blown crisis.

Frank Jefkins gives a graphic illustration of seventeen different types of crisis which could afflict Big Ben, the clock tower above the Houses of Parliament in London, dividing them into possible and impossible crises.

Possible crises

1 Could be struck by lightning.

2 Could be hit by aircraft.

3 Could be blown up by terrorists.

4 Could collapse on House of Commons.

5 Could collapse in river Thames.

6 Could be destroyed by wartime bombing or rocketry.

7 Clock could be stopped or time changed by fanatic.

8 Could be daubed or have banners hung on it.

9 Bell could disintegrate.

10 Belfry could be invaded by thousands of starlings.

Impossible (?) crises

1 Could be stolen by false contractors removing, like previous London Bridge.

2 Could be occupied by demonstrators or other fanatics.

3 Could have time mechanism distorted by some electronic or laser device.

4 Could be privatised by Mrs Thatcher [then Prime Minister], and BBC etc. charged royalty for reproducing sound of Big Ben.

5 Destruction could be threatened by IRA, Libyans, Palestinians, etc. if prisoner not released.

6 A kidnapper could hold a victim in the clock chamber.

7 Legislation could be passed to have the bell silenced.

(Jefkins 1988: 295–6)

He goes on to consider how many, if any, of these potential crises may have been considered by Big Ben's custodians, and what measures might have been taken to deal with such crises happening. This is an example of the first step in any crisis management programme: asking the question 'what if?'. Once an organisation has got to the stage of thinking about the kinds of crisis which could affect it, it is well on the way to setting up a crisis management plan.

This brings us to the ten principles of crisis public relations which form the backbone of this chapter and which are summarised in Figure 6.1.

These principles have been distilled from the extensive literature on crisis public relations and from personal experience. They can act as an aid in crisis public relations planning and a reminder during a crisis. How organisations handle crises affects their reputation with the public as well as their future relationships with journalists. Let us look at the principles in more detail.

1 Be prepared

We can subdivide this further.

Scenario planning

Successful scenario planning needs to involve staff from different parts of the organisation and different levels in the hierarchy, so as to bring as much experience and as many views to bear as possible. It is often helpful to have a facilitator – a management or public relations consultant – to help the process along. By brainstorming, a lengthy list of everything that could possibly go wrong can be compiled and worked through. When all possible topics have been covered, a good consultant will probably come up with a

Principles of crisis public relations | **Figure 6.1**

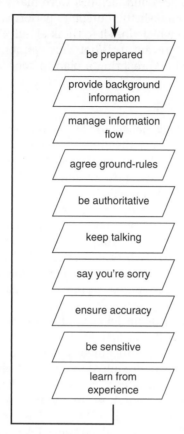

be prepared

provide background information

manage information flow

agree ground-rules

be authoritative

keep talking

say you're sorry

ensure accuracy

be sensitive

learn from experience

few more from his or her own experience. These scenarios can then be worked on, asking the question 'what if?', and refined. For example, what if there were a fire at the company's headquarters? And what if the managing director and head of public relations were respectively on holiday and off sick? What if it happened over a bank holiday weekend? What if the fire destroyed the computer system? What if the entire senior management of the company were away on a team-building exercise and their boat capsized?

It is important if such brainstorming is to work successfully that every scenario is considered, however improbable it may seem. Try this.

What if a jumbo jet exploded and fell out of the sky? Suppose it had only just taken off and so was full of fuel. What if it landed on a small town in a remote region? Suppose it was just before Christmas, freezing cold and pitch dark. What if the wreckage completely severed the main road link between England and Scotland? What if the hundreds of casualties came from over 20 countries? If this is beginning to sound unrealistic, cast your mind back to December 1988, Pan Am flight 103 and the town of Lockerbie.

You might reasonably expect an airline to have considered the elements of the Lockerbie disaster. But there was no particular reason why the local emergency services would have done so, nor the local authority, Dumfries and Galloway, whose offices and facilities were many miles away. Scenario planning, however outlandish the outcome, performs the vital function of getting the organisation which does it to think about what could befall them so that they can try to prevent it. What they cannot prevent becomes the subject of our next section: preparing a plan to cope with the crisis.

Crisis management planning

Scenario planning will have helped to identify not only what could happen, but who the most important individuals would be at a time of crisis. From that stage it is a relatively straightforward matter to choose a crisis management team, with clear responsibilities at both the planning stage and the time of crisis. The team will almost certainly include the managing director or equivalent, the head of public relations or whoever is assigned responsibility for communications, one or two press officers, someone from the finance department, and the person responsible for buildings maintenance and security. Each organisation will have its own version of a crisis management team, and it may be appropriate in some organisations to include staff from the computer section, the legal department and the switchboard.

The team should take responsibility for drawing up a plan which can be taken down from the shelf and activated when required. This means the plan needs to be clear and unequivocal so that whoever uses it can understand what it is they are required to do. But it also needs to be flexible enough to be adapted for whatever crisis occurs. There is little point, for example, in stipulating exactly how many telephone lines need to be available in a specified room which will be used as a press centre, when the crisis may happen miles away and portable telecommunications will be needed. The important thing is to make clear whose job it is to ensure that a press facility is made available, and that that person knows how to provide such a facility at a moment's notice.

Members of the team should meet regularly even when the crisis plan has been drawn up. It is important that they keep in touch and that the plan is continually reviewed and updated to take account not only of changes in personnel and within the organisation, but to keep up to date with media contacts and improvements in technology.

Rehearsal

Once a crisis management plan has been formulated, the only way to test it is to rehearse. It is too late to practice when the crisis happens. The emergency services, the utilities, high-risk companies in the chemical and similar industries and the major transport undertakings regularly run practice exercises. Every organisation with a crisis management plan should do so, to test that the plan works, to keep it up to date and to keep everyone concerned on their toes.

It is often a good idea to let a specialist crisis management consultant or trainer loose on the organisation's plan, giving him or her *carte blanche* to create a scenario and 'ambush' the organisation. An example of how this was done is given in Case Study 6.1.

Crisis planning
Porsche: Leonard Saffir

Leonard Saffir, in a chapter on the secrets of crisis management, gives a nail-biting account of an accident involving a school bus and a Porsche sports car, driven in excess of the speed limit by a Porsche executive, at the time of a high profile advertising campaign focusing on the high-performance aspects of the car. The first Porsche knew of the accident was when a local television reporter rang the company to ask for a comment. Saffir goes on to say:

> It was a dramatic story, with tremendous media appeal and serious national implications. And yet very few readers of this book have ever heard anything about it. The reason? The accident which triggered these events never happened. [It was] part of Project Ambush, a crisis management fire drill for Porsche Cars North America.

> (*Source*: Saffir 1993: 82. Used with permission of NTC/ Contemporary Publishing Group)

---

2 Provide background information

When a crisis occurs everything happens at once, and very fast. It has been estimated that at Lockerbie the media outnumbered the entire Dumfries and Galloway Constabulary – part of whose job was to protect evidence in what would be Scotland's largest ever murder investigation – within 24 hours. It is not uncommon for over a thousand reporters, photographers, sound recordists and camera crew to be present at a large-scale disaster. They all have to get back to their news editors with something – the picture, the story, the inside story, the human interest angle. The public relations officer who can imagine what it is like for the journalist can help the journalist do a better job.

One of the problems at crisis time is that often the public relations officer can say nothing at all to help the journalist with the story. Perhaps the public relations officer knows nothing yet, the situation is still unclear, or the lines of communication have not started to unwind. Perhaps the public relations officer is prevented from saying anything by legal advisers. But if the journalist goes away empty handed, a story will come from somewhere to fill the column inches or the broadcast minutes – from an unreliable 'eye witness' who heard something, or from a disgruntled ex-employee with an axe to grind, from someone who wants to be famous for 15 minutes by being on the telly, or as a last resort from the journalist's own imagination.

If the public relations officer has plenty of usable background information at the ready, this will go at least some way to filling the gap. In any case it is vital to have material to hand about the organisation, giving essential facts and figures, names, dates, locations, operations and so on, together with good quality black and white photographs of the premises, the products and appropriate members of staff.

Media coverage of the shipping industry following the sinking of the roll-on roll-off ferry Estonia in 1994 provides a good example. Reporters all over the world wanted to know how safe were the ro-ro ferries operating on their patch of water. British ferry operators were prepared for the media onslaught, co-ordinating their response through the Chamber of Shipping's director of marine services, Walter Welch. He appeared on numerous radio bulletins and gave interviews to every newspaper in the country. 'By answering every question, we've been able to convince the press we've nothing to hide', he said. 'We stand by our record.'

Journalists were provided with figures which showed that UK ferries carried 14 million cars and 51 million passengers on 84,000 sailings in the previous year. They were also given briefing sheets, in user-friendly question and answer format, on ferry design and operational practice, so that they could more easily and accurately compile their stories.

As the crisis unfolds there will be times when there is not much to be said between one press conference and another when a fund of human interest stories can be generated. Perhaps someone has been very brave or selfless; there may need to be an appeal for food, clothes or shelter; a VIP is coming to visit the injured: these can all provide stories for the media and fill the gaps between set-piece releases of real news. Where a disaster is the subject of legal inquiries and the organisation cannot know whether or not it will be held responsible, it is even more important to ensure that there are plenty of other things to talk about.

Following the disaster at Hillsborough football ground in Sheffield, when 96 people received fatal injuries during a soccer match between Liverpool and Nottingham Forest, a public inquiry was announced almost immediately. However, it took almost two years before the inquiry and inquests were completed, and it was not until then that the council knew they would not be held responsible for the deaths and injuries. In the meantime, reporters wanted to know everything about everything, and most particularly about safety inspections and safety certificates, something which was *sub judice* until the inquiries were complete. The press team at Sheffield council had to deal with this problem. They did so by establishing a regular flow of information to reporters, trying to ensure that they never went away empty-handed, even if there were some topics on which the council could not provide the answers the journalists were looking for.

3 Manage the flow of information

In a crisis situation events move fast and in a haphazard fashion. Sometimes the first the organisation affected knows about the crisis is when a reporter telephones or turns up on the doorstep to confirm what is happening. In such a situation it is vital that the organisation takes immediate control of the information process. This is vital for three reasons.

Why?

First, the organisation will look foolish, incompetent or even negligent if it gives the impression that it does not know what is going on. If it appears to know but refuses to say, the organisation will look shifty, secretive and untrustworthy. When the spotlight is on you, it is impossible to keep a low profile. In any case, keeping a tight hold on information and saying 'no comment' merely creates a vacuum, into which will fall speculation, rumour and gossip, all totally outside the organisation's control.

Second, it is important that the organisation in crisis speaks with one voice. There may be different experts acting as spokespeople for the organisation, but the media and the general public will be sensitive to any inconsistencies or different interpretations within the organisation. Thus it is more important than ever when the heat is on that these should not surface publicly. The discipline of good, well-organised internal communication really shows its worth at a time of crisis and helps the staff to do their job better at a time when they may be feeling nervous and unsure.

Third, managing information properly makes for greater clarity. Staff know who is to speak on what issue, and what is to be said. Journalists know who to approach, how and when, to ensure they get their stories and pictures. A well-organised response to a crisis can even make the event itself less newsworthy.

How?

Remember the crisis plan you drew up, perfected, rehearsed and updated? This should have covered how you will manage the flow of information. You may have classified potential crises and have a different response for each level of incident. Unocal UK, operators of a north sea oil platform, uses the following system. Incidents are classified as *A* (possible serious injury or damage to installations), *B* (fatalities and/or serious damage to an installation requiring shut down) and *C* (potential catastrophe). In each case, implications for the media response team are considered. For an *A* incident it would be inappropriate to bring in a media response team or an external public relations consultant, but media inquiries would be handled by a designated individual within the company, and inquiries from relatives by the personnel department. A level *C* incident would call for the full media response team with public relations co-ordination (McDonald 1990: 195–6).

Some crisis plans may allow for only one designated spokesperson, who needs to be on-call at all times. This person will almost certainly have a public relations adviser close by. Describing the aftermath of the Hillsborough disaster in Liverpool, Paddy Marley of the social services department said:

one person, the director of social services for Liverpool, was appointed as the media spokesperson for all five local authorities on Merseyside and all contact was directed through him. He was relieved of his normal departmental role which was taken on by his deputy. He was given the full time services of a senior public relations officer who advised on presentation, content of briefings and so on. All the media were informed that there would be only one general press conference per day and all the facts and figures available would be disseminated then. This provided the basic structure for information giving and both the city council and the media could plan accordingly.

(Marley 1999: 147)

Sheffield Council approached things differently.

Every morning before the normal day's work began, a group of council officers met briefly to clear who was responsible for saying what on a number of issues. From the news and information perspective, the purpose of these sessions was twofold: to bring everyone up to date on what had happened over the past 24 hours and to predict what was thought likely to crop up during the coming day. The meetings were usually over with in less than half an hour, when everyone could go about their business confident that they were clear about who was the authoritative source on each issue. The system also made clear organisationally that certain named individuals had the responsibility of talking to the press, so that everyone who did not could get on with their jobs.

(Harrison 1999: 162)

However an organisation decides to manage the flow of information, all the experts agree that whoever speaks on the organisation's behalf must be properly trained to do so. The ability to deal calmly with a battery of cameras and a scuffle of reporters is a learned skill which takes practice.

4 Agree the ground-rules

Interested parties

Forward planning for a crisis should enable the organisation to identify other parties with an interest in any crisis that might affect it. Such interested parties may include the organisation's insurers, its legal advisers, its subsidiaries, its suppliers, other organisations operating in the same sector (a poorly handled crisis in a chemical company affects the reputation of the entire chemical industry), and the emergency services serving the organisation's local area. The organisation's public relations advisers will certainly have an interest.

It is helpful to have agreed with these interested parties beforehand what the ground-rules will be when the crisis breaks. This might include agreeing what can and cannot be said publicly without reference to the organisation concerned, so that the various spokespeople can avoid unnecessarily getting in each other's way, or passing the buck, or blaming each other.

Others may try to dictate the ground-rules. For example, insurance companies and lawyers are usually insistent that no one say anything at all following an accident. Every motorist is familiar with the advice from the insurer: exchange names and addresses but do not say anything about the accident. The chief executive officer of the organisation has to consider whether or not this is reasonable, and thus whether to take the insurer's advice. In one of the most celebrated examples of good crisis public relations practice, the Kegworth air crash, British Midland's spokesman, Sir Michael Bishop, made himself instantly available to say as much as possible about the accident and the circumstances surrounding it. It is hard to believe that the company's insurers would have advised such an approach, but there is no doubt that it was the right one to take.

The media

Paddy Marley (1999: 147), recalling his bitter experience with national newspaper reporters in Liverpool, is adamant that 'responses to the media are organised and controlled and rules of engagement are agreed'. Any reporter failing to abide by these rules would forego privileges, such as entry to the daily press briefing. While this may seem a hard line to take, he reached his conclusion after having to issue 300 social services staff with new identification cards because unscrupulous reporters had obtained the original cards and were attempting to gain access to the bereaved by posing as social workers.

The ground-rules do not necessarily have to be about excluding the media, however. Controlled access can be helpful to all concerned. One way of controlling access is by the pooling system. In such a case, representatives of the media – a national press reporter and photographer, a local reporter, a crew from ITN or BBC television and both local and national radio reporters – are selected. The representatives are then taken to the site of the disaster and allowed to take pictures, do interviews and get relevant material. They are then required to pool their material with all the other members of the media. Clive Ferguson, Home Assignment Editor for *BBC TV News*, gives:

> a word of warning, though: if you do decide to organise a pool, do not try to set it up yourself. Leave it to the broadcasters to sort out. We do it all the time, and it means that we will only have ourselves to blame if it all goes wrong – and you can emerge untarnished, and still be friends with everyone.
>
> (Ferguson 1999: 43).

Another way is to select volunteer victims or eye-witnesses who are willing to talk to the media under controlled conditions. This will give the reporters and photographers their stories and pictures while taking the pressure off other victims who are unwilling or unable to take the glare of publicity. For those who can do so, it is thought that talking about it in public can be a helpful experience in dealing with the trauma of a disaster. That is certainly the view of Paul Corley of Carlton Television, who justifies the making of a documentary series *The Day I Nearly Died* thus: 'survivors of Hillsborough, King's Cross and the Manchester air fire believe it can help by bringing these stories out into the open – one major traumatising effect of disasters is that victims and relatives bottle up emotions and do not talk about it' (Corley 1994).

This view is not universally held, however, and there may be different considerations for interviews conducted immediately following a disaster, before survivors have had time to be de-briefed and counselled. The sole British survivor of the Estonia ferry disaster gave a number of lengthy news conferences immediately after his ordeal, describing in detail how he survived for several hours in the freezing waters of the Baltic. But when reporters asked how he felt about what happened he was hurried away by medical staff. It is believed to be damaging to record what survivors say about their feelings immediately following a disaster, as they may be deeply distressed to be reminded of it at a later stage, when they have had chance to reflect and come to terms with what has happened to them and to those who did not survive.

Writing in an internal newsletter in 1993, Mike Granatt and David Dowle of the Metropolitan Police's directorate of public affairs explained how making the ground-rules clear worked in one instance for the victim's relative, the police press officers and the media:

> Reporters do understand the need to work sensitively with victims, and if the playing field is level for all of them, they behave with appropriate care.
>
> In a recent case, the wife of a murder victim agreed to meet the press at New Scotland Yard for a few minutes. More than 50 of the media set themselves up around the table where she was going to speak, and waited uncomplaining in a very hot room for an hour until she arrived. They were silent for most of the short time she was present, leaving it to one selected woman reporter to ask most of the questions.
>
> The ability to make such arrangements depends on the credibility and professionalism of those making them. It is in no one's interest to get it wrong; trust and clarity of purpose and procedure are vital.
>
> (Granatt and Dowle 1993: 26)

5 Be authoritative

By taking the initiative from the very beginning, it is possible to establish the organisation's press team as the authoritative source of information about what has happened and what the organisation is doing about it. If the journalist wants to know, he or she will have to ask the organisation's press officers or public relations consultants.

Of course, any reporter worth the name will find eyewitnesses to talk to, may get opposing views from local residents or pressure groups who have a view on your organisation's business, behaviour or practices, and will be looking to find a new angle on the story, aside from the organisation's official line. But it is important that the organisation is willing and able to act as the single source of clear information at the time of the crisis and subsequently.

Authority may come from a number of causes. The organisation may be the only source of information; or it may be the only credible source because other sources do not have access to property, records or staff. Authority may spring from the status or demeanour of the organisation's spokesperson: is it the chief executive officer or an anonymous 'company spokesman'? Does the person exude confidence, *gravitas*, expert knowledge?

The breadth of knowledge required to handle the information requests is likely to be staggering. When the Piper Alpha oil platform burst into flames a huge number of questions arose, ranging from numbers and nationalities of people on board (dead and alive) and of rescue vessels; through the history of the platform and of north sea oil exploration; comparisons of Norwegian and UK safety regulations; safety equipment and arrangements; likely public inquiry and its remit, chairman, location, duration; history of disaster funds; history of trade union complaints about safety; and 'how to spell Red Adair and the likely size of his bank balance' (Granatt 1999: 116–17).

When agreeing roles during the planning process it is crucial to decide who speaks for the organisation. The media's preference is for the most high profile, most senior person – the managing director, say, or chief executive, or a figure-head. While they may not mind being briefed by a press officer, the public relations officer is not likely to get many requests to be interviewed. It may be that the person who is most expert on the subject or the best performer in a television studio is a better bet from the organisation's point of view than the most senior person. Certainly there is an issue here about forward planning: whoever is going to face the press, the microphones and the cameras needs to be fully equipped to do so – equipped in every sense. If that means sending the boss off on a series of training courses, so be it.

Media training	Case Study 6.2

EU Directorate General XII: Goldwyn Associates

The European Commission arranged for scientists working in its Directorate General XII to receive media training from television production company Goldwyn Associates in April 1999. The scientists work on projects such as genetically modified (GM) crops which, at the time, were a major subject of debate throughout Europe and beyond. Companies with a financial interest in GM foods were promoting the advantages of growing such groups, while environmental groups were doing the opposite, with emotional campaigns dubbing the products 'Frankenstein foods' capturing the media's and the public's attention.

The straightforward scientific facts were not easily got across by technical people accustomed to using jargon not readily understood by the public. Goldwyn's brief was to train the scientists to communicate without jargon, focusing on content and style. The scientists, including directors of GM laboratories and project leaders from research programmes, learned how to address chief executives, public authorities, journalists and members of the public.

The developing crisis of confidence in GM foods in Europe had meant that the fruits of EU-sponsored research were being ignored by European public authorities and companies, and were instead being snapped up for commerical development by US and Japanese investors. The EU hoped by investing in media training for its scientists to reverse this trend.

(*Source*: *PR Week* 1999d)

Authoritative spokespeople, who are properly briefed and trained, and a well-managed information process, controlled by experienced and practised press officers, will be able to slake the thirst of the media and the public for information and stories, so long as proper planning has been done beforehand.

6 Keep talking

This advice echoes the earlier point: provide background information. If everything is *sub judice* it is a mistake to say nothing, or to say 'We have no comment to make'. Rightly or wrongly, silence is always construed as secretiveness. If you are not saying anything, what have you got to hide?

So, what can you say? The best advice is to explain why you cannot answer questions about the specific matter in hand, to give out your carefully prepared background material and talk about something else. Journalists need to have something to take away.

> There are no empty newspaper columns or silent or pictureless broadcasts. If hard, accurate information is unavailable, something far less desirable will fill the space. If no organised vantage points are made available, the pictures will have to be taken from somewhere else.
>
> To quote a Lockerbie relative speaking about a desperate TV reporter: 'I realised that nobody sent this guy 3,000 miles for him to say "I can't get the story"'.
>
> (Granatt and Dowle 1993: 24)

'Keep talking' does not, though, equate to 'ramble on at all costs'. If there is really nothing to say, say so in clear terms, but offer some hope for the future. An example may be: 'We cannot tell you anything more at the moment because there is nothing to say. But there will be a news conference at 12 noon today and I promise we will bring you up to date with developments then'.

'Keep talking' is not an invitation to provide additional information which is of no help to the organisation. The media do not know as much about the organisation as the organisation knows about itself and half a story may lead to all sorts of spurious connections being made. When product recalls are announced in the press, notice that the company always specifies the batch number or other identifying factor of the product. This is not solely to prevent its retailers being swamped unnecessarily with non-faulty goods: it is at least as important to disassociate all other products and brands from the one which is faulty. So when Johnson and Johnson had to deal with the massive media response to news that their Tylenol painkillers had been tampered with, causing death by cyanide poisoning, they 'restricted the discussion to Tylenol, did not discuss other products and guarded the corporate reputation' (Bernstein 1986: 231).

7 Say you are sorry

This is a tricky one, and other experts on the subject of crisis management may disagree. Certainly the cautious lawyer or insurer will advise against saying 'sorry', but there is a view that expressing regret is a different matter from making an apology, and that expressing sorrow at a disastrous or tragic event is perfectly proper behaviour. The airline El Al surprised many by taking full-page advertisements in the Amsterdam press to express their sorrow at the carnage caused when one of their planes crashed in a residential suburb in 1992: they did this long before it was possible to tell whether they could ultimately be held responsible.

If in fact there has been cause for concern about the organisation's behaviour, this will surface anyway, and it can be helpful to pre-empt unnecessary criticism by being open at the very beginning. Sam Black deals briskly with the problem of legal advisers who urge companies to refrain from saying sorry.

> An opportunity to gain some advantage from an unfortunate accident arises from the way in which relatives of the dead or injured are treated. This is an occasion for hospitality to be extended without stint and for maximum sensitivity to be exercised. If a lawyer is present, there may be pressure on the company to avoid any expression of sympathy lest this be taken to imply liability. Any suggestion of this kind must be resisted and in some circumstances the offer of *ex gratia* payments may be part of the way in which sympathy can be expressed in practical terms. Lawyers must be told that the consequences to the company of not communicating and showing sympathy in practical terms are sure to be much worse than if an open policy of full information and generosity is adopted.
>
> (Black 1993: 143)

8 Ensure accuracy

This advice falls into two areas: always make sure that the organisation is giving out accurate information, and ensure that what is printed is accurate.

Tell the truth

A public relations practitioner's personal moral code or the company's code of ethics may require this. However, those whose ethical standards are not so scrupulous should remember that telling the truth is not solely an ethical issue. It is practical. First of all it is easier than concocting complicated lies, and second, there is no danger of being found out if you tell the truth. Journalists are generally pretty good at getting to the bottom of an unsound story. While you do not need to volunteer information which is not asked for, it is always wise to ensure the accuracy and truthfulness of what you say. Information may need to be given out on the initiative of the organisation, especially if it discovers something which could be damaging in the hands of the media. Case Study 6.3 gives an example of how an organisation prevented the spectacle of being unmasked as negligent, simply by releasing material to the media instead of letting it be 'found out'.

Case Study 6.3

Crisis management

Bradford City Football Club fire: Bradford Council

In the spring of 1985 during one of the last games of the soccer season, a catastrophic fire destroyed the stand at Bradford City Football Club, causing many deaths and injuries. The stand was made of wood and, in hindsight, was an accident waiting to happen.

West Yorkshire Metropolitan District Council had written to the football club a few months before the fire with a warning about the stand. 'The timber construction is a fire hazard' the letter said, and 'a carelessly discarded cigarette could give rise to a fire risk'. The club was then in the third division and so did not need to have a general safety certificate, but when the fire happened they were due to be promoted to the second division, when a certificate would be required. In fact, West Yorkshire and Bradford councils, the police and the fire service had a meeting planned to discuss the safety certificate for the Wednesday following the match on the Saturday. The stand itself was in any case due for demolition two days after the match.

Copies of the letter warning of the fire risk had been sent to Bradford Council at the same time as the football club received theirs. The implication could easily have been made that the warning had been ignored.

Three days after the disaster, the chief executive of Bradford council issued a press statement acknowledging receipt of the letter and explaining why the council had been powerless to act: responsibility for ground safety and the issuing of a safety certificate was not yet theirs. A press officer said later 'It was very much the right thing to do. We owned up right away, as soon as we knew we had done something which could be seriously criticised'.

The statement was duly printed in the local press without comment. The national press did not want to follow up a non-story, and that was the end of that particular angle on the fire. It is not difficult to imagine the kind of story that could have been printed if the council had attempted to cover up or deny that they had received advance warning of the safety problem.

(*Source*: Bradford Council 1986)

Accuracy is vital for several reasons. Most important, it would be wicked as well as stupid to give out the wrong information about casualties or to speculate about causes. Getting it wrong will make the organisation look incompetent and untrustworthy. The media are also concerned with accuracy, especially when it comes to vital details like the flight number of a crashed plane, the telephone number for relatives to call or the precise description of a vehicle or location of an accident.

Monitor coverage

The organisation may be scrupulous about ensuring honesty and accuracy in the information it provides. But this information may become distorted in the telling, knowingly or by accident. Although some sections of the media suffer deservedly from a poor reputation for honesty, the vast majority of reporters want to get an accurate story. If an organisation finds it has been seriously misrepresented, it needs to do something about it straight away. It can only do so if it has arranged to monitor coverage of the crisis in all the relevant media. The crisis plan should make clear who will be responsible for monitoring coverage and how they will do it. This may be a job for a sub-contractor, but it is vital that reports on coverage go frequently to the public relations officer in charge so that untrue allegations or misrepresentations can be dealt with immediately.

If the organisation is misrepresented there are a number of ways of dealing with the problem. The choice will depend on several factors such as the seriousness of the misrepresentation, the speed with which it needs to be put right, and the need to stay on good terms with the media concerned. Ways of dealing with it include a telephone call or fax to the radio station or newspaper; a letter to the editor (clearly marking whether or not it is for publication); a written complaint to the proprietor or the newspaper's ombudsman (if it has one); a complaint to the broadcasting regulator or the press complaints commission; a solicitor's letter requiring a retraction or recompense and an injunction to prevent the publication or broadcasting of further details. In choosing which path to follow, it is wise to remember the purpose: to ensure accuracy of information, not to give added publicity to an inaccurate story.

9 Be sensitive

Good public relations officers have an understanding of their publics as well as of the organisations they represent. In the normal course of his or her work, the public relations officer is sensitive to the use of language and appropriateness of style or design of the public relations messages the organisation transmits. At a time of crisis, when the opportunities to adopt the wrong tone are legion, it is vital that the public relations officer's crisis team remembers and acts according to the rule: be sensitive. This means taking care over the tone and content of what is communicated externally, as well as noticing and responding to the needs of the organisation's own staff.

External audiences

Those who are directly affected by the crisis may be suffering worry, grief, fear, guilt and anger. The general public may be feeling sympathetic, concerned, anxious to help, or merely curious. The information they all receive will be filtered through the organisation providing it and the media reporting it. The chances of upsetting someone are many. Planning and careful thought, however, can prevent some of the most insensitive communications.

A graphic example is provided by Paddy Marley, who was grateful to be given permission to re-print a leaflet published following the Bradford City Football Club fire, containing very helpful advice to those affected by disaster. Thousands of copies of the leaflet were printed and distributed through drop-in centres, libraries and other public places in Liverpool and Sheffield to help those affected by the Hillsborough disaster to understand how they felt, so that they would be better able to acknowledge that they needed help. He explains how the leaflet ends.

This is what it says.

'Don't hesitate to seek help. No problem is too big or small for us to help you deal with. **Everyone** needs help – it is nothing to be ashamed of. Anything you say will be totally confidential.

FINALLY, REMEMBER – you're the same person you were before this tragedy. There **is** a light at the end of the tunnel.'

Where did most of the victims of Hillsborough die? In the tunnel on the Leppings Lane terraces.

(Marley 1999: 149)

In the planning phase before a crisis any material of this kind should be closely read to ensure that it does not contain expressions which may sound quite wrong in the aftermath of the crisis.

The importance of media training for those who may have to act as spokespeople cannot be underestimated. Interviews and press conferences may be transmitted live or heavily edited: in any case, it is important for the spokesperson both to strike the right note, and to ensure that what is said cannot be misunderstood. This may mean the interviewee has to consider changing tack on a subject which the crisis has made particularly sensitive. For example, immediately before the Hillsborough disaster the government had been considering the use of identity cards for football supporters. Sheffield's Conservative MP, Irvine Patnick, supported his party in the view that identity cards would help prevent hooliganism. Less than 24 hours after the event, he was pictured at Hillsborough claiming that, had identity cards been in operation, they might have prevented the tragedy. The remark was particularly ill-considered as neither hooliganism nor impersonation were factors in the disaster.

But it is not only language which needs to be watched. Sheffield's crisis public relations team prevented at the last minute the spectacle of a fleet of bin lorries carting away cherished mascots, poems and letters of sympathy and thousands of bouquets and wreaths from the Hillsborough ground. These were tokens of deeply felt grief, but after some weeks they were also 'litter'. In the end, they were removed discreetly, incinerated, and the ashes taken to Liverpool's football ground at Anfield.

Internal audiences

The organisation's crisis planning may have been so effective that all members of staff are comfortable with their roles and there are no internal difficulties with communication flow. Sensitivity is still called for, however, in ensuring that staff can cope with their work, that they have adequate rest, that their emotional needs are cared for and that they are not expected to behave like heroes for days at a time. When a crisis involves serious injuries or loss of life, it is sometimes necessary to change responsibilities, and even to rely on volunteers for some of the work: those who are best able to cope with the emotional upheaval may not be those whose names are on the rota.

It is also important to remember that 'the professionals' are not immune to the stresses and strains of working in a highly charged and emotional environment. The hard-bitten press officer, the experienced police officer, the cynical journalist and the gung-ho fire-fighter may well feel the need to shed a few tears or talk over their feelings with a counsellor. It is a feature of crises that, once the staff for the press office are in place, they are reluctant to take rest breaks or indeed to go home at all. It may be a mistake to insist that they do so: first, it might have a bad effect on their morale, and second, the problems of hand-over and continuity are reduced. However, no one can work at full stretch for very long and it is important for whoever is in charge to be able to identify those who need to take a break, have a hot meal or whatever, and make sure they get one. It is vital to be able to spot those who are unable to cope with the stresses and strains of the incident itself: such staff must be taken off the work and given something else to do. While this must be done with sensitivity, it must also be done promptly and firmly.

Conversely, in a large organisation where the crisis is the province of a very small number of members of staff, the rest of the organisation may be needing to get on with the work in hand. Those not involved can feel left out, especially when the heroes of the crisis team are applauded for their sterling work, get to have sherry with the managing director and have their pictures in the paper. The unsung heroes may be those members of staff who were never in the public eye but who made sure that the day-to-day running of the organisation and its routines were undisturbed. As the person with responsibility for internal communication in normal times as well as during a crisis, the public relations officer needs to ensure that this is handled sensitively at the time of the crisis and in its aftermath.

10 Learn from your experience

As a postscript to the crisis, the crisis team can use the experience it has gained to enable the organisation to be better prepared next time. By keeping a log of what happened in the run-up, during and after the crisis, and by proper de-briefing for all concerned with the crisis team, conclusions can be drawn and lessons learned which will be of value in the future. When the crisis plan is re-visited, those lessons will be invaluable in revising the arrangements for the future.

A thornier problem is how far organisations can learn from others' mistakes. It is not generally considered good business practice to tell everyone about the mistakes you made in developing a product, so why should it be a good idea to come clean on the lessons learned from poor crisis management? This is a question that each organisation will have to consider for itself, but the principle of disseminating best practice throughout one's sector seems to be just as important in the management of crisis as in dealing with safety issues.

It may be that the legal implications make it difficult to discuss the lessons learned in situations of crisis. If, for example, out-of-court settlements are reached, with conditions about no further disclosures being made, public discussion of the crisis itself may be limited. However, the press team at Sheffield were helped by the advice received from other local authorities who had been involved in disasters in recent years, and it does seem important to be able to learn from others and not have to re-invent the wheel every time something goes badly wrong.

Summary points

✔ A crisis is a dramatic change, usually for the worse, which may arise as a result of an accident, through someone's negligence or because of criminal behaviour such as product tampering or sabotage. Crises, disasters, scandals and emergencies are the very essence of hard news and always receive extensive coverage in the media.

✔ How organisations deal with crises affects their reputation with the public and their future relationships with journalists.

✔ Planning for a crisis is vital. This can take the form of brainstorming possible scenarios, planning the public relations response and rehearsal. Part of the planning process involves ensuring that potential spokespeople are thoroughly trained and that relevant background information is available.

✔ The flow of information during a crisis must be controlled by the organisation's crisis public relations team. This may involve agreeing certain ground-rules with the media and with other interested parties.

✔ Openness is generally the best policy. 'No comment' or silence are generally construed as secretiveness and distrusted. It is helpful to try and find other things to talk about if it is not legally permissible to discuss the crisis itself.

✔ The public relations officer should have mechanisms in place to ensure that accurate information is given. Media reports need to be monitored so that, if inaccuracies appear, they can be immediately corrected.

✔ The crisis public relations team needs to be especially sensitive to the feelings of others at a time of crisis and try to prevent any blunders which may be hurtful. Expressing regret and sorrow on behalf of the organisation is a sensitive and reasonable course of action, and need not imply that the organisation is responsible for what has happened.

✔ Crises and disasters affect those working in the press office and elsewhere in the organisation. The effect on staff needs to be recognised and action needs to be taken promptly to ensure that staff are deployed appropriately.

Questions for discussion

1 Advances in technology mean that news and pictures of disasters can be half way round the world before the organisation concerned knows that something is wrong. What implications does this have for crisis public relations planning?

2 Choosing a company or other organisation which you know well, consider what situations could arise and make a list of probable, possible and improbable crises. Would the same personnel make up the crisis management team for each crisis situation?

3 The GM foods issue became a subject for wide international debate and controversy in a relatively short period. Organisations such as food retailers, manufacturers, growers of GM foods, restaurant owners and cooks, envioronmental groups and food writers all became involved. Could any organisation in such a situation ensure that it takes the lead? How could it do so?

Recommended further reading

There are many books and articles describing and analysing crises and disasters which have taken place in the UK and elsewhere, such as Deppa (1993) on the Lockerbie air disaster. Appropriate chapters on crisis and issues management can be found in Kitchen (1997), Seitel (1995), Caywood (1997), Newsom et al. (1993) and Hendrix (1998).

Berge (1988) provides a useful guide to dealing with a crisis in the immediate aftermath. Barton (1993), Mitroff and Pauchant (1990), Pinsdorf (1987) and Irvine (1987) are all general texts on the USA experience of crisis management while the contributors to Harrison (1999) give a UK perspective.

Toft and Reynolds (1994) and Allinson (1993) take a general management approach, the latter focusing on management ethics.

 ## References

Allinson, R. (1993) *Global Disasters: Inquiries into Management Ethics*, New York: Simon and Schuster.

Barton, L. (1993) *Crisis in Organizations: Managing and Communicating in the Heat of Chaos*, Cincinatti, OH: South Western Publishing.

Berge, D. T. (1988) *The First 24 Hours: A Comprehensive Guide to Successful Crisis Communications*, Oxford: Blackwell.

Bernstein, D. (1986) *Company Image and Reality*, London: Cassell.

Black, S. (1993) *The Essentials of Public Relations*, London: Kogan Page.

Bradford Council (1986) *Out of the Valley: Bradford MDC's response to the Bradford City Fire Disaster 1985–86*, Bradford: Policy Unit.

Caywood, C. (1997) *The Handbook of Strategic Public Relations and Integrated Communications*, New York: McGraw-Hill.

Corley, P. (1994) 'Letter to the Editor', *Guardian* 20 April.

Deppa, J. (1993) *The Media and Disasters: Pan Am 103*, London: David Fulton.

Ewing, R. (1997) 'Issues Management: Managing Trends through the Issues Life Cycle', in Caywood, C., *The Handbook of Strategic Public Relations and Integrated Communications*, New York: McGraw-Hill.

Ferguson, C. (1999) 'Television News', in Harrison, S. (ed.), *Disasters and the Media: Managing Crisis Communications*, Basingstoke: Macmillan.

Granatt, M. (1999) 'A Central Government Perspective', in Harrison, S. (ed.) op. cit.

Granatt, M. and Dowle, D. (1993) 'Managing the Media Needs at Major Incidents', *Metropolitan Police Journal* (issue unknown) 23–7.

Harrison, S. (ed.) (1999) *Disasters and the Media: Managing Crisis Communications*, Basingstoke: Macmillan.

Hendrix, J. (1998) *Public Relations Cases*, 4th edn., Belmont, CA: Wadsworth.

Irvine, R. (1987) *When You Are the Headline: Managing a Major News Story*, Homewood, IL: Dow Jones Irwin.

Jefkins, F. (1988) *Public Relations Techniques*, Oxford: Butterworth-Heinemann.

Kitchen, P. (ed.) (1997) *Public Relations Principles and Practice*, London: International Thomson Business Press.

Marley, P. (1999) 'A Tale of Two Cities: Liverpool', in Harrison, S. (ed.), op. cit.

McDonald, J. (1990) 'Accidents do happen: an emergency response plan for Unocal', in Moss, D. (ed.), *Public Relations in Practice – A Casebook*, London: Routledge.

Mitroff, I and Pauchant, T. (1990) *We're So Big and Powerful Nothing Bad Can Happen to Us*, New York: Carol.

Newsom, D., Scott, A. and Turk, J. (1993) *This is PR: the Realities of Public Relations*, 5th edn, New York: Wadsworth.

Pinsdorf, M. (1987) *Communicating When Your Company is Under Siege*, Lexington, MA: Lexington Books.

PR Week (1999d) 'Campaigns' 30 April.

Saffir, L. (1993) *Power Public Relations*, Lincolnwood, IL: NTC Business Books.

Seitel, F. (1995) *The Practice of Public Relations*, 6th edn., Englewood Cliffs, NJ: Prentice Hall.

Toft, B. and Reynolds, S. (1994) *Learning From Disasters: A Management Approach*, Oxford: Butterworth Heinemann.

7 Internal communication

Key Issues

The aim of this chapter is to explain the role and functions of internal communication within organisations. The key points covered are:

▶ the relationship of internal communication to overall organisational communication and to the corporate culture;

▶ communication flow within organisations and how it can be managed;

▶ the content of internal communication;

▶ the organisation of the internal communication function.

Throughout this book there have been references to internal audiences or publics. Although the practice of internal public relations is sometimes seen as rather routine in comparison to dealing with external audiences, good internal communication is vital as an underpinning to the success of an organisation's communications overall.

The scope of internal communication is wider than simply the employees of an organisation. If you look back at Chapter 3 and the audiences shown on Bernstein's wheel, you will see that the staff may fall into every category, except 'the trade'.

Staff are almost certain to live nearby and therefore to be members of the *local community*.

As individuals, staff may be active in *pressure groups* which wish to exert an influence on their employer's business or sector.

Members of staff may be active in local or national *politics* and may be parish or district councillors whose decisions could have an effect on the organisation.

Staff will generally read the papers, local and national, and take note of what they see and hear in the broadcast *media*.

Companies which offer pension schemes, cheap loans or staff share ownership deals find that their staff also form part of their *financial audience*.

Members of staff may be *customers* of the organisation, in that they buy its products or services as other member of the public do, and in addition they may be *internal customers* of other departments within the organisation.

Finally, the staff and their families and friends are part of the *general public*.

Clearly, communicating with the staff, who fall into such diverse publics, is not simply a matter of dealing with personnel issues such as pay and conditions of work. Before we look at the way in which communication works inside organisations, and the likely content of internal communications, let us start by finding out why people do it at all.

What do organisations and employees want from each other?

At a very simple level, the organisation wants people to come to work, do a good job and go home. Staff want a fair day's pay for a fair day's work.

The organisation

Looking in more detail at what the organisation wants, it may not be as simple as that. It probably does not want 'people' in general working for it, but drivers, sales staff, charge-hands, accountants, cleaners and secretaries. These people may need to have very specific skills such as the ability to speak French or Urdu, drive a car or an HGV, operate complicated machinery, use chemicals safely, identify and sort out bugs in computer programs.

The organisation may not want them to come to work at all: it may want freelance or home-based workers. Or it may not want them to come to work today or this week, perhaps because it needs to lay-off staff during a quiet period, or perhaps because it would prefer them to be on strike and not to have to pay their wages, or even because there has been a sudden emergency and the workplace is temporarily closed.

Staff

Staff generally want to be paid and not be exploited. However, there is more to it than that for most people. Job satisfaction, a sense of doing something well, or the chance to get a better or easier job in the future can all be motivating factors. Some people go to work because they like the social atmosphere and their job itself is not so important as the friendships, while for others the pay packet is the most important feature of their job.

On the whole, though, people would rather do a good job than a poor one, and like to know that someone up there in the organisation's hierarchy has noticed.

Communication flows

Information flows around organisations whether or not they try to control it (Figure 7.1). In a typical hierarchical organisation, with the manage-

| **Figure 7.1** | *Communication flows* |

① ——→ downwards	⑤ ——→ group–group (up/down)
② ——→ upwards	⑥ ——→ individual–individual
③ ——→ within group	⑦ grapevine
④ ——→ group–group (same level)	

ment at the top of the pyramid, communication flows downwards (1) in the form of instructions and information, and there may be an upward flow through suggestion schemes or some other form of feedback to management (2).

Each working group has its own communication system: people who work in the same office or in the same part of the factory communicate between themselves (3). Group communicates with group both at the same level (4) and across the hierarchy (5). In addition to these information routes, which may be formalised within the organisation, there are plenty of informal communications between individuals who happen to be friends or relatives of other members of staff (6). The grapevine, which flourishes in every organisation, ensures that information, accurate or not, reaches every outpost (7).

It is important to get a feel for the scale of information washing around in organisations before thinking about the why, what and how of internal communication. It is also important to remember that, organisational charts notwithstanding, staff do not fit neatly into boxes but have their own person-to-person networks.

Why communicate?

If communication happens anyway, why should organisations have to do anything about it? Successful organisations know it is worth investing in internal communication for these sound business reasons.

Effective employee performance

Staff are more likely to perform effectively if they are clear about what their jobs are, how to do them, who to report to, what constitutes good or poor work and how they can improve their performance.

Manageability

Well-managed communications mean that staff know what they need to know but are not overwhelmed by unnecessary information. Receiving piles of memos, newsletters and information sheets about things which are nothing to do with the recipient only devalues the material, so that when something important and relevant does arrive it gets thrown out or ignored. Junk mail can be just as much a feature of working life as home life: managing information properly avoids this problem and saves money.

Sharp-end feedback

Organisations have an immense research resource in their front-line staff. Those working at the sharp end – the receptionists, the sales assistants, the service engineers who go into customers' houses to do repairs – all obtain valuable information in the course of their work about how the organisation, its products and services are viewed by the public. By creating a formal channel of communication for staff to feed this information back, products and services can be improved, complaints dealt with effectively and the organisation will benefit accordingly.

Motivation

Properly managed internal communication systems will improve staff motivation and help build morale. Giving a group of staff the opportunity to explain their work to others can give them a sense of pride in their job and help them to realise their importance to the company's business overall.

Team spirit

A group of staff communicating together is well on the way to becoming a team, all using individual skills to work towards the same goal. Internal communications programmes which recognise this may include incentives and competitions to engender and reinforce team spirit within the workplace.

Crisis preparation

A crisis may never happen to the organisation, but if it does, that is not the time to be trying to put good internal communication systems in place. If such systems are functioning well, they can cope with the extra demands at a time of crisis, ensuring that staff know what is going on, even though the focus may be on external communications at the time.

Participative staff

Giving good and relevant information is a pre-requisite for the next stage: consultation. Organisations which consult their staff generally have better industrial relations than those who do not. Consultation is one of the building-blocks on the way to participation. Staff who participate, who are actively involved in their organisation instead of simply doing their job, are much more valuable to the company.

Case Study 7.1

Participative communication

The 'Excellence' study

James Grunig's massive study on excellence in public relations (Grunig 1992) found that excellent organisations have symmetrical internal systems of communication and decentralised management structures that give their employees autonomy. A real estate company identified this as 'Very open a very supportive environment which will allow people to take on jobs which aren't in their job descriptions', where people are allowed to make mistakes and still feel supported. Thus job satisfaction is high.

Excellent organisations have a participatory culture; less excellent ones are authoritarian. Participatory culture provides a conducive environment for excellent communication programmes.

(*Source*: Grunig 1997: 296, 298)

Good relations with its public

Think back to the definitions of public relations we looked at in Chapter 1. If good public relations aims to foster mutual goodwill and understanding, it needs a well-managed internal communication system to address its public: the staff.

Corporate culture

The general principles listed above need to be looked at in the light of the culture of the organisation concerned. We touched on this in the section on 'Corporate connections' in Chapter 5.

An organisation's culture is made up of a mixture of its values and the way it expresses them, and the management styles prevalent in the organisation.

Management styles

Smythe et al. (1992: 62–4) identify five different styles of internal communication (Figure 7.2). These are as follows.

Instructional

This style ensures that staff are given the information to do their jobs only. It is one-way and information flows only from superior downwards.

Informative

This style aims to help staff understand what they are doing and how it fits in with the rest of the organisation, by keeping people informed – but only about what management thinks they need to know. Again, it is one-way, downwards.

Consultative

This is a more personal style which provides for interaction between management and staff and thus is a two-way form of communication. Staff

Management styles | **Figure 7.2**

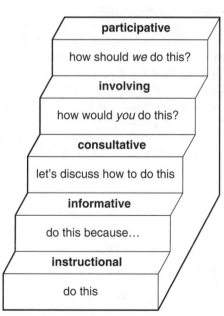

Source: adapted from Smythe et al. 1992: 62–4

have the opportunity to be involved in discussion about the organisation and their work and to put forward their own views.

Involving

This two-way process is the first of the five styles to reverse the flow of communication: it is upward flowing, or 'bottom-up'. Involvement gives junior staff the chance to share their expertise with their seniors so that the organisation can maximise the benefit of its accumulated experience.

Participative

This two-way, symmetrical style guarantees that staff views will be taken into account because staff are required to participate in the decision-making processes of the organisation. Many other European countries achieve participation by requiring companies to have worker-directors on their boards or require their boards to work with Worker Representative Councils.

How does it feel?

It is a straightforward matter to analyse the way communication flows in an organisation and to identify the communication styles adopted by the management. It may be harder to gauge what staff feel about their jobs and their employers, but their perception will act as a filter through which all communication reaches them.

The process of surveying how communication works in an organisation is sometimes called a communications audit. The aim of an audit undertaken for the organisation Family Service Units (FSU) was 'to analyse all existing communications within FSU and provide recommendations for an efficient and effective internal communications structure'. Extracts from the report are shown in Figure 7.3. You can see how research was conducted and the results analysed, what items of internal communication were reviewed and how this led to three proposals for a revised communications plan.

There is no shortage of management consultants and internal communication specialists who will go into a company and survey staff attitudes. They may use focus groups, self-completion questionnaires mailed to work or home addresses, individual interviews or a combination of these methods. Here are some examples of the kind of material which may be used:

For each of the following statements, indicate whether you agree or disagree on a scale of 1 to 5 (1 = strongly disagree to 5 = strongly agree).

1 People support each other in getting the job done.

2 There are rules for everything.

3 People have to work very hard.

4 There are plenty of opportunities for training.

| *Extracts from a communications audit report contents page* | **Figure 7.3** |

6.0 METHODOLOGY
    6.1   Background research
    6.2   Competitor research
    6.3   Qualitative/quantitative research plan
    6.4   Qualitative research
    6.4.1   Structured interviews
    6.4.2   Group discussions
    6.5   Quantitative research
    6.5.1   Postal questionnaire
    6.6   External research
    6.6.1   Social Services Department – Hampshire visit
7.0 ISSUES AND CONSTRAINTS
8.0 RESEARCH RESULTS
    8.1   Organisation environment
    8.2   Competitors
    8.3   Public relations within FSU [Family Service Units]
    8.4   Future developments
9.0 REVIEW OF INTERNAL COMMUNICATIONS
    9.1   Written communications
    9.1.1   Unit briefing
    9.1.2   Letters/memos
    9.1.3   Social policy update
    9.1.4   Training update and calendar
    9.1.5   Events chart and deadlines
    9.1.6   Minutes
    9.1.7   Index of services and Profile Report
    9.1.8   Staff induction pack
    9.2   Oral communications
    9.2.1   Meetings
    9.2.2   Staff support/specialist groups
    9.2.3   Organisation flow
    9.2.4   Current technology and uses
10.0 COMMUNICATIONS PLAN
    10.1   *Proposal A*
    10.2   *Proposal B*
    10.3   *Proposal C*

Source: adapted from LMU (1994: i)

5 People are often critical of other sections or departments.

6 Junior staff are very wary of management.

7 The main emphasis is on quality.

8 We have to follow rigid procedures.

In a long questionnaire questions such as 2 and 8 would probably appear further apart. Their purpose is not only to find out whether or not staff agree with the statement, but also to cross-check that a similar answer has been given to both, i.e. that the respondent has actually considered the issue, and not merely put random marks in the boxes.

A communication audit of internal communication should include a report on how staff currently perceive the culture of the organisation and the way in which it communicates. Knowing how people feel to start with makes it more likely that an appropriate style of internal communication will be recommended in the future.

Smythe et al. illustrate this well with the following case study.

Case Study 7.2

Conflict and confusion in internal communication

Team briefing: The Royal Mail

In order to create a shared understanding about the objectives of communication programmes, choosing the right style is vital.

In 1989, Britain's Royal Mail Letters tried to improve communication in its workforce by refining an existing team briefing process. Managers met their staff regularly to pass on core messages that had cascaded down through the structure, as well as to relay local information. But whereas management saw the team briefing as information dissemination, the staff saw it as a consultation which was aimed at involving them. The confusion led to conflict with the trade unions, communication blocks, legal action and eventually – and inevitably – a loss of credibility for team briefing inside the Royal Mail.

The reason team briefing failed in the Royal Mail when it was first introduced was because of the confusion about what it was trying to achieve. The organisation was not yet ready to launch a consultative communication approach. Staff were used to getting the real stuff from their unions and managers felt uncomfortable communicating information which they themselves did not fully understand, and they quickly viewed the team briefing process as ineffective.

(*Source*: Smythe et al. 1992: 64)

What to communicate

We have looked at the reasons for internal communication programmes and the culture of the organisation in which they might operate. Now we can begin to think about the kinds of messages an internal communication programme might consider. When considering the content of messages, it is useful to remember that the recipient is likely to be most interested in what directly affects him or her, and what is seen to be near rather than distant. Although it may be helpful to give a sketch of the grand design to everyone, people generally are less interested in policy and more interested in the effects on their own patch. Table 7.1 gives the results of a survey undertaken among employees to find out what interested them most.

The content of internal communication could include any of the following.

Subjects of interest to employees

Table 7.1

Rank Subject		Scale (1–10)
1	Organisational plans for the future	8
2	Job advancement opportunities	7
3	Job-related 'how-to' information	7
4	Productivity improvement	6
5	Personnel policies and practices	6
6	How we're doing vs the competition	6
7	How my job fits into the organisation	6
8	How external events affect my job	5
9	How profits are used	5
10	Financial results	4

Source: IABC study quoted in Center, A. and Jackson, P. (1995: 39). Reprinted by permission of Prentice Hall.

News

Departmental, company and industry-wide news about research and new products, human interest stories about members of staff and items about performance could all make newsworthy material.

Information

Increasingly, internal communication focuses on providing information rather than attempting to burnish the organisation's image. It may be product information, details of new procedures or operations, sales information or financial reports. Organisations are likely to target information more closely than used to be the case, producing different types of information, aimed through different media at niche audiences.

Policy

Policy changes and updates need to be communicated. It can be helpful to spotlight policy-in-practice, so that staff can understand what their company policy means. For example, company policy on pollution and the environment, or sexual harassment, or equality of opportunity may be at best meaningless and at worst misunderstood as negative practices unless the reasoning behind them is understood by staff.

Recruitment

The process of recruitment and selection, including the induction of new employees, is an important area of internal communication. How existing employees treat new staff and how potential recruits feel about the organisation can greatly affect its performance. Are staff encouraged to apply for new jobs or promotions within the company before they are advertised externally, or in competition with outsiders? What messages do actual and potential staff get from the recruitment process?

Staff development

An organisation which wants to help its staff to develop, views training and development as an investment. It must not neglect to communicate this to its employees in a way which includes all those eligible for a staff development programme. Development opportunities such as secondments, job-swaps and time off to study need to be made clearly accessible to staff: these are big steps for an employee to contemplate.

Conditions

Proposed changes to conditions of service, such as increased holiday entitlement or amended bonus payments, need to be explained well in advance of their implementation. An internal communication programme might provide the means of consulting on such changes.

Success stories

Once the staple fare of house magazines, success stories have now gone rather out of favour as material for internal communication programmes. They became devalued as a result of their use in blowing the company's trumpet, in the days when a 'bad news' story would never have made it into company material. However, there is a place for success stories: certainly, those members of staff who have worked their socks off to win an award for quality, or the person who won the incentive-scheme's top prize will want to read about it in the company newspaper. Stories of personal success against the odds also make good human interest copy.

Announcements

Another staple ingredient, announcements can be social (the paint shop's ten-pin bowling team is meeting at the Red Lion for an end-of-season party), personal (Fred and Maureen from printing are getting married) or staffing (Jo Smith is joining as finance director, Joe Jones is retiring as canteen supervisor).

How to communicate

The overriding principle in determining what methods of communication to use, is that they should be appropriate – to the audience, to the message and to the organisation and its culture. If the method chosen is inappropriate, the message will lack credibility or simply be ignored.

Methods of internal communication can be loosely divided into spoken, written/visual and multi-media, although some methods do not strictly fall into one category alone.

Spoken

Individual briefings

One-to-one, face-to-face individual briefings give the sender and receiver of information the opportunity to take part in the process, allow for feedback and, in theory at least, minimise the chance of misunderstanding. However, such briefings are time consuming, and where the same message has to be passed several times, there is the risk that inconsistencies may arise when the message is not repeated in identical fashion.

Team briefings

A more common practice, team briefings allow one person to communicate with a team. Team briefings can form part of a cascading process, in which information is cascaded down through an organisation by each manager or supervisor briefing his or her own team, the members of whom go away and brief their own teams. So a message about what the senior management team has been discussing may be relayed via the team of department heads to their teams of section heads, who in turn brief their own sections. Properly managed, this can work very well, but there is always the danger of noise creeping into the process, so that the message received by the last person may bear little resemblance to what the management team had to say in the first place.

Staff meetings

The entire staff of a department or company may meet together from time to time. While this may lead to problems, such as who is minding the shop, it does give everyone the opportunity to see everyone else and to hear the same message at the same time. Feedback can be hard to obtain from a large group, as people are often diffident about asking questions or making comments in front of a crowd, but there are techniques to make it easier to get feedback, such as written questions or splitting into smaller groups with a spokesperson or facilitator per group.

Conferences

A company conference may be called to debate a new idea, to discuss relocation of premises, or to launch a new product or corporate identity. Conferences are usually one-off affairs as opposed to staff meetings, which may be programmed into the working year.

Walking the job

Sometimes known as Management By Walking About (MBWA), walking the job involves the manager walking round the workplace to get a feel for how things are going, and to allow staff to raise any issues they see fit. The culture of the organisation is all-important to the success of MBWA as a technique. If the staff are suspicious of management, MBWA will only encourage the feeling that they are being spied upon by their boss. If it is a non-hierarchical company, where the boss is approachable and staff are accustomed to seeing managers getting their hands dirty, MBWA is a logical step.

The above are all forms of personal, spoken communication. Advances in technology have fostered an increase in impersonal spoken communication through the following channels.

Television

Closed circuit television (CCTV) has been used for some years within large companies. It enables staff to see and hear messages from management on their workplace television sets. Open-access CCTV allows staff to make their own programmes to be shown to their colleagues and can provide a graphic way of explaining their role. Business television (BTV) is a newer concept. Pioneered by BT, BTV uses satellite to transmit live broadcasts on issues of the day. Many of the major financial services companies use BTV, including the Halifax group which launched Halifax Television beamed by satellite to its 1,600 sites across Britain, and the Abbey National, with Abbey Vision delivering a 20-minute weekly news and information programme. Some BTV programmes aim for interaction with staff, such as supermarket group Sainsbury, whose BTV SMART Network runs phone-in shows (*PR Week* 1999a: 17–19)

Radio

Company radio has been a feature in business since bakeries first started piping Music While You Work-style programmes through the factory loudspeakers, to drown out the noise of the machinery. Nowadays local radio stations may provide the background music, while company messages are interspersed with the programmes as required.

Video

The Body Shop was a notable pioneer of video as an internal communications tool. It is particularly useful for an organisation such as this, where franchised outlets are located all over Britain and abroad. The weekly programmes contain news, sales tips, features on product ingredients and use, and updates on company campaigns such as the 're-use, re-fill, re-cycle' campaign. Each programme, hosted by Body Shop staff, is edited on Thursday for viewing in-store on Monday morning. Staff can call a hot-line with their views on programme content, and to make suggestions about topics they would like to see in future programmes. Other companies may use video bulletins for special occasions, such as end-of-year results, or they may form part of a training package.

Company video

TNT: Jacaranda

When the distribution and logistics firm TNT decided to go for a listing on the London Stock Exchange it undertook a major internal and external communication programme to revamp its image and reposition itself as the global expert in its field. It decided on the use of video to keep its 55,000 employees worldwide up to date on what was happening. The production company Jacaranda made three video films to be shown in the more than 200 countries (dubbed where necessary) where TNT had a presence. All staff saw the films between April and June 1998.

The first film showed why the company needed to change, the second explained the rationale for the new corporate identity and the third unveiled the corporate identity at its launch in Belgium, relating it to the company's new advertising campaign.

The internal communication programme also included information packs and local events, but feedback from staff indicated that there was a particularly good reaction to the videos. The company's management felt that the film enabled them 'to develop a monolithic brand which would embrace all our different activities and bring them together on a business, social and visual level'.

(*Source*: *PR Week* 1999a)

Teleconferencing and video-conferencing

This allows a number of individuals to have a meeting by telephone or, increasingly, by telephone with video link. It saves time and money by obviating the need for everyone to leave their desks and travel to a meeting place, but it gives the opportunity for everyone to have their say in real-time. It may be too expensive an option for many companies, but hotel chains are now beginning to see the benefit of offering the service on a for-hire basis. Instead of everyone converging from different parts of the world on a hotel in London, Paris or New York, they simply pop down to their respective local Forte or Holiday Inn and video-conference from there.

Hot-lines

A company may set up a hot-line for a specific purpose, or it may have a permanently dedicated service. A hot-line gives staff the opportunity to make phone calls, to speak to someone about a specific concern; to leave a message on tape, anonymously or not; or to hear a recorded message about an item of interest. Unsurprisingly, BT has a hot-line service for its UK staff. They can ring an 0800 number for immediate three-minute reports on company developments, and it receives up to 15,000 calls a week.

Visual/written

House journal

The typical house journal of the past, an all-purpose affair with lots of photographs of men in suits, giving the message that your organisation is a great one to work for, is now more or less moribund. Today's house journal may be a glossy magazine with inserts specifically tailored to sectors of the organisation – managers, those working on one particular site, or computer specialists. BP, with 62,600 employees in 70 countries, has an enormous internal communication challenge. One sector, BP Exploration, produces a monthly publication, *BPXpress*, in four editions from four locations: Aberdeen for Europe, Houston for North America, Bogota for South America and London for the rest of the world. Using BP's computer network, editors can pick and mix stories for their own editions, so that each issue combines local stories with the feeling of being part of an international organisation.

Newsletters

Quick, cheap and easy to produce, newsletters can satisfy the demand for truly local news. In large organisations, a locally produced newsletter which is made up and distributed within a small section, can help overcome the feeling of working in a monolithic and impersonal company. With the advent of cheap and user-friendly desk-top publishing systems, sections of a department can take it in turns to produce the departmental newsletter, putting their own personality and slant on to the publication. The team-building effect of doing this can be an important spin-off.

Direct mail

Organisations sometimes use direct mail to ensure that all targeted members of staff receive their own personal copy of a message. Where direct mail is appropriate, the management needs to decide whether to mail to the employee's home or work address. How and where it is received colours the message.

Electronic mail (email)

In organisations where everyone has a computer terminal, email is an effective way of reaching all staff at a time convenient to the person receiving the message. Typically, the user finds a message that email is waiting on logging on to the terminal; it is then up to the user to read the message, print it off if required, or ignore it altogether.

Intranet

Many organisations which are linked by email have also developed an Intranet system for internal communication. Web pages which can only be accessed by staff within the organisation can provide up to the minute news, information, useful services (such as cafeteria opening times or the local weather forecast), and opportunities for comment to everyone with access to a computer. Useful information which needs regular updating, such as the staff phone book, can be placed on the Intranet and downloaded or consulted as necessary, thus saving time, paper and money. The staff newsletter is usually also available on-line.

Pay inserts

Companies take a policy decision as to whether or not they will allow messages to be inserted into staff pay-slips. Some organisations help defray their payroll costs by allowing outside bodies to advertise on their pay-slip envelopes, or to put inserts into the envelopes themselves. Increasing computerisation and automation of payroll has made this easier in some respects, and more difficult in others, but it is as well to bear in mind that many people do not like the idea of someone tinkering with their pay advice slips, and may not receive too kindly any message that comes in the same envelope as notification of a tax increase.

Staff annual reports

Some organisations produce an annual report specifically for their employees. It may contain much of the same information as that which appears in its annual report to shareholders, and certainly the information in both will be consistent. The staff report, however, may look different, and should have a different emphasis if it is to be of interest to employees.

Notice-boards

A neglected medium of communication in many organisations, notice-boards can be a valuable tool or a disaster. The unbreakable rules are that notice-boards must look good, be up to date, and contain interesting material. A notice-board which claims to show pictures of everyone who works there is no good if it does not. An untidy board means that the important notice about Christmas close-down is lost and unread among the scraps of paper offering second-hand tents for sale or babysitting. A board which displays a yellowing copy of the Offices, Shops and Railway Premises Act and what to do if you hear the fire alarm may be glanced at once by a new employee, and forever after ignored. Simply ensuring that someone is responsible for updating and keeping notice-boards tidy is a start. Using eye-catching devices, such as coloured borders, or a magnetic arrow to point to today's bulletin, can liven up a notice-board and make it required reading. Positioning a departmental notice-board by the coffee machine instead of in a dark corner makes a big difference to how many people read it.

Displays

The foyer of a company is sometimes used to display material on the range of the organisation's activities, but the use of displays as an internal communication mechanism is less common. They can be very effective in the right setting. An eye-catching series of posters, showing ordinary people doing their jobs, with a few lines of text in which they explained in their own words the satisfaction they got from their work, made a lively and appropriate display in one local authority's training centre. Displays by staff to explain their role to other groups or teams can also work very well, and can form the basis of internal open days. Producing displays can act as a morale-booster and engender pride in the staff involved.

Suggestion schemes

Sometimes these work well, sometimes not. Staff need to be encouraged to take part in suggestion schemes, as their alternative name of 'Speak Up! schemes' indicates. Good ideas may be forthcoming, as may critical comments about current practices. The organisation must acknowledge suggestions and explain how it is going to act on them, or why it is not going to do so, if that is the case. Suggestion schemes are sometimes linked to incentives and competition, and there may be a range of prizes for the best, next best and so on each month.

Multi-media

There are other internal communications techniques, which use written, spoken and visual material. These include the following.

Exhibitions and presentations

An organisation may put on an exhibition to communicate to its staff about a specific issue, such as relocation of the company. The exhibition could include displays of photographs, maps and sketches, there could be available brochures with inserts specific to different groups of staff, management may be on hand to discuss the implications with individuals, or to run workshops with teams, and there may be presentations from the new area's tourism, education and housing experts. An exhibition may be used to provide a background for the annual report, where material from all over the company can be displayed. Staff may find that they can understand better how they fit into the whole if they can see a graphic representation of their organisation.

If the organisation is considering a new corporate identity, an exhibition inviting views on potential designs will be of help to staff and management in taking account of opinions of those who will be working with the new material.

Launches

The launch of a new corporate identity to its staff can be a major multi-media event for any organisation, giving the opportunity to unveil the new identity, to show how the identity is to be used (and how it is not), and to explain why it is important that the implementation of the identity follows an agreed plan. If such a presentation is a success, staff will have a greater sense of ownership of the new identity and will be more inclined to use it in the correct way. There will be fewer chances of gripes about what a shocking waste of money the changed identity is.

Internal launches may cover other areas too. New product launches may be made to an internal audience before they go public, to ensure that staff know what they are making or selling and how it will be presented to the outside world. This can, incidentally, be a good opportunity for rehearsal before a sales launch to customers. An internal launch can be motivating for staff, and fire them up with enthusiasm for the new product or service.

Social activities

This is an area of internal communications often ignored by organisations, but it can be very useful. When an organisation provides or even merely encourages social activities, it is showing its staff that it cares for their welfare out of hours, as well as during work time.

Social activities can range from a Christmas party, paid for by the firm, to the provision of sports fields. The employer may give staff time off, with or without pay, during working hours to engage in company social activities. Some companies provide very good facilities for social activity on the premises, such as staff clubs. Others may include the families of staff by holding sports days with children's events or barbecues and garden parties. Others provide holiday homes, either free or at a reduced price: these may be 'won' in competition with other staff, or randomly allocated in a staff draw.

Social activities are sometimes tied in with an organisation's sponsorship programme, and may be an opportunity for staff to participate in the company's sponsoring activity. They may also be a community activity: some firms give staff paid time off and resources to organise parties for pensioners or for disadvantaged children.

Responsibility for internal communication

It is clear from the types of activity involved in internal communication programmes that the public relations department of an organisation is likely to be the lead department in this area. However, activities such as recruitment of staff are usually seen as falling within the personnel or human resources department. Firms may choose to contract-out the internal communication function, wholly or in part, to specialist consultants.

Sometimes tensions exist in organisations as to where the responsibility lies for internal communication. In a survey published in 1990, Smythe Dorward Lambert (1990: 3–4) interviewed 54 organisations from public and private sectors to find out their views on internal communications. Their findings included:

▶ responsibility for managing internal communications varies from company to company, but generally falls between the public relations and personnel departments;

▶ although many companies devolve responsibility for internal communication to departments, there is seldom a corporate policy, nor do guidelines on quality exist.

Roger Haywood (1991: 109–10) believes that personnel and public relations should work closely together to ensure that best use is made of everyone's skills.

> The personnel world is not an arena to be played in by amateurs. The public relations professional will have to work extremely hard to earn respect from his [*sic*] personnel colleagues and ensure that there is an understanding of each other's roles at all levels.
>
> It is vital that they work closely together. If not, there is a danger that a cautious personnel department can allow a communications vacuum to develop; this may rapidly become filled with unhelpful speculation or gossip. Alternatively, an over-enthusiastic public relations operation can create unnecessary problems for the personnel professionals, for example, through not being sensitive to all factors involved in human relations negotiations.

On the subject of negotiations, Haywood is adamant that 'managers must manage' and not abdicate their responsibility for employee communications to the trades unions, whose interests he perceives as very different from those of the company.

> The company may well be concerned about other factors for example, the return on investment, manpower costs, improved productivity, market-place competition, introduction of new technologies and so on. Why do some companies allow vital information relating to these changes to be communicated via the very group of people who are intent on resisting such change?
>
> (ibid.)

An alternative view is to see the internal communication specialist as an information broker rather than simply as a mouthpiece for the management. This may make managers uncomfortable, but it encourages openness and aims closer to the participative style of management. Case Study 7.4 gives an example.

Case Study 7.4

Even-handed internal communication
Working for Sheffield: Sheffield City Council

During one particularly tricky period of industrial unrest at Sheffield Council the editor of its staff newspaper, *Working for Sheffield*, had to conduct his own series of delicate negotiations before he could publish what he felt was needed: a double-page spread giving management's case on one side and the unions' case on the other. Both were presented in simplified form so that the reader could grasp the essentials without being distracted by jargon. For most members of staff it was the first and only time they could weigh up the merits of the arguments, literally on both sides.

The editor's salary and the costs of the newspaper were funded by the personnel department, who represented management's view, but the editor himself worked in the public relations department and was responsible to the head of public relations. This gave him a little more licence to rock the boat, and the organisation benefited from a newspaper produced for staff rather than by management.

(*Source*: author)

The subject of the final case study in this chapter found themselves in a potentially explosive staff relations situation when they needed to introduce 5,000 redundancies. The way in which British Aerospace developed an internal communication programme won the company an IPR Sword of Excellence award.

Case Study 7.5

Redundancy handling

Turning adversity into advantage: British Aerospace

Background

In 1991 the Military Aircraft Division of British Aerospace was undergoing radical upheaval as traditional demand was shrinking and competition becoming more intense. In early 1991 it was announced that 5,000 jobs would be lost over the next 12–18 months, when two major sites were to be closed. An employee attitude survey showed that managers were seen as secretive, remote and uncaring; 80 per cent of respondents thought the company must change to survive; and employees most wanted information on Military Aircraft's current performance and future business plans.

Objective

To support the change process, informing and motivating the 20,000 workforce as effectively as possible.

Strategy

This was expressed as a number of strategic goals:

▶ enhancing the flow of focused information;

▶ helping to create a climate of openness within a business which necessarily had a history of working on a 'need to know' basis;

▶ getting everyone on the payroll to understand and commit themselves to the key business objectives;

▶ developing wider opportunities for upward communications;

▶ involving the Military Aircraft 'family' as far as possible;

▶ doing all this cost effectively.

Communication plan

Project Sony: a briefing programme to explain the redundancy and site closure programme, including liaison with the local community and counselling for individual employees.

Prosper 2000: Intensive seminars for the top 500 managers to get their commitment to the change process.

Visible management: Managers became first-line deliverers of key messages using 'Team Talk', business plan briefings, cascade messages, hosted lunches, discussion forums, listening groups and walking the job.

Business plan: Every member of staff received a copy of the business plan, containing data on targets and their achievement/non-achievement, on competitors, and a market analysis, with critical success factors identified for each area of business.

Revamping the team briefing system: refocusing Team Talk and continued training of managers in delivering briefings.

Use of electronic media: using computer-disseminated faxes, cutting time required to get a message to all employees from one day to 20 minutes.

Upward communication: formerly non-existent in the military/bureaucratic structure. Now encouraged through listening groups, Team Talk, senior management walkabouts, involvement-based suggestion schemes, quality improvement groups, random sampling, opinion surveys, cross-functional project teams, feedback question-naires, letters pages and manager-hosted lunches.

Refocusing publications: several periodicals have been replaced by one: *Fastrack*; local issues are addressed through site newsletters; communications are themed so that a different key priority is addressed each month.

Sharing best practice: demonstrating and helping spread the know-ledge of best practice from the use of IT to the introduction of natural work groups in manufacturing and concurrent engineering on the European Fighter Aircraft.

Involving families: introducing a new magazine, *Lifestyle*, which reinforces business messages through leisure activities; open days for the whole family; employee visits to other sites; and becoming involved with the wider community through activities such as soccer schools and photographic awards.

Evaluation

Against the six key objectives:

► employees and managers have more information of the right kind at the right time;

► openness will be measured in the attitude survey, but evidence is visible;

► research on the effectiveness of the business plan roll-out shows that employees have a better understanding of business imperatives and their role in achieving business goals;

▶ upward communication improvements will be measured in the attitude survey, but the *Financial Times* has already described Team Talk as 'one of the UK models for two-way communication';

▶ over 2,500 readers and their families responded to the first issue of *Lifestyle*;

▶ £100,000 was saved by rationalising periodicals, the communication team has been reduced by five because managers are now responsible for first-line message delivery, and the communication spend has been halved.

In addition, the board has demonstrated its confidence in the internal communication team by extending its remit to cover the division's external public relations.

(*Source*: IPR 1993b)

Summary points

✔ Good internal communication forms a vital underpinning to the organisation's communication overall, and to the ultimate success of the organisation, by improving employee performance, making information more manageable, providing feedback to managers, improving participation and team-spirit, and as a preparation for crisis management.

✔ Staff are not simply the internal public of an organisation. As individuals they are members of several different publics.

✔ Communication flows in different directions within organisations and this flow can be managed.

✔ Internal communication needs to be conducted in the light of the corporate culture, a mixture of the organisation's values and management styles.

✔ The content of internal communication may include news, information, policy, personnel material, success stories and announcements. The form may be spoken, written, visual and multi-media.

✔ The organisation of the internal communication function varies from company to company but generally falls within or between the personnel and public relations departments.

✔ A good internal communication programme can turn adversity into advantage.

Questions for discussion

A major bank has decided to relocate its head office from London to Nottingham.

1 How and at what stage might the company introduce consultation into the decision-making process?

2 Staff could opt to move to Nottingham, stay in London but transfer to a branch, or take voluntary redundancy. What would be the best ways of presenting these options to staff? You might like to consider the form and content of the messages to be presented.

3 In addition to staff, who else might have an interest in the relocation? How might the bank communicate with these other target publics and what might they say?

4 Consider the effect on the host city. What kind of communication plan might the bank consider for publics in Nottingham?

 ## Recommended further reading

Bland and Jackson (1992) is a straightforward handbook on internal communication. Smith (1991) provides advice and case studies on improving trust, teamwork and performance through good internal communication in US companies. Smythe et al. (1992) focus on the UK experience, briefly analysing some cases where internal communication was not suited to the circumstances in addition to the success stories.

Grunig (1992) reviews theories of organisational communication and advises on how internal communication can be made symmetrical. Puchan et al. (1997) illuminate the concepts of organisational culture and structure using numerous examples and exercises.

D'Aprix (1996) and Quirke (1996) are both human resources specialists who link internal communication with business success.

Clampitt (1991) uses findings from behavioural research to give a highly readable account of effective internal communication.

 ## References

Bland, M. and Jackson, P. (1992) *Effective Employee Communications*, London: Kogan Page.

Center, A. and Jackson, P. (1995) *Public Relations Practices: Managerial Case Studies and Problems*, Englewood Cliffs, NJ: Prentice Hall.

Clampitt, P. (1991) *Communicating for Managerial Effectiveness*, Newbury Park, CA: Sage.

D'Aprix, R. (1996) *Communicating for Change: Connecting the Workplace to the Marketplace*, San Francisco, CA: Jossey Bass.

Grunig, J. (1992) 'Symmetrical Systems of Internal Communication', in Grunig, J. (ed.), *Excellence in Public Relations and Communication Management*, Hillsdale, NJ: Lawrence Erlbaum Associates.

Grunig, L. (1997) 'Excellence in Public Relations', in Caywood, C. (ed.), *The Handbook of Strategic Public Relations and Integrated Communications*, New York: McGraw-Hill.

Haywood, R. (1991) *All About Public Relations: How to Build Business Success on Good Communications*, 2nd edn, Maidenhead: McGraw-Hill.

IPR (1993b) *Sword of Excellence Awards, 1993*, London: IPR.

LMU (1994) 'Communications Audit' (final year PR degree project), Leeds Metropolitan University, Leeds.

PR Week (1999a) 'Business Television', 19 February.

Puchan, H., Pieczka, M. and L'Etang, J. (1997) 'The Internal Communications Context', in Kitchen, P. (ed.), *Public Relations Principles and Practice*, London: International Thomson Business Press.

Quirke, W. (1996) *Communicating Corporate Change*, London: McGraw-Hill.

Smith, A. (1991) *Innovative Employee Communication*, Englewood Cliffs, NJ: Prentice Hall.

Smythe Dorward Lambert (1990) *Your Employees – Your Edge in the 1990s*, London: Smythe Dorward Lambert.

Smythe, J., Dorward, C. and Reback, J. (1992) *Corporate Reputation: Managing the New Strategic Asset*, London: Century Business.

8 Community relations and sponsorship

Key Issues

The aim of this chapter is to introduce the concept of community relations as a key element in public relations policy. The key points considered are:

▶ the social responsibilities of companies;

▶ planning and implementing community relations programmes;

▶ the role of sponsorship in community relations and in other applications;

▶ what can be sponsored and how it is done.

In Chapter 7 we saw that staff, far from falling into the convenient pigeon-hole of 'internal public', may be members of many different publics. The same can be said of 'the community' as a public.

'The local community' is usually taken to mean those people who live near to a company's office or factory, but what about organisations which operate from a number of sites? Marks and Spencer's local community is clearly not restricted to a few streets near its head office in Baker Street, London: there is a separate and specific local community for each of its stores and distribution depots. Each community may have its own views about Marks and Spencer, based on proximity to the company's outlet and the effect the shop or warehouse has, for good or ill, on the individual's life. It may be convenient to shop there, or inconvenient to have lorries delivering or shoppers parking outside your home or office.

Defining and listing an organisation's local communities can be quite a lengthy and complicated business, but it is a necessary one. The local community may include customers; suppliers; competitors; staff, former employees and potential recruits; pressure groups, opinion formers and others with influence; shareholders; the local authority; the local member of parliament; the local media and representatives of the national media; and the financial and business community.

Using the planning model in Chapter 4 we could construct a public relations plan to achieve specific objectives with different sectors of the local community as our publics. The public relations programme which resulted might include activities such as sponsorship of local community events, adopting a local school or playground, giving or lending products, services or employees for service to the local community, or even changing working practices so as to improve the environment for the community. These are all activities which could be considered to fall within the social responsibilities of business.

The social responsibilities of companies

This sounds very worthy. However, some readers of this book will no doubt be thinking, the business of business is – business. It is all very well to behave in a philanthropic manner, but how does it satisfy the bottom line, pay the dividends, keep the company in business? Perhaps the best way is to see the two as interrelated. It is not an issue of philanthropy or appeals to the good nature of business that we should be concerned with here, but rather that it makes sound business sense to foster good relations with the community.

Len Peach (1987: 191–3) likens the impact of an organisation on its communities to that of a stone being dropped into a pond, with the ripples going outward (Figure 8.1).

A company at level one fulfils the basics: it pays its taxes, observes the law, deals fairly and honourably with staff, suppliers and shareholders. At level two, a company takes account of its effect on the environment and seeks to minimise the negative effects by, for example, containing pollution and avoiding product misuse. This type of organisation will typically act in the spirit rather than to the letter of the law and will be in the forefront in

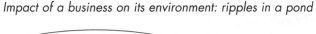

Impact of a business on its environment: ripples in a pond | **Figure 8.1**

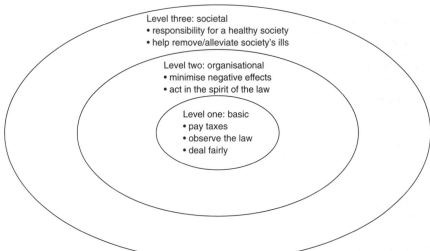

Source: adapted from Peach 1987: 191–3

anticipating trends in legislation and consumer awareness. These two levels cover most of what respectable companies think is their responsibility to society and the communities on which they have an impact.

The level three company has a different outlook. It sees that the healthier the environment, the better the company's prospects, and is therefore concerned to do something about the ills that constrain the healthy development of society. Although third level activities are not so common, Peach argues that they are not a luxury add-on to help a company's conscience. They should guide the company into a new way of thinking about all aspects of its activities. Figure 8.2 shows how certain organisational functions could be looked at anew through the filter of corporate responsibility. These are: research and development, manufacturing, finance, marketing, personnel, distribution and public relations.

If we take the stakeholder approach, we can see that public relations is vital to an organisation's corporate and social responsibility, which can be defined as: 'the responsibility to plan and manage an organisation's relationships with all those involved in or affected by its activities, or those who can affect the ability of that organisation to operate effectively [i.e. its stakeholders]' (Peach 1987: 192).

Figure 8.2 | *Some examples of corporate responsibility: issues for consideration by individual departments*

Organisation functions in terms of corporate responsibility

✔ **Research and development**
animal testing
socially useful product development

✔ **Manufacturing**
processes – waste
methods – de-skilling

✔ **Finance**
where raised
share availability
where invested

✔ **Marketing**
methods
audiences

✔ **Personnel**
recruitment and selection policies
training
personal development

✔ **Distribution**
environmental considerations
social utility

✔ **Public relations**
strategic objectives
programme methods

Planning and managing an organisation's relationships with its stakeholders, or publics, is what public relations is all about. How companies behave and how they are reported, talked about and thus perceived by their publics, is arguably the greatest factor in the management of their reputation.

A company may take the view that it is important for it to be able to recruit from a well-educated pool, and may therefore serve its own interests by providing educational resources or opportunities. Companies in the information technology business can only sell their products and services to customers who are IT-literate, so it makes sense for them to ensure that society becomes familiar and comfortable with computers and their uses. A local authority housing department, wanting to improve relations with its black tenants, may strive to recruit black housing managers: in Sheffield Council's case, the housing department encouraged black youngsters to train as housing managers so that the department would have a more representative pool of potential recruits.

Many successful and highly profitable companies spend large amounts of time and money on fulfilling their social responsibilities. They may do so purely for commercial reasons, because they want to raise their profile and improve their reputation through being associated with 'good works', because they know that what is good for society is good for business, or out of altruism.

Geoffrey Mulcahy of the Kingfisher group defines two of the benefits to spring from community involvement as improved corporate reputation, and the personal and management development of staff through equal opportunity action and secondment schemes. He says: 'There are considerable mutual benefits to well-managed community involvement programmes. For example, directing attention towards social problems, which themselves affect profitability of business, such as crime prevention, helps contain a major problem' (Clutterbuck et al. 1992: 10).

He believes such benefits can add up to a significant competitive advantage for a company. Properly managed empoyee volunteer schemes provide a win-win-win situation for those involved: the charitable or voluntary body which receives the volunteer, the volunteer and the company all benefit in numerous ways (Bunta 1992: 38).

Community relations

Fostering good community relations requires the organisation first to identify its local communities and then to plan its relations with them in line with the organisation's corporate objectives. A community relations programme which is unrelated to the organisation's objectives will fail because neither the staff, shareholders nor the local community itself will understand why it is being undertaken, unless it is only intended to make the organisation look good. Figure 8.3 gives some examples of the community relations programmes adopted by companies based in the UK, the USA and France covering both their domestic operations and those elsewhere in the world.

| **Figure 8.3** | *Some examples of community involvement and community relations programmes* |

Community Relations

Eli Lilly and Company
Global pharmaceutical company based in the United States.
   'As Lilly touches the lives of people worldwide, we recognise that we have a particular responsibility to be a good corporate citizen of the communities in which we operate and to help preserve the environment for the generations to come'. The company's activities include employee volunteer programmes, financial grants, and donations of product and equipment. 'In 1997, Lilly contributed more than $102 million in cash and product . . . to charitable organisations around the world and joined the circle of companies in America with the most generous records of giving'.
   Information provided on http://www.lilly.com/info/citizenship/

KPMG UK
The UK arm of the global professional services firm.
   'KPMG's Community Broking Service focuses on volunteering programmes supporting education, employment and enterprise as well as children and young people'. Programmes include the Head Teacher mentoring programme – KPMG share their financial management and organisational skills with head teachers; Roots and Wings, a programme of mentoring for secondary-school children; education – KPMG sponsor several chairs in accounting and management at UK universities; and charitable donations (£506,000 to UK charities in 1995–6).
   Information provided on http://www.kpmg.co.uk.

Danone Group
International food manufacturer and distributor based in France.
   'As a people-oriented company, Danone believes in encouraging social bonds, sharing and community. Through our investments in partnerships, development and education, we prove that new forms of solidarity can succeed'. Examples of activities include:

   A Baker in Every Village: grants aimed at providing financial support to young artisan bakers who establish a bakery in a [French] community of fewer than 200 inhabitants . . . In keeping with Danone's commitment to promote sharing and solidarity, Britannia, the Group's Malaysia-based subsidiary, invests in programmes such as the construction of a home for abused and abandoned children.

Re-Vivre, founded by Danone in 1995 to turn the waste of unsaleable products (for example those with misprinted labels) into food for the needy, distributes food and provides employment and rehabilitation to the chronically unemployed. In 1999 Re-Vivre collected 800 tons of food for distribution to 350 associations in France.
Information provided on http://www.danonegroup.com/

Marks and Spencer Plc
International retailer and financial services company based in England.
The company's objective is to:

   support the communities in which we operate, thus creating a more prosperous and self-sufficient society. Being a good corporate citizen and sharing our success with charities and other voluntary sector organisations is as important to us as the principles we hold on quality, value and service . . . Our Community Involvement programme is one of 'enlightened self-interest'. By supporting those communities where we operate, we bring added value, create safer living and working environments, better educated young people, more effective small businesses, and an enriched cultural life and a healthier nation. In turn, this creates a more prosperous and self-sufficient society, which is obviously good for business.

Marks and Spencer's community involvement consists of staff secondment, donations, sponsorships, gifts in kind, support of employee fund-raising and a number of other schemes. The company's total commitment in 1997–8 was £10.1 million, with £14 million projected for 1998–9.
   Information provided at http://www.marks-and-spencer.co.uk

Source: company information on websites

It is also important for the organisation to consider the needs of the communities it identifies. Are these in line with the type of support which the organisation is willing to offer?

This leads to consideration of the resources which an organisation is willing to commit. Some companies may limit their community involvement to staff time, others may give or lend materials, some may give grants and others may offer their facilities. Community involvement may be long term or for a specific period.

Organisations may plan their community relations programmes according to an agreed policy. For example, acting on the principle that the company wants a happy, healthy and well-educated pool of youngsters from whom to choose its future workforce, it may decide to allocate community relations resources according to certain criteria. Here are some hypothetical criteria:

▶ assistance will only be made to local organisations;

▶ staff may only be seconded to youth and community projects;

▶ resources such as computers will only be provided to certain schools;

▶ grants will be made to set up new initiatives, not to fund ongoing projects;

▶ support will be reviewed annually and will not normally last for more than three years.

Thus the organisation can act consistently in making decisions about what it will support, and the community has a clearer idea of their chances of success in applying for support. Some companies consult representatives of the local community when deciding their policy. Many publish their policy and allow for applications to be made at specific times of year.

Another way of formalising community involvement is by joining or setting up a scheme. The Association for Business Sponsorship of the Arts, Business in the Community and the Per Cent Club are all examples. The latter is a group of businesses each of which guarantees to spend at least 0.5 per cent of its pre-tax profits on community initiatives.

The responsibility for implementing community relations policy may lie with the public relations department or elsewhere in the organisation, and possibly in a dedicated, separate community relations department or unit. A survey conducted in the USA found that the proportion of respondents working in such a department had increased from 16 per cent in 1987 to 22.3 per cent in 1995 (Boston College 1995, cited in Baskin et al. 1997). In any case, it is important that ultimate responsibility is taken at the highest level. Although an organisation may contract its community activities out to a consultancy, this level of ownership within the organisation itself needs to be maintained.

Let us now consider the activities which an organisation might consider in formulating its community relations programme, whether carried out by its own staff or by a consultancy.

Grants

Within its community relations policy, an organisation may make provision for giving grants to local groups such as a mother and toddler group, a residents' association or the village brass band. An important consideration is whether or not these are one-off gifts or whether the group can rely on financial support on a regular basis. Sometimes companies will give grants for pump-priming only, to help a group get started, and expect the recipients to fund themselves in the future. Grants are sometimes given through charitable foundations or trusts set up by companies as a separate operation from their normal business, as shown in the example of Dreyer's ice cream.

Case Study 8.1

Community involvement

Dreyer's Foundation: Dreyer's Grand Ice Cream Inc.

The company was founded in 1928 and in 1987 it set up the Dreyer's Foundation to provide support to children and young people from kindergarten to grade 12 (ages 5 to 18). The Foundation:

> supports public education in communities throughout the US where Dreyer's employees are involved. Its mission is to promote family, school and community environments which enable young people to develop individual initiative and talents in order for them to become contributing members of their communities and contributing members of their communities' values and ideals for the next generation. We believe that any young person, given the tools and information for learning, will ultimately develop his or her own potential and, through trial and error, his or her own 'excellence'.

The company puts 2 per cent of its pre-tax earnings into the Foundation, which runs two main programmes: Grand Expectations and Dream the Dream. The former supports programmes and projects which promote excellence in young people and establish high expectations of them; the latter rewards young people who design a programme or project which improves the quality of life for their neighbourhoods or communities and helps young people to 'learn how to learn'.

The Foundation focuses its support on the geographical area near to its headquarters in California, but it does make donations to organisations in other areas where its products are sold (small grants) or where its employees are involved (large grants). It does not make donations or grants to individuals, nor does it support sectarian or political causes.

(*Source*: company information)

Equipment

Companies may have a policy of donating surplus, out-dated or even new equipment to the local community. This may be a regular gift or the company may take applications as it receives them. Sometimes companies give equipment, usually their own products, as raffle prizes for charitable events. Equipment gifts, together with grants, may form part of a sponsorship package.

Staff secondments

An organisation may choose not to give cash or materials but may instead lend staff to work on community projects. The company sees this as a form of staff development, from which mutual benefit will accrue. Some companies second staff into their organisations or offer them the chance to swap jobs – a teacher may change places with a supermarket manager, for example. The organisation continues to pay members of staff on secondment as if they were still working for it. Staff may be able to opt to work for their pet project. The company benefits from the wider experience – and sometimes from a different perspective – which seconded staff bring back to the organisation. Companies increasingly offer their staff as mentors, as the examples of KPMG and Marks and Spencer in Figure 8.3 show.

Training

Members of the local community may be given free or cheap training by the organisation in everything from book-keeping for voluntary bodies to computer skills for the unemployed. Many companies now have their own dedicated training section as part of the human resources department, and offering this resource to the community can help the staff development of the trainers, as well as fulfilling other company objectives.

Projects

Becoming involved in a local community project, such as providing a wildlife garden at a local hospital, may involve the organisation in giving grants, equipment and staff time. Tackling a discrete project can be helpful in providing a clear focus for community involvement for the company's staff. It can also act as a toe-in-the-water before the organisation considers community involvement on a wider scale.

Use of facilities

A company may make its sports facilities, its canteen or even its photocopying facilities available to the local community. It is a way of introducing local people into the firm and helping them to see the company as a resource rather than a nuisance.

Visitor centres

Companies are increasingly opening their doors to visitors, not only on special occasions but all the year round. This can fulfil a number of objectives. It can show that the organisation is open and has nothing to hide, as the British Nuclear Fuels visitor centre at Sellafield has attempted to do. A case study of this centre is given by Richard Varey (1997). It can give visitors an understanding of the philosophy behind the company, which the Body Shop's centre aspires to. Or it can act as a self-financing or income-generating tourist attraction, such as Cadbury's World, sited close to the company's chocolate factory at Bourneville near Birmingham. Visits to see working factories, craft workshops or farms are becoming increasingly popular with the public. Sometimes visitor centres, with their associated shops and cafes, create new employment opportunities for the local community, as well as acting as a leisure attraction and possibly an educational resource, in the form of school trips.

Open days

Open days have a long history as a method of improving community relations and they can still be highly successful. Anything which involves wearing a hard hat or climbing on to a huge piece of machinery will usually be very popular with children: fire stations, bus garages and generating stations have discovered this. Staff often get a great deal of pleasure, as well as the opportunity to improve team-working and to express their creativity, out of organising and running open days. Such events can act as a recruiting ground for new staff, an opportunity to show how the company operates, and a way of showing what the company brings to the community in which it is based.

Environmental improvements

Once a company has its own house in order in terms of its policies and practices on the environment, it can become involved in environmental improvements in the local community. This may range from putting money and equipment into cleaning up a local eyesore to developing a new environmental corridor. The Five Weirs Walk, alongside the formerly heavily polluted River Don in the east end of Sheffield, is now a flourishing nature trail, supporting populations of kingfishers and even the occasional trout. The riverside walk has been created largely as a result of the money, land, labour and goodwill donated by the companies operating close to the river. Elsewhere, staff interests and environmental improvements came together when ten divers from IBM's sub-aqua club restored and mapped an underwater nature trail at the Purbeck Marine Wildlife Reserve in Dorset, following heavy storms.

Public speaking

Some organisations have a speakers' panel: a group of trained staff who can go out to pensioners' lunch clubs, business dinners, residents' meetings or other professional and community groups to speak about the organisation. They will have prepared material to show, such as slides, video or a photographic exhibition; they may have leaflets, brochures or even free samples to give away. Members of a speakers' panel must always be thoroughly trained and kept up to date, and it is vital that they do not give conflicting messages about the company even if their styles differ.

Media relations

The local media forms a very important public for local community relations. The media will report on what the company does and can take a cynical or a positive attitude to the organisation. The organisation needs to bear this in mind when it is planning its community relations programmes, and to ensure that it keeps in close contact with the local media and with local representatives of the national media. This may be important in order to gain maximum coverage for what the company is doing, but it may simply be in order to ensure that a good flow of information to the media is maintained.

Case Study 8.2

Corporate philanthropy

Investing in the community: IBM

IBM has three main strands to its policy of corporate philanthropy, each of which it sees as investing in the community. These are education; adult education and training; and arts and culture. Some examples of recent activities are shown under these headings below.

Education

In Australia, the company provided cash and equipment to refurbish an exhibit, Mathematica, at the National Science and Technology Centre of Australia. The exhibit was seen by 1.5 million visitors during its tour round Australia and then set off for a tour to other countries in the Asia-Pacific region. Classroom kits and software in appropriate Asian languages accompanied the exhibit. In Canada, IBM donated computers and software to upgrade and expand seven technology rooms at Cambrian College's Special Needs Regional Resource Centre.

Adult education and training

As a contribution to solving the problem of mass unemployment in Europe, IBM organised a Pan-European session for training practitioners and policy makers to look at problems in the training sector. This resulted in the company's funding six not-for-profit training centres in Denmark, Ireland, France, Portugal and the United Kingdom.

Arts and culture

IBM has been involved in digitising paintings in Brazil in order to improve inventory control and help a museum to undertake restoration of paintings; has helped the Vatican Library to archive its illuminated manuscripts; designed the first 'virtual art gallery' in Latin America, based on the collections at Mexico's Monterrey Museum; and is helping archaeologists in Peru to restore ancient temple figures with a computer-aided graphic reconstruction system.

Employee giving is a major element of IBM's corporate philanthropy. In 1997 donations reached $30 million through the IBM Matching Grants programmes and the Employee Charitable Contributions Campaign. In addition to the company's substantial investment in paid employee secondments, IBM employees donated 3.8 million hours of their own time to philanthropic activities during 1997.

IBM-UK's Director of Corporate Community Involvement believes that the most effective support, both for IBM and for the community organisations concerned, seems to be employee involvement.

(*Sources*: company information and Portway 1995: 226)

Sponsorship

Throughout this chapter there have been references to sponsorship as a community relations activity. It is given separate treatment here, rather than appearing in the list of activities, because sponsorship can be undertaken for a variety of reasons, not all of which may have anything to do with relationships with the community. One approach is to look at reasons for sponsorship by asking what objectives a sponsorship programme might have, or to put it simply, why use sponsorship?

Why sponsor?

Here are five reasons why an organisation might consider sponsorship.

To familiarise the name

This may be necessary either because a brand or company is new, because a product has been launched under a new name or a company has changed its name, because it has always had a very low profile, or because people are wary of using the name, perhaps because it is hard to pronounce or it has undesirable connotations. Two examples will show how name familiarisation was achieved by sponsorship.

Cornhill Insurance

Twenty years ago the world of insurance was a shadowy one to most people, who bought their insurance through a broker or from someone who came to the door to collect their premiums by weekly instalments. Research showed the Cornhill Insurance company that less than 2 per cent of their target population knew their name. Following Cornhill's sponsorship of test cricket, name awareness went up to 16 per cent.

The choice of test cricket was an interesting one. It was in the news because some of England's best players were being tempted overseas by offers of more money than the Test and County Cricket Board (TCCB) could afford. Cornhill was the first company to sponsor test cricket, so this was a newsworthy event in itself and one which generated a good deal of coverage. An additional spin-off was that Cornhill was admired for having come to the aid of a national institution, the TCCB, in its hour of need, when traditional test cricket was being threatened by Kerry Packer's World Series. Cricket was also the sport most likely to appeal to opinion leaders in the financial community and other important publics.

Durex

Although the name of the London Rubber Company's condoms was familiar to its publics, it was rarely used in the days before safer sex campaigns, when merely to utter the word 'Durex' could be shameful and embarrassing. Instead, customers would ask for 'a packet of three', or refer to 'french letters'. Durex wanted people to be comfortable using their brand name and chose sponsorship as the ideal way in which to get their name 'normalised'. By sponsoring a car involved in motor-racing, a sport televised by the BBC, they hoped that viewers would get used to seeing the name and commentators to using it, and that this would gradually remove the taboo and normalise their name.

In fact, the BBC initially refused on the grounds of taste to televise rallies in which the Durex car was taking part. This generated massive press coverage, largely sympathetic to the company, and this of course was of immense benefit to Durex, thus helping to normalise their name and even to make it acceptable in the morning newspaper over the breakfast table.

To reinforce corporate identity

Sometimes the holding company or parent is hardly known, while its brands are famous. It may be that a company has the same name as others in different fields, and needs to differentiate itself. Here are examples of both, and how sponsorship was beneficial to the companies concerned.

Canon

This is the name of a company which was quite well known for making cameras, but not so well known for its photocopiers, and certainly not as well known as its competitors in the office equipment business. They decided on a very high-profile sponsorship by taking on the football league.

Canon sponsored the football league for three years. Their name was used every time matches were played between the 92 teams in the league, and it appeared every time the football results were shown on television – several times a week. By the end of their period of sponsorship it is estimated that hardly an office remained in Britain without a Canon copier.

Seagram

This is an example of a company whose brands (Glenlivet whisky, Sandeman port) were more famous than the wine and spirit manufacturer which made them. They chose a high-profile sporting event to sponsor: the Grand National, together with the Derby, probably Britain's most famous horse race. The Grand National was in financial trouble and under threat of disappearing altogether when Seagram's sponsorship, taking a leaf out of Cornhill's book 'saved' it for the nation.

To demonstrate goodwill

Sponsoring charitable or arts events is a way for a company to demonstrate goodwill and thus be looked upon kindly by its target publics.

Yellow Pages

In 1998 Yellow Pages sponsored Make A Difference Day, the UK's largest day of national volunteering run by Community Service Volunteers (CSV). The Day supported 400 different volunteering activities and was well reported in the media.

The Rice Bureau

The long-term public relations campaign by the Rice Bureau won an IPR Sword of Excellence in 1994. Included in its campaign was sponsorship of the artist Vong Phaophinit, whose work 'Neon Rice Field' was short listed for the Turner prize. The work was shown at both the Serpentine and Tate Galleries and was the subject of an unusual video news release.

When advertising is not an alternative

The television advertising ban on cigarettes means that the only way a tobacco company can get brand name exposure on the small screen is by sponsoring an event which is covered by television. These have often been sporting events, although the continuing debate about the linkage of healthy activities with that of cigarette smoking indicates there will be a ban on this activity before long. Even for products where no outright ban exists, the rules about advertising a product on television may make sponsorship a better bet.

Tobacco companies

Embassy cigarettes have sponsored the World Snooker Championship for some years. Unlike cricket, which is an outdoor game for which the players have to be demonstrably fit, snooker is associated with smoky rooms; hence there has not been quite so much controversy over the cigarette company link. However, the event still regularly attracts protesters. In the USA Philip Morris, forbidden by law to advertise their cigarettes directly, sponsors tennis tournaments such as the Virginia Slims women's event.

Lil-lets

One of the last taboos of polite society, mentioning sanitary towels or tampons in front of a mixed audience, seemed finally to be on its way out when so-called 'sanpro' advertising began on independent television. However, the rules still ban showing such advertisements at a time when children might be watching, and individual campaigns have been banned because they describe the product too vividly. Lil-lets decided to use sponsorship instead, paying £750,000 to sponsor a six-week season of prime-time feature films. The films, under the banner Leading Ladies, featured strong, confident characters played by actors such as Sally Field, Sigourney Weaver and Melanie Griffiths. Lil-lets' credit, a 'pastiche of heroic women from the old movies' according to its producer, was shown before and after each film and during each commercial break.

To attract media interest

Sponsoring an event which is in itself interesting to the media ensures that the sponsor will get some media coverage merely by being linked to the event. However, a controversial linkage, or one which is particularly apposite, or humorous, will probably result in greater coverage for the sponsor. Similarly, choosing an event which is itself making news will attract more media interest.

Chupa Chups

The lollipop brand Chupa Chups supported No Smoking Day in the UK on 10 March 1999. The company had been using two drag queens in its campaign to increase sales in the 18–35 year-old market: they inspired the theme of Chupa Chups' involvement in No Smoking Day – The Last Drag. The drag queens drove around London in a jeep decorated with the message 'Don't Smoke. Suck'. They offered free lollipops to smokers in exchange for the cigarettes they were smoking, handing out 5,000 in the day. Chupa Chups chose an innovative way to gain media attention by linking themselves with the good cause of No Smoking Day and also raised their profile with the target audience they were hoping to reach.

What can be sponsored?

As we have seen above, there are numerous vehicles for sponsorship. When considering sponsorship opportunities, a company needs to consider how it will meet the company's objectives, as we have already noted. An important consideration is that the target audience for the sponsored activity should be the same public which the organisation is trying to reach. This may seem obvious, but the days when sponsorship activities were undertaken on the chairman's whim or on behalf of someone's favourite good cause, are by no means over.

In addition the sponsorship programme must be relevant or appropriate in some way to the organisation doing the sponsoring. This can be as simple as the two parties sharing a name, such as Royal Insurance sponsoring the Royal Shakespeare Company. The link may more directly connect product and event, such as the high-energy Mars Bar and the London Marathon. (Interestingly, the race was subsequently sponsored by Flora, connecting the healthful pursuit of running with the spread which is alleged to be a healthy food.) There may be a visual link, such as the insurance company Legal and General's logo, an umbrella, and their sponsorship of the local weather forecast.

It is worth listing for the sake of completeness the vehicles which companies have used for sponsorship.

Sport

This has to come first in any listing. More money is spent on sports sponsorship than any other category and it has become a crowded field in which to take up sponsorship activities. Sports include football, cricket, athletics, tennis, yacht racing, motor racing and golf. Some sports are attractive to sponsors because those who follow them form a tightly drawn target audience; others because of their wide international appeal and for the opportunity to get television coverage.

The arts

Sponsorship of the arts, such as underwriting the costs of travelling art exhibitions or putting on an opera season, is often seen as the more philanthropic end of sponsorship, undertaken primarily for goodwill. However, the appropriateness of the target audience is often the prime consideration. This explains why financial institutions such as banks and insurance companies regularly sponsor the arts.

Performers

Orchestras, theatre companies and individual artists and artistes can be sponsored. Spin-offs include the use of corporate hospitality for the sponsoring company and its clients, and such media as CD boxes and theatre programmes for acknowledgements. As with any sponsorship activity, though, the performance can go horribly wrong. The rock-star who succumbs to the overuse of drugs on tour will reflect very badly on his or her sponsor.

Books

The publication of books is sponsored by such companies as Guinness, with the Guinness Book of Records series; Michelin with their restaurant and hotel guides for motorists; and Rentokil, who have sponsored a library of books on pest-control. A company may sponsor a single book, such as the

Kingfisher group's sponsorship of a book on corporate social responsibility. Or it may sponsor a training manual, such as Barclays' sponsorship of the St John Ambulance first-aid course notes. Sponsorship of publications is usually part of a wider marketing or public relations campaign.

Exhibitions and shows

The *Daily Mail* has for many years sponsored the Ideal Home exhibition, while the Royal Horticultural Society's sponsorship of the Chelsea Flower Show is inextricable from the event itself. Trade shows are often sponsored by the industry sector concerned, while overseas trade missions may be sponsored partly by participating businesses and partly by government funding. They may be self-funding or income-generating, as well as providing the opportunity to conduct business and offer hospitality.

Expeditions

Single-handed voyages round the world, treks to the North Pole and character-building youth expeditions have all been sponsored. These offer the chance to sponsors to associate themselves with celebrity, and also with the virtues of ruggedness, pioneering and healthy activity, so long as no disastrous accidents occur. An added benefit can be the use of sponsors' products on an expedition, both to test them in harsh conditions, and to use the results for subsequent product endorsement.

Charities and voluntary bodies

This may range from supporting staff who are raising money for charity to sponsoring a charity's event. Roadline sponsored the collection of charity parcels on behalf of the children's television show, *Blue Peter*, and the British Heart Foundation has attracted sponsorship from a manufacturer of diet foods for its annual Slim-In. Barclays contributed £50,000 to the Breath of Life campaign, run by St John Ambulance to encourage members of the public to learn the technique of resuscitation. Charitable sponsorships are usually undertaken for goodwill, for staff motivation or for their ability to reach a specific target audience.

Awards

The Booker company and brewers Whitbread both sponsor literary prizes, which are well reported in the media. The IPR's Sword of Excellence awards are sponsored category by category, some by public relations consultancies such as Shandwick and others by firms such as Mercury and Vickers. Glenfiddich, the whisky distillery, sponsors awards for food and drink writers and Diners Club sponsors an award scheme for young chefs. The details are shown in Case Study 8.3. This type of sponsorship offers the opportunity for escalating media coverage as the heats of the competition progress, and coverage of a major event, complete with photogenic celebrities and hospitality opportunities, at the end.

Case Study 8.3

Sponsorship

The Roux Diners Scholarship 1993: Vital Public Relations for Diners Club International

This was a small scale but highly focused sponsorship project. The client's brief was to increase awareness of Diners Club among establishments which already take the Diners Club charge card and those which do not. The consultancy went for a three-strand strategy: to generate awareness among the catering, hotel, restaurant and regional press of Diners Club and its work for establishments; to position Diners Club alongside the best in terms of young chefs and their establishments; and to support the establishments for their loyalty and further to develop young culinary talent throughout the UK.

The vehicle chosen to accomplish these objectives was a national scholarship held for young chefs between the ages of 22 and 27 to enhance their skills through a unique training scheme. The Roux Diners Scholar has the opportunity to train for three months with a 3-star Michelin chef anywhere in the UK or the rest of Europe, while the runner-up is offered the chance to cook under the supervision of one of the Roux brothers at Le Gavroche or the Waterside Inn for two weeks.

Audiences were identified as restaurants, hotels, pubs; hospitality and catering bodies; restaurant group associations, e.g. Soho Restaurateurs Association; catering colleges; suppliers and associated organisations, e.g. Wedgwood.

The project ran from September, with the launch of the scholarships in the trade press, through the winter while the judges conducted the contest through to the regional finals on 3 March and the grand final on 23 March. There was extensive regional press, television and radio coverage and trade press coverage.

(*Source*: *Vital Public Relations*)

Community events

These have been discussed in the earlier section on community relations. Another example is that of Henry Boot, the building firm, which provides local churches with a large, well equipped and very beautiful setting for their annual garden party in the grounds of its headquarters building.

Educational activities

This includes the award of scholarships and grants, sometimes by companies to individual students, who may be expected to work for the company during the vacations and following graduation. Some organisations sponsor specific areas of research, such as that provided for medical research by charities such as the Imperial Cancer Research Fund. Other companies may sponsor a chair, such as the London Business School's Chair in Business Ethics and Social Responsibility, sponsored by the high-street retailer, Dixons. Educational material may be sponsored and both the sugar industry and the nuclear industry have made free material available to schools on this basis.

Advisory services

While these are sometimes thinly veiled sales pitches, a number of companies sponsor advisory services which offer the public sensible and impartial, free advice. Trade associations sometimes offer a service to help people in making a decision on, for example, the purchase of financial services. The supermarket chains banded together to set up a food-advisory service following concerns about salmonella and listeria in prepared foods: callers were given advice on the storage and preparation of such foods, rather than a sales message about the retailers' lines. On the theme of food poisoning, Domestos, makers of household bleach, sponsor a hygiene advisory service which in its turn sponsors the Pre-school Playgroups Association.

Television sponsorship

This is a relative newcomer in the UK, although it has been common for many years in the USA. In the UK, television sponsorship falls into two types.

The first is the sponsorship of off-air material, which sprang from the community units set up in the 1980s by television stations. These units typically run seminars, competitions and road shows, requiring sponsorship to help pay for the cost of associated information booklets and packs for schools. Companies such as British Gas, BT, ICI, Lloyds Bank and Sainsbury's have sponsored this kind of material. Although on-air sponsorship was not permitted until recently, sponsors of off-air material could have their names reported on-air.

The sponsorship of television programmes has been permitted since 1991. Early takers were Beamish stout, sponsors of the Morse television series, featuring a beer gourmet as lead character; and Croft port with its sponsorship of Rumpole of the Bailey, whose eponymous hero was everyone's idea of someone who would enjoy port. Television sponsorship has the advantage over television advertising in that the viewer tends to associate the product with the 'editorial' content rather than with the paid-for advertising slots, thus giving the sponsors' message more credibility.

How does it work?

Once an organisation has decided that sponsorship is an appropriate vehicle to achieve its objectives it needs to get the activity underway. Responsibility for making it happen may lie with the personnel department, with the head of public relations, in the marketing division or with a dedicated member of the board of directors.

Making the link with an appropriate body which is looking for sponsorship is quite straightforward. There are specialist consultancies and agencies who deal solely with sponsorship, and some bodies which specialise further, dealing only with, for example, football sponsorship. Publications such as *PR Week* carry columns of classified advertising giving details of sponsorship opportunities, and there are a number of directories and yearbooks which give similar information.

Organisations seeking sponsorship can use agencies and directories, but will often contact companies, whom they believe to be sympathetic, direct. Some companies have forms to be completed and make their decisions on sponsorship at a special committee meeting once a year.

In spite of what has been said about the strategic nature of sponsorship decisions, it is true that in the real world some decisions are made on the basis of the boss's interests or preferences. When it comes to a decision, the difference between sponsoring the opera and a golf tournament may rest on the personal tastes of the chairman. Justification for the choice may have to come later.

In the same way, contacts for sponsorship deals are still often made through the so-called old boys' network. The immensely successful Eureka! museum for children is a good example. The museum is situated in Halifax, a closely knit community in west Yorkshire. The pillars of society in a small town such as this are likely to be well known to each other: the Halifax Building Society, the local newspaper, the town's civic leaders among them. Eureka! is very much a hands-on museum, with exhibits that children can operate and play with, and the majority of these exhibits are sponsored by companies who are either locally based or who have significant branches in the area. So the supermarket is sponsored by Marks and Spencer, and has diminutive trolleys into which the shoppers of the future can load their corn on the cob and packets of lasagne. While all of the companies who have provided products or services to Eureka! will certainly have considered their sponsorship as part of their strategic planning process, the initial contacts with the major sponsors were all made through the offices of one of the town's great and the good – who contacted her friends.

However the links are made, it is clearly important to both sides that proper arrangements are agreed for the sponsorship deal. A contract needs to be prepared and agreed. It is particularly important that the organisation being sponsored knows exactly what support it can expect and for how long. Some sponsors feel it is very important that the sponsored body does not rely totally on handouts from a sponsor, and the conditions under which grants are made must be clearly understood.

A further consideration is that of the position of multiple sponsors. A fun run may seek a number of sponsors, offering them different vehicles according to a price-list: £5,000 gets the sponsor's name above the race name and onto the certificates; £1,000 sponsors the runners' numbers; £500 sponsors the clock; £250 sponsors the stewarding; £100 puts the company's name in a roll of honour in the programme; £25 gives the company a mention. It is important in such a situation that everyone is open and above board about the arrangements.

Costs

A local trader may sponsor the Brownies' annual sports day for £100, while some television sponsorship deals run into six figures. Sponsorship can cost as much or as little as the sponsor is prepared to pay.

Sometimes sponsorships are self-liquidating: they raise at least as much money for the sponsor as the sponsor has put in. This is more likely to be the case where goods are sold as part of a sponsorship deal – tee-shirts are a prime example.

In the case of the *Liverpool Echo*, it is a little more risky. The newspaper sponsors the purchase of a racehorse every year and offers its readers the opportunity to buy a stake in the animal. This offsets some of the cost of sponsorship and gives the readers the opportunity to go into the owners' enclosure when 'their' horse is running. The sports pages of the paper cover the horse's every move throughout the season and at the end of the year the horse is sold. A division of the spoils takes place, with all 'owners' getting their share of the prize money and the sale price: as often as not, there is a profit for everyone, including the newspaper itself.

Evaluation

Following the public relations planning model we discussed earlier, evaluation should take the form of measuring effectiveness of the sponsorship package against the objectives it was set to achieve. This may involve monitoring coverage in the press and broadcast media for volume, quality and appropriateness. Case Study 8.4 gives an example of how this was achieved.

Evaluating effectiveness of sponsorship

	Case Study 8.4

The 40th anniversary Everest expedition: DHL

Global carrier DHL's major objective in sponsoring the 40th anniversary Everest expedition was to capture the imagination of the media and increase awareness of the company to a general audience by achieving a high volume of positive media coverage. In getting the news from the world's highest mountain to the desks of editors all over the world, using a combination of Nepalese runners, helicopters and satellite solar telephone, DHL was able to demonstrate its skill as a global carrier. Everest was particularly appropriate to a company whose advertising message is 'Ain't no mountain high enough'. Although Everest had been climbed before, this expedition was especially newsworthy for the attempt by Rebecca Stephens to be the first British woman to reach the summit. The company estimated that they received media coverage equivalent to over £17 million.

In evaluating its Everest 40 sponsorship deal DHL not only totted up the number of mentions, translated into readership and viewers, but they also looked at how many front pages, and how many lead items on the television news the expedition received. Their research indicated that all the coverage was positive and that the company's competitors received no positive editorial in the national press during this period.

(*Source*: IPR Sword of Excellence awards)

A name awareness campaign using sponsorship requires the company to undertake research before, during and after the event to track awareness of the sponsor's name and see whether or not it can be linked to the sponsorship activity.

In some cases sales may be monitored. If the objective is to increase sales, or sales leads, and no other activity is going on at the same time, it is fairly straightforward to make the connection.

Summary points

✔ It makes good business sense to foster good relations with the community. Each organisation has its own community publics to consider.

✔ Companies have social responsibilities. Fulfilling these is not merely a question of altruism but can be of great mutual benefit and can give a company a competitive edge.

✔ Organisations should plan their community relations in line with their corporate objectives and be clear and consistent in applying their policy.

✔ Elements of a community relations programme may include giving grants or equipment, staff secondments, offering training or the use of other company facilities, becoming involved in local projects, opening a visitor centre, organising open days, improving the environment and setting up a speakers' panel. Local media relations are also important.

✔ Sponsorship is sometimes undertaken as part of a community relations programme. It may be used, in addition, to familiarise a name, to reinforce corporate identity, to demonstrate goodwill, because advertising is not a suitable alternative or to attract media interest.

✔ There are numerous vehicles for sponsorship from sport to television series. Sponsors and those seeking sponsorship find each other through direct contact, through directories or advertising, or through specialist consultancies. Sponsorship arrangements need to be thoroughly costed and evaluated.

Questions for discussion

1 Imagine yourself in the position of volunteer public relations officer for your favourite charity. Consider ways of raising money from the general public and the business community.

2 Who are your target publics and what events and activities do you think will most appeal to them?

3 How will you communicate with your publics? What are your objectives? Are they the same for each public?

4 Now imagine you are the community relations manager for a large engineering company. What are your criteria for supporting community activities?

5 Consider how you would react to requests for assistance from the charity above.

Recommended further reading

Public relations and ethics, incorporating the notion of corporate social responsibility, is a very wide field. McElreath (1997) bases much of his book on ethical decision making in public relations practice. Seib and Fitzpatrick (1997) is a short volume on the subject of public relations ethics. Harrison (1997) in Kitchen looks at why organisations should consider their social responsibilities.

Koten (1997) in Caywood looks at sponsorship, cause-related marketing and events management in the context of corporate philanthropy as exercised by USA corporations. Seitel (1995) has a good chapter on community relations, focusing on multicultural communities. Center and Jackson's (1995) Chapter 5 on community relations is also worth looking at.

The practicalities of sponsorship are covered in Sleight (1989), in Wragg (1994) and among the cases in Hendrix (1998). Hendrix also has a useful chapter on community relations illuminated by three very different examples of community relations programmes.

References

Baskin, O., Aronoff, C. and Lattimore, D. (1997) *Public Relations the Profession and the Practice*, 4th edn., Chicago, IL: Brown and Benchmark.

Boston College (1995) *1995 Profile of the Community Relations Profession*, Chestnut Hill, MA: Center for Corporate Community Relations at Boston College.

Bunta, R. (1992) 'Employee Volunteerism: A Complement to Corporate Philanthropy', *Journal of Corporate Public Relations* 3.

Center, A. and Jackson, P. (1995) *Public Relations Practices: Managerial Case Studies and Problems*, Englewood Cliffs, NJ: Prentice Hall.

Clutterbuck, D., Dearlove, D. and Snow, D. (1992) *Actions Speak Louder: A Management Guide to Corporate Social Responsibility*, London: Kogan Page/Kingfisher.

Harrison, S. (1997) 'Corporate Social Responsibility: Linking Behaviour with Reputation', in Kitchen, P. (ed.), *Public Relations Principles and Practice*, London: International Thomson Business Press.

Hendrix, J. (1998) *Public Relations Cases*, 4th edn., Belmont, CA: Wadsworth.

Koten, J. (1997) 'The Strategic Uses of Corporate Philanthropy', in Caywood, C., *The Handbook of Strategic Public Relations and Integrated Communications*, New York: McGraw-Hill.

McElreath, M. (1997) *Managing Systematic and Ethical Public Relations Campaigns*, Chicago, IL: Brown and Benchmark.

Peach, L. (1987) 'Corporate Responsibility' in Hart, N. (ed.), *Effective Corporate Relations*, London: McGraw-Hill.

Portway, S. (1995) 'Corporate Social Responsibility: the Case for Active Stakeholder Management', in Hart, N. (ed.), *Strategic Public Relations*, Basingstoke: Macmillan.

Seib, P. and Fitzpatrick, K. (1997) *Public Relations Ethics*, Fort Worth, TX: Harcourt Brace Jovanovich.

Seitel, F. (1995) *The Practice of Public Relations*, 6th edn., Englewood Cliffs, NJ: Prentice Hall.

Sleight, S. (1989) *Sponsorship: What It Is and How to Use It*, London: McGraw-Hill.

Varey, R. (1997) 'External Public Relations Activities', in Kitchen, P. (ed.), *Public Relations Principles and Practice*, London: International Thomson Business Press.

Wragg, D. (1994) *The Effective Use of Sponsorship*, London: Kogan Page.

Specialist public relations

9

Key Issues

The aim of this chapter is to bring together the main specialist areas of public relations practice that are not separately covered in the book. The specialisms briefly covered are:

► media relations;

► lobbying;

► central and local government public relations;

► international public relations;

► investor relations;

► public relations for marketing support.

As an introduction to public relations, this book aims to give the reader a basic grounding in the subject. It does not pretend to give comprehensive coverage of the theory and practice of public relations. Books which do can be found in the bibliography. So far we have looked at topics of general interest: anyone involved in public relations needs to know what the subject is about, how it arose, its theoretical basis and the importance of planning. The four specialist chapters, on corporate and crisis public relations, internal communication and community relations respectively, have been included because they are likely to be of value to most readers. In this chapter we will complete the picture by looking at a number of other specialist areas: media relations, lobbying, central and local government public relations, international public relations, investor relations, and public relations for marketing support.

Media relations

While most public relations people list media relations as one of their activities, the press officer performs a very specialised function: that of conducting relations with reporters on behalf of his or her employer or client. To fulfil this role, the press officer needs to have a good understanding of how the respective media work – their interests, resources, deadlines and so on; the ability to produce and transmit properly written and targeted news releases; and the kind of temperament to get on well with journalists. Press officers are often trained and experienced journalists who have decided for one reason or another to make a career change. Incidentally, the term 'the media' is used for convenience when referring to broadcasting as well as the printed word, but it is as well to remember that journalists, especially in the press, do not much like the term, and refer to themselves as 'the media' very seldom. Similarly, the term 'media relations officer' has never caught on in the public relations profession, and 'press officer' is much more common, even though the incumbent is just as likely to be dealing with the local radio station as with the evening paper.

Press office

Many organisations with in-house public relations staff run their own press office. This may be simply a desk in the public relations department staffed by a duty press officer whose job is to answer the phone when it rings and deal with any questions, requests for information or photographs, or set up interviews or visits. More commonly, the press office is there to act positively, or pro-actively, on behalf of the organisation, and this means taking the initiative in contacting the media, rather than simply reacting to calls.

Large and complex organisations sometimes have a number of press officers so that they can provide a round-the-clock service. In such offices, while every one of the staff is capable of running the press desk, each press officer may have a specialised area of expertise and his or her own special list of media contacts. In a large local authority, for example, it makes sense for a number of press officers to specialise, one in education, another in leisure, a third in social services or planning for example. The education press officer, while fully competent to deal with any queries about the authority, will be especially knowledgeable about issues to do with schools, colleges, careers and training, and will have good contacts in the local media, as well as with the education correspondents of the national newspapers and the education supplements.

Media relations is not by any means the province only of the in-house press officer. It can be provided by a public relations consultancy, and there are some consultancies which specialise in this type of work. An organisation based outside the capital may choose to sub-contract its relations with the national media to a London-based consultancy because of the consultancy's proximity to, as well as contacts with, the influential reporters it wants to reach. Alternatively it may have a London outpost: the Equal Opportunities Commission, whose public relations office is based at headquarters in Manchester, has a press office in London.

What makes news?

This is an interesting question which we could begin to answer by, for example, listening to all the radio and television news bulletins during the course of a day, and scanning the lead stories in the newspapers. On any given day this might lead us to say that murder, war, famine or other catastrophe is what makes news. But sometimes murder, war and famine do not make it on to the front pages, even though they continue to exist. In the British press, news may be the reported behaviour of a television star (in other words, gossip); a diatribe against the EU (in other words, editorial comment); or an exhortation to vote for one party or another on election day (political propaganda). Clearly, what makes news depends on the vehicle which presents it and the pressures which drive those vehicles. It is important to remember that news is a product, that newspaper publishers need to sell copies of their paper and that the broadcasting companies need to be able to reach large numbers of viewers and listeners with their news programmes.

It follows, therefore, that every editor is looking for a different angle on a popular story, an exclusive, something which will differentiate his or her product from everyone else's. Reporters and the public have a low boredom threshold: hence the tendency to try and make a story more interesting, sometimes at the expense of accuracy. Conversely, the press officer may want to play down a story which reflects badly on his or her organisation, and may try to give the impression that it is not at all interesting, in fact, it is not a story at all. The example of game theory given in Chapter 3 includes this scenario. Unless the press officer and the journalist have a relationship of mutual trust and respect, this approach is likely to be wholly counter-productive.

The media are looking for novelty, interesting stories which will appeal to their readers, listeners and viewers, and which are obtainable without too much difficulty. Resources are limited, and the television station will not send out a crew to cover an item which is of little importance or where the pictures or sound will not be of broadcast quality.

The news is not solely made up of material which journalists gather themselves, however. It comes from a number of sources: the diary, the wire services, news and picture agencies, freelances, tip-offs and public relations departments and consultancies.

Diary

The news-desk keeps a diary, which lists what is happening and what might need to be covered on a given day. For a local newspaper or radio station this might include items such as: the new wing of a hospital is to be opened by a member of the royal family; there is a lunch-time seminar for regional business leaders; it is sports day at the local primary school. Most of the items in the diary will be there because a public relations officer has sent prior notification to the news-desk, in the form of a news release or list of forthcoming events.

Wire services and agencies

The Press Association (PA), based in London, transmits national news stories to its subscribers, the national and local newspapers. The fastest way to get a story out to all newspapers is to tell the PA, who check it and then transmit it electronically to every news-desk. Once received, it is up to the individual news editor to follow up the story with the paper's own reporters. Reuters performs the same function with news from overseas.

News-desks also receive material from agencies and pay for what they want to use. Most large towns have local news agencies which offer a service nationally, and some agencies specialise in certain topics. Picture agencies and photo libraries are also available to provide news editors with photographs to accompany their stories on payment of a reproduction fee. Foreign news agencies also sell material and this often appears as short paragraphs in a column such as 'News from around the world'. UPI and AP are American news agencies who distribute such material, and whose initials can often be found on the foreign news pages.

Freelances

Freelance journalists are often highly respected experts in their field, supplying stories to news editors on specific topics, sometimes to order. At the other extreme are the freelances who give journalism a bad name by adopting dubious methods to get stories and pictures which they can then sell on to the tabloid press: the freelance remains anonymous and does not have to face the victims of an untrue or biased story, unlike, for example, the local newspaper reporter, who has to live in the community and who is likely to be more sensitive.

Tip-offs and leaks

This is rather more the stuff of movies than reality, when the 'scoop' does not happen so often. However, calls do come from all kinds of people: a disgruntled or concerned employee, worrying about safety at their factory; a member of the public who happens to have seen something interesting, or someone with an axe to grind. When an individual or organisation wants to float an idea in the press to gauge public reaction, or wants to draw public attention to something which (they believe) is wrongly being kept secret, they may leak the information to the press. A reputable journalist receiving a tip-off will always want to check with the official source for a comment, but if none is forthcoming, the story may be run anyway, with the damaging 'XYZ company refused to comment on the allegations' leaving readers to draw their own conclusions.

Public relations sources

Print and broadcast media rely to a greater or lesser extent on material which they receive from public relations sources. This may come in the form of a printed or video-format news release, material provided at a press conference or reception, interviews arranged or pictures supplied by the public relations officer, a facility visit, or simply a press briefing given in person or over the phone by the public relations officer. Some of the free-sheets rely very heavily on public relations sources for their content. Such newspapers and magazines sometimes run unedited product information which has dropped on to their desks, forgetting to remove contact telephone numbers or to change pronouns appropriately.

Generally, however, if public relations people want their material to be taken up by the media, the material itself must be of interest to the media concerned, must be properly presented and usable. Numerous books and training courses exist which explain how to compose a news release, how to target it and how to get it distributed.

Dealing with media inquiries

Press officers generally divide their time between generating news and information on behalf of their client or employer and dealing with inquiries from the media. (Some press officers also act as journalists for their own in-house newspapers and magazines.) To do the job properly, the press officer must know, or easily be able to find out, anything and everything about the organisation for which he or she works. Press offices often keep files of information on their organisation and its senior management, including up-to-date photographs (black and white as well as colour) of key personnel and products, bromides of the company logo, and all manner of facts, figures and statistics about the sector in which the organisation operates. Some press offices keep folders at the ready so that appropriate material – photographs, off-prints of articles, a news release, maps or plans – can be sent to journalists on request.

Inquiries from the media usually come by phone, and the press office needs to be properly resourced to deal with queries: enough lines are needed so that one can be dedicated to receiving calls and another can be connected to the fax machine, with other links for computer modems and Internet connection a possibility. It is vital that media inquiries are dealt with efficiently and promptly. If the press officer cannot give the answer straight away, the call must be returned within the time-scale agreed with the journalist. Whether the journalist's deadline is eleven o'clock in the morning or nine o'clock at night, the press officer needs to be aware that a query answered too late means an opportunity missed. It is far better to contact the journalist by the time agreed, even if only to say 'I couldn't find out the information', than to leave the query unanswered.

This is all part of building a relationship of trust between the press officer and the journalist. It can only be achieved if the two parties are honest with each other and reliable in their dealings.

Whole books have been written on the practice of media relations, and this brief section is intended simply to give a flavour of the work involved.

Lobbying

The UK public relations industry defines lobbying as 'the specific effort to influence public decision making either by pressing for change in policy or seeking to prevent such change' (IPR 1994). In the USA lobbying is seen as the branch of public affairs which is most closely tied to legislation: lobbying's objective is to influence governmental decisions and particularly legislative votes. Although there has been some movement towards the registration of professional lobbyists in the UK, they are subject only to a voluntary code and are not required publicly to disclose information about their business. There are state and federal laws in the USA which require the registration of lobbyists: all those earning over $5,000 in any six month period from lobbying activities must register under the Federal Lobby Reform Act 1996, and companies which spend more than $20,000 in six months on lobbying must also report details of their activities. Lobbyists are required to report their income and expenses, who they have been working for and on what issues. There are estimated to be 100,000 people working in the lobbying industry in Washington. Comparable figures are not available for the UK, where there is no reliable means of estimating the numbers involved. Moloney (1994), however, found that in the UK about £25 million was spent simply in hiring professional lobbyists in 1993–4.

There are two conflicting views about lobbyists and their activities. One says that, in a pluralistic society, competing interests balance each other out, and that lobbying is a part of this process, ensuring a healthy democracy where everyone has their say. The alternative view is that, because only the rich and the powerful can afford to run sophisticated and sustained lobbying campaigns, these special interests have an unfair influence over government decision making. In the worst case, such special interests may manipulate politicians for their own ends, using corrupt practices to do so.

Legitimate lobbying can take a number of forms. Miller (1996) describes two of them: 'representations based on careful research, usually followed by negotiation in short, working the system and mobilisation of public and media opinion in short, pressure'. In the former case, the lobbyist uses contacts with government, either with politicians or with civil servants, to ensure that information helpful to the client is put before those responsible for making decisions. Legislators cannot hope to become expert in every field which their decisions affect. They are often grateful to lobbyists for providing them with sufficient background information to enable them to take a position on proposed legislation. Lobbyists may directly target the Secretary of State or Minister in the government department which is leading on the legislation, or they may do so indirectly by making their case with the civil servants in the department, the permanent staff responsible for giving advice to the politicians concerned.

In the latter case, what Miller calls 'pressure' can be applied by two means: grass-roots lobbying and media campaigns. The objectives of both are to create awareness of an issue, to sway public opinion in the direction required by the lobbyist, and to galvanise the public or the media into action. Grass-roots action could be a letter-writing campaign from constituents to their parliamentary representatives (in the UK or in the European parliament) or congressmen (in the USA); it could include public demonstrations, sit-ins or a day of action. Media campaigns are aimed either at persuading an influential news provider to take up the lobbyist's case, or can include letter-writing to the editors of newspapers, provision of information and photographs in support of the lobbyist's case, and taking out advertisements in the media to put one's views across.

Case Study 9.1 gives examples of most types of lobbying activity in both areas: working the system and pressure.

Case Study 9.1

Lobbying
The banana wars: Europe and the USA

In 1993 the European Union voted narrowly to adopt the Banana Trade Regime (BTR), a measure to restrict the import of bananas into Europe. Those in favour of the BTR wanted to protect the growers in Africa, the Caribbean and the Pacific (former colonies of the supporting countries concerned) from the effect of large quantities of cheap bananas grown by American companies in Latin and South America.

A media campaign spearheaded by the Caribbean producers' striking spokesperson, Dame Eugenia Charles of Dominica, put the issue firmly on the public agenda and attracted the attention of European interest groups in Europe. These were groups who would not necessarily have been interested in the commercial arguments, but who, once they perceived the BTR as a 'third-world' issue, took up the cause. Thus pressure from the grass-roots began to be put upon decision makers in Europe.

There was also plenty of behind-the-scenes activity before the final vote was taken, with a range of interests making their views known to Ministers. The Dutch minister was reportedly subject to campaigns by influential Dutch groups concerning the effect on the poor banana growers of the Windward Islands. Both Portugal and the Netherlands switched sides between the first and second votes in Council. Although the 'liberal' side had many advantages and at least as good a case against the BTR, it could not in the end generate enough momentum to ensure support and the BTR was approved.

The European Union won the battle, but not the war. The banana wars between Europe and the USA continued to rumble on. The World Trade Organisation ordered the EU to drop its restrictions on imports with effect from 1 January 1999. When the EU failed to comply, the Office of the US Trade Representative retaliated by targeting 17 European exports to the USA for 'punitive tariffs'. They were chosen on two counts: products were to come from Britain, France or Italy, the prime movers in the original EU decision; and they should have the minimum impact on Americans.

This latter criterion brought USA lobbyists out in force, as they could see an opportunity here to improve their position by banning competitive imports. Thus USA pork producers managed to ensure that the Italian ham, prosciutto, was on the list, though Dutch and Danish pork products were not (these countries having voted against the BTR). Cheesemakers in the USA, a country not known for the excellence of its cheeses, were unable to get Greek feta cheese or the

Italian hard peccorino cheese included on the list because of the immense popularity of these cheeses among American citizens. Washing machines were originally on the list but were dropped at the last moment when USA manufacturers pointed out that European washing machines are made largely from USA-manufactured components.

(*Sources*: adapted from Pedler and Van Schendelen 1994; *New York Times* 1999; *Time Magazine* 1999)

Although lobbying at the highest levels may mean mixing with the famous and powerful, most lobbying activity is not so exciting. It involves painstaking research of some of the world's dullest documents; monitoring the progress of legislation; keeping track of developments; providing written briefs for meetings, conferences and committees; analysing attendance and voting behaviour of parliamentary representatives; and generally keeping on top of all the minutiae necessary. As Harris and Lock (1996: 31) point out: 'the most powerful form of lobbying is the supply of information on your case, and the issues surrounding it, on a regular basis to those within the decision process'. To this we might add the concepts of timeliness and clarity. Lobbyists must know the timetable of the process they are trying to influence and they must present their case with absolute clarity, especially if they need to distinguish their position from that of an opposing lobbyist.

Lobbying is a very specialised activity within public relations practice, but it is also very widespread: for example, a lobbyist could work for a commercial lobbying firm on whatever accounts the company won, or in-house for a large corporation, defending and protecting its commercial interests. Lobbyists also work in-house in the not-for-profit sector, for charities, voluntary bodies and campaigning groups. Some organisations are set up specifically to look after the interests of their members, such as the European Federation of Pharmaceutical Industry Associations (EFPIA), which was set up in the 1970s to see off the threat of regulation of its members from the World Health Organisation (EFPIA managed to get this dropped in return for a code of self-regulatory practice).

The tools which lobbyists use are those of other public relations professionals: news releases, reports, conferences and special events, newsletters, 'issue' advertising and so on. You will find some suggestions for further reading on the practice of lobbying at the end of this chapter.

Central and local government public relations

Here is another big topic, which will only be touched upon briefly here for two reasons. First, there are a number of other books which go into these specialised areas more deeply; and second, there has recently been very rapid change in the way both central and local government public relations officers operate. This change continues apace, and whatever is written today may be history rather than current practice when this book is read. In this brief section, we will look at what central and local government public relations officers do and how their work differs from that of private sector practitioners; and at some of the issues currently facing the public sector.

First it is important to point out that government public relations encompasses the activities undertaken *on behalf of* government, local or central, unlike lobbying which is, as we have seen, *directed at* local or central government decision makers. It is also important to note that local and central government public relations are undertaken on behalf of the local authority or national government of the day, and not on behalf of a political party. The political parties have their own public relations arrangements. Local and central government public relations officers are public servants who are required to explain and inform the population about the policies and actions of their employers, regardless of their political complexion.

In the UK, central government public relations is conducted largely through the Government Information and Communication Service. Local government public relations is the province of individual local authorities, each of which has its own arrangements – or none.

The move towards competitive tendering and other policy decisions have made it harder to distinguish between the practice of public and private sector public relations. Practitioners who used to operate solely in one sector now find themselves able to work in either, as the concept of the free market has entered the public sector, and the provision of public information is increasingly seen as important by private sector clients.

Central government public relations

As we saw in Chapter 2, the British government has used public relations techniques to provide information to the public about its policies for well over a hundred years. The establishment of press and information officers in government departments really occurred in the late 1940s when information divisions were set up to advise and assist departments with their public relations needs. Now all government departments have their quota of press officers and public affairs specialists.

The job of the senior public relations professional in a government department is a key one. The press secretary or chief information officer in a government department advises the minister of state on all public relations matters, provides comments and quotes to the media, and sometimes writes speeches for the minister. It is important to remember, however, that the public relations staff are non-partisan. They are not there to perform the function of image-maker to a politician. Ministers have their own 'special advisers' to undertake that role.

In the USA, there is a constant fear that the president will use the government's public relations machine for the purposes of political propaganda (Baker 1997: 453). There are certainly plenty of foot-soldiers: the federal government employed 10,000 public information or public affairs personnel, with a budget of $1 billion in, 1993.

The rationale for expenditure such as this on central government public relations is three-fold: a democratic government should encourage the flow of ideas and information between itself and the country's citizens; the government should be accountable to the people it serves; and taxpayers have a right to get information about what the government is doing or planning to do with their money (Baker 1997: 456).

Government departments organise their public relations provision as they find appropriate, but there is usually a divide between the press office and the publicity or promotional activities. The latter may include devising and mounting campaigns such as 'Belt up in the back!', a campaign to encourage the wearing of rear seat-belts by children in cars. In addition, regional offices look after visiting foreign dignitaries and journalists from abroad, as well as organising on-the-ground media facilities to cover royal and prime ministerial visits. The regional offices also have a role to play in assisting with public information at a time of disaster or emergency.

Local government public relations

Although the first public relations practitioners in Britain came from local government, there were no more than a handful in the early days. Since the 1970s, however, four major developments have led naturally to the establishment of the public relations function in nearly all councils. These are first, a greater politicisation of local government; second, a move towards more corporate and professional management in local councils; third, substantial changes in the names, identities and functions of local authorities in all parts of the country; and fourth, the increasingly competitive nature of funding programmes from central government. This latter development requires the successful council to be able to differentiate itself from others, position itself appropriately, and produce persuasive material to influence decision makers.

The day-to-day work of a local government public relations officer varies depending on the type of authority, the size of the deparment or unit and the character of the authority itself. The status of the public relations function within the authority also affects the type of work a local government public relations officer does. Increasingly appointments are being made at the strategic level, at director or assistant chief executive level for example, mirroring the trend in private sector companies. It is becoming more common for the public relations officer to have:

> direct access to the chief executive, chief officers and leading members, and a place at the table in the boardroom or chief officer group. In that way the PRO not only knows what's going on but has the clout to promote PR strategies first hand and to give advice and influence decisions before they become irrevocable.

(Raine 1996: 2)

That said, the public relations officer or team in a local authority will almost certainly be involved in media relations, campaigns (though they are excluded from running party political campaigns by law) and the production of publications. There will usually be at least one press officer and there may in addition be individuals or sections dealing with council publications (possibly including a civic newspaper or magazine); tourism, destination marketing and conferences; photography, design and printing; community liaison; and the council's international or twin-town links.

Some authorities operate a central public relations department, which is responsible for corporate and departmental communications, while others have a de-centralised system of public relations officers in each department. In recent years, some authorities have started to employ marketing officers to promote their services, in addition to or instead of their public relations staff.

Chief executives are advised by their professional body (Society of Local Authority Chief Executives, or SOLACE) to employ properly qualified public relations help. Sir John Boynton, former chief executive of Cheshire County Council, puts it this way

> Whatever the personal role of the chief executive he should never let public relations slip in his priority list. It is the activity of ensuring that the authority's policies, objectives, problems and achievements are known and explained to all concerned.
>
> (Boynton 1986: 106)

Local authorities have since the mid 1980s faced many changes, and a diminution in both their power *vis-à-vis* central government, and in their financial resources. Their public relations departments have often been cut back or even disbanded, with the work contracted out to consultants. As a result, local government public relations officers increasingly try to work like private sector consultants, with whom they are already in competition. However, the picture is not one of total retrenchment. The IPR Local Government Group estimates that almost a thousand public relations professionals work in local government, producing 60,000 items of publicity a year and spending £250 million; they generate over 100,000 news releases annually, with coverage running into miles of print. The doings of the local council form the mainstay of regional and local press and broadcasting throughout the country.

Local government public relations officers tend to work rather more at the public information than the promotional end of public relations. However, they do run campaigns in their own areas, especially on issues such as road safety and issues concerning the environment. Easington District Council hit the headlines with a campaign to shame dog owners into clearing up after their defecating pets. Not only did the posters (Figure 9.1) hit the streets, but the hard-hitting nature of the campaign made news in itself, appearing not only in the local media but being taken up by Sky TV, the Press Association and Channel 4. The campaign went on to win the Excellence in Communication award of the IPR's Local Government Group and featured as a case study in *PR Week*.

Some further examples of local government campaigns are shown in Case Study 9.2.

| Figure 9.1 | *'Dog fouling. It's every owner's business': an award-winning campaign by Easington District Council* |

Source: Easington District Council publicity material, 1994–95. Copyright: District of Easington. *Design*: Elmwood, Leeds.

| Local government public relations | Case Study 9.2 |

Local government public relations

Campaigns: London Borough of Brent and Worcester Council

The London Borough of Brent has campaigned steadily on the issue of collecting local taxes since 1991, when it was castigated for having managed to collect only 61 per cent of the taxes due. Each year's campaign has had a different theme so that the campaign will not become stale and be ignored by the target audience. Themes have included shaming non-payers by printing their names in the newspapers; offering discounts for prompt payment; and accepting payment by credit card. By 1996 the collection rate had increased to 87 per cent.

Worcester Council made a modest investment of local authority funds – £860 – to show its support for Car Free Day, a national initiative. The council persuaded the local newspaper that it was in its interest to back the campaign and gave it extensive coverage. The event received £60,000 of media coverage and, more importantly, achieved an increase of 10 per cent in the numbers who walked or cycled on Car Free Day.

(*Sources*: *PR News* August 1996 and April 1997)

International public relations

The practice of international public relations falls into two separate types: public relations programmes conducted for domestic clients and aimed at audiences in other countries; and public relation activity for foreign organisations (typically, foreign governments) aimed at the domestic audience.

The rise of the multi-national conglomerate and the shrinking of world markets into the global village marketplace have created the need for international public relations. Organisations which operate in more than one country need to consider their public relations strategy in the international context, although it may be delivered nationally or locally. Even organisations which operate only in the domestic arena may need to take account of the international dimension. In the business world, regulations affecting manufacturing and the environment in one country may soon be taken up by another; a corporate identity symbol or colour used in one part of the world may have another, very different meaning elsewhere; and the internationalisation of the media means that news stories can be picked up in one place and reported in many others very rapidly.

International public relations, while remaining a specialised area of expertise, is becoming more relevant to all public relations practitioners, and it is worthwhile to look at some of the more specialised texts on the subject.

Organisation

There are a number of ways of achieving good public relations in an international context. First, a company can retain the services of an international consultancy which has branches all over the world, or at least, in the parts of the globe the company wants to reach. The consultancy may be British or American based, for example, but have branches abroad, with its staff moving around the world from office to office. Alternatively, the parent company may have taken over a number of national consultancies in the countries in question, retaining the staff in each, so that they retain a more intimate knowledge of the areas in which they operate. Second, it can use as consultants a firm which is part of an international network. In this case, the 'home' consultancy may take the brief and pass it on to other members of the network, who will be independent consultants, in the appropriate countries. There are other variations on the theme of international networks which are more tightly or loosely drawn, but these are the main options. For an in-house operation, the company needs to have its own in-house department in each country in which it wishes to operate, with some clear way of co-ordinating the work of them all.

Issues

The main issues to be considered in this very brief overview are those of language and culture; consistency of messages; and practical considerations such as shipping and timing.

Language and culture

A company must consider the way its messages will be received by audiences abroad – through the filter of a different culture and possibly a different language. It is preferable to have written and spoken material composed by a native speaker rather than to have it written in English and translated. By the same token, a local person will be much more in tune with the local culture and thus better at judging how messages will be received.

Consistency

Giving autonomy to the local office or consultancy means that there must be more attention paid to ensuring consistency: if messages are generated locally, they must still be consistent with the corporate message. How this is managed depends on the way in which the company chooses to have its international public relations delivered, but it must not be neglected.

Practical considerations

Each organisation will be able to compose its own list of practical considerations which need to be taken into account when operating in an international context. One which will figure on everyone's list is timing – the difference in time zones around the globe may be of vital importance.

The perfect timing of an announcement in one country may lead to all kinds of problems in another. Simply contacting the office in Singapore from headquarters in Manchester during normal working hours is a problem when there is a time difference of eight hours. A related problem is that of moving materials around the globe. Electronic communications are more or less instant, but getting exhibition panels and samples of goods from one country to another, not to mention the customs and other formalities, can take a long time and cost a lot of money.

The global carrier DHL used research it had commissioned on the problems at border crossings to put together a campaign which won the Shandwick International Award in 1998. The details are given in Case Study 9.3.

International public relations

Case Study 9.3

The DHL Customs Report: The Red Consultancy

Goods held back at border crossings are a real problem for Western companies dealing with Central and Eastern Europe. They are also an enormous problem for DHL Worldwide Express and its clients. The company wanted to create pressure for improvement without itself alienating the customs authorities in the countries concerned. The Red Consultancy did this by commissioning research into the effect of customs hold-ups on inward investment.

The report showed that 89 per cent of exporters based in the EU and exporting to Central and Eastern Europe had experienced major delays serious enough for half of them to have lost revenue as a result. DHL produced two versions of the report: one for external audiences and a separate report detailing the problems for policy makers. The 'public' report was launched via one-to-one media briefings with international news agencies and was also sent to the international business media, creating sufficient interest to generate 300 inquiries. The campaign addressed at opinion formers involved meetings with bodies such as the International Monetary Fund and the Organisation for Economic Cooperation and Development.

As a result, DHL is seen as the expert in the field, with company representatives regularly participating in international conferences on the subject, and the company contributing regular articles on customs issues to the World Bank's publication *Transition*. One country has already liberalised its customs legislation and others are considering following suit.

(*Source*: *PR Week* Awards 1998)

Investor relations

As we saw when looking at corporate advertising in Chapter 5, organisations need to keep in touch with the people who provide them with the resources to stay in business: their shareholders (individuals, pension funds, insurance companies), financial institutions who lend them money, and in the case of non-commercial organisations, donors, the government, the charity commissioners and so on.

Day-to-day financial public relations

The area of financial and investor relations is complex and specialised and there are a number of books covering the subject in detail. Although financial specialists often work in-house in the larger companies' public relations departments, there are many successful financial public relations specialist consultancies.

Whoever is charged with doing the job, the 'investor public' needs to be addressed. In some cases that public will consist of a handful of people: the influential fund managers and financial analysts who advise those with big money to invest. The media list for financial public relations in a company may consist of two or three names – reporters for the *Financial Times*, the *Daily Telegraph* and the *Investors Chronicle*, for example. In other companies, investors may include the entire workforce (as the staff, or partners, in the John Lewis Partnership, a UK retailer which operates with its staff as partners) or the general public as a whole (for nationwide charity appeals). Perhaps the only form of corporate communication common to them all is the annual report.

Annual report

All limited companies must produce an annual financial statement and report. Charities and voluntary bodies usually have to satisfy some similar regulation. In the public sector, local authorities have to publish annual performance indicators as well as financial reports. Schools, colleges and universities, hospital trusts, the utilities, all produce some kind of annual report, willingly or reluctantly.

Many annual reports are very similar in style, making it hard to distinguish the business of the organisation producing it. This style is characterised by beautiful graphic design, an overview from the Chairman which makes multiple use of the expression 'We are confident' and the company's mission statement shown prominently. If it is the report of a manufacturing company it will have moody photographs of a factory with the setting sun behind it, if it is a high-tech company it may have a picture of an astronaut with the world reflected in his or her visor. A recent fashionable development is to feature photographs and quotes from so-called ordinary members of staff.

By taking the strategic approach and planning carefully, an organisation can ensure that the annual report takes its place as a valuable communications tool. For example, it may be that more than one report needs to be published. The annual report for investors, containing relevant detailed financial information, may not be suitable for employees' use, so a staff report, giving a different emphasis to the review of the year, may be more appropriate.

As part of the RSA's Tomorrow's Company Inquiry, Alan Benjamin produced an annual report for the fictitious Prototype plc as a model of reporting business performance to stakeholders. This pays attention to the concerns of customers, employees, shareholders, suppliers, the financial community and local communities, as well as reporting on the company's education and environment programmes. Figure 9.2 shows some sample pages.

Many companies provide their annual report on their websites, where they can take advantage of sound and moving pictures. The added advantage to the reader is that there is no need to plough through the entire report: it is usually possible to download simply what is of interest. Lowe's Companies of North Carolina had this idea long before widespread use of the web. Their solution to overload was simply to send out a fill-in-the-blanks postcard to investors (see Figure 9.3), with the promise of the annual report in due course. For those who wanted everything, the company would send out a set of five books detailing everything about the company and why people invest.

Take-overs, acquisitions and mergers

Companies need to be in regular touch with their financial publics, but this is never more important than when take-overs are in the wind. The company is asking investors to put up more money or to resist the offer of more money from a competitor, and the future of the company itself is at stake. The value of the reputation which the company has built up and cemented through its day-to-day investor relations is paramount. Competing and even conflicting information is being presented to investors, who have to decide which company's message they trust. The target company has to try and portray itself as strong and independent to the City and its investment communities and possibly also to the Competition Commission (formerly the Monopolies and Mergers Commission).

There is a strict code on take-overs and mergers, with a clear timetable for contested bids, and rules about the timing and format of campaign material. Companies which do not normally retain specialised financial public relations advisers usually find it necessary to do so when threatened by predators.

Public relations for marketing support

As this book has shown, public relations is employed for a wide variety of purposes. The last one we will look at is public relations used in support of marketing. Marketing textbooks usually list public relations in the Index, and most will devote a chapter to the use of public relations as part of the marketing communications mix.

Uses of public relations

Marketing professionals are inclined to see public relations as simply a tool in the mass-promotion kit, but public relations can support marketing in a

| **Figure 9.2** | *Extracts from Prototype plc's annual report* |

MANAGEMENT'S VIEW – 1996

The stewardship of Prototype plc has been a challenging task during 1996. We have found international competition to be competent and well resourced.

CUSTOMERS

We have given a great deal of detailed attention to our customers this year and our relationships with them have grown and are richer in both form and content. Increased sales indicate success. Over 40% of our customers have been buying from us for five years or more, a pleasing result for our customer retention programmes. Our three year plan, begun in 1995, seeks to improve this ratio to 60%.

EMPLOYEES

Our long term plans have seen real progress, with significant education and training investment programmes inaugurated. Our employees remain less than satisfied with progress, but we are communicating well and believe that the investment will pay in productivity and quality over the next two years. Morale is pleasingly high. 30% of our employees are female and over 70% met their training programme objectives – a figure we are not yet satisfied with. Employee turnover rose to 8% – slightly above our plan for the year. We plan to bring our production and distribution costs per employee up to benchmarked best performance in our industry by the end of 1997. Over fifty employees now operate from their homes using information technology to perform their functions. We expect this to exceed 100 in the next two years.

PROVIDERS OF CAPITAL

Shareholders have expressed satisfaction with their increased dividends and the strength of our share price. Dividends rose 8% in 1996 and the stock market values our shares more than 30% higher than in 1995. Over 30% of our shareholders are long term (over five years) holders and are members of our Long Term Shareholder Association which enjoys corporate privileges. It is our intention to raise our long term borrowing ratio to 30% of paid in capital in the coming year, to cover new automation investments. We have therefore secured credit for £5 million to assist with the company's development and training investments and our bankers have accepted the business automation plans for the next three years. Productivity improvements, technology acquisition and our balanced approach to stakeholder expectations are reflected in favourable five year financial trends.

SUPPLIERS

In recent months our supplier research development and technology programmes have developed strongly. We have launched no fewer than six product development and enhancement programmes, where facts and knowledge are shared with nominated, long term suppliers. Two brand new products will be launched in 1997 as a result of these programmes which include interoperational database sharing and on-line access by Prototype to its suppliers' information bases, and vice versa.

LOCAL COMMUNITIES

During 1996 we inaugurated three new projects with the local communities which are adjacent to our main business operation centres. With a principal theme of helping disabled people, the company is seconding eighteen personnel to projects designed to provide information technology support to those in need. It is hoped that future recruitment will include candidates from among this group of people. We continue to communicate with local community leaders to understand better the impacts of our business presence.

EDUCATION

The company now participates in eleven joint research and development programmes with universities and schools. Our goal is to seek academic and innovative qualities in our research for new products and services, while supporting and encouraging industry/academic links. Although new and not yet sufficiently advanced to create growing enthusiasm, we are confident that these links will yield beneficial results to our partners as well as the company.

ENVIRONMENTAL INTERESTS

We have significantly reduced the waste products emerging from our production processes. We have worked with environmental health experts radically to improve working conditions for our employees. In particular we report better air quality and reduced noise levels in all our premises. We have a consistent seminar programme of employee communication relating to environmental risks and invite our suppliers to participate. We plan to increase our investment in pollution reduction by 20% per annum over the next three years.

ACCORDINGLY, WE REPORT INCREASES IN THE FOLLOWING KEY PERFORMANCE MEASURES

	Over 1 year (%)	Over 5 years (%)
FOR CUSTOMERS		
Turnover	22	14
Market share	1.3	4.9
Retained accounts	6	21
FOR PROVIDERS OF CAPITAL		
Dividends	8	15
Percentage of long term shareholders	3	8
FOR EMPLOYEES		
Value of knowledge bank	66	40
Training investment	16	20
Reduced noise levels	9	16
		(3 years)
FOR SUPPLIERS		
Co-operative budget	62	81
Volume of shared data	92	241

STAKEHOLDERS' VIEW – 1996

Independent research has been carried out by IR Ltd to seek the views of key stakeholders to gain **their** perceptions of our performance throughout 1996. We report verbatim a summary of these views from the independent research company. All stakeholders are welcome to a copy of the full report.

CUSTOMERS

Customers perceive significant improvements in product range and quality but consider key German and Italian competitors offer equally attractive products. Customers also indicate that support activities outside the UK are now comparable with those of continental competitors.

EMPLOYEES

Employees are generally pleased with new investment in training programmes especially those which enable them to train at their own pace through distance learning. They are not yet satisfied with the quality of instructional material in the learning programmes and have brought to Prototype's attention systems in use by competitors in Germany which are apparently more appropriate and have improved technical content.

PROVIDERS OF CAPITAL

Shareholders are generally satisfied with the company's ability to provide a competitive overall rate of return on their investments. Prototype's bankers have indicated that they do not believe it takes sufficient advantage of borrowing facilities which are available compared with some competitors' activities.

SUPPLIERS

Suppliers have expressed the view that Prototype has inaugurated its co-operative product research programmes later than its chief competitors in the UK and France but are considerably ahead in bringing together these efforts across all 6 countries in which it operates. They have also reacted well to improvements made in the automation of payment systems and arrangements for smaller companies.

LOCAL COMMUNITIES

Local communities adjacent to Prototype's business locations perceive its support for disabled people as valuable but insufficient. It has been suggested that activities should be combined with those of other local companies for more effective use of resources. It is reported that there have been instances of extraordinarily valuable support by named Prototype employees in several locations, but which are uncoordinated.

EDUCATION

Prototype is perceived as one of the few companies which has a well-developed strategy for working with academic institutions and aligning its new product development with the technological strengths in such institutions. Students of universities consider Prototype communicates its policies and programmes well, although they have criticised our pay levels.

ENVIRONMENTAL INTERESTS

Health and Safety officials have indicated that Prototype is addressing environmental issues in a constructive and focused manner. Employees suggest that the company could allocate more resources to problems of noise reduction but are pleased with the company's attempts to involve them in solutions to such problems.

Source: adapted from Prototype plc with permission from Alan Benjamin

---

| **Figure 9.3** | *Lowe's 'generic' annual report* |

Date *March 1, 1994*

Dear Investor:

- We want you to be the first to know *Lowe's* results for *1993*

- Sales were $ *1.43* (billion, ~~million~~).
  This was a (record, ~~near record~~, ~~not a record~~).

- Earnings were $ *50.6* (~~billion~~, million).
  This was a (record, ~~near record~~, ~~not a record~~).

- Per share earnings were $ *1.40*
  This was a (record, ~~near record~~, ~~not a record~~).

- Dividends paid were $ *.32* per share.

- Share price in the year (increased, ~~decreased~~) by
  12 %

- Prospects for the new year look to be (~~great~~, good,
  ~~about average, not so good, poor, just plain awful~~).

- Full Annual Report will be mailed about *April 25*

Chairman *Robert L. Strickland*

President *Leonard G. Herring*

Source: Baskin, Aronoff and Lattimore 1997

number of ways: building and maintaining awareness, re-positioning, and overcoming negative perceptions.

Building awareness

Common sense dictates that you cannot sell something that no one wants, but how can the prospective customer want something that he or she has never heard of? If this were really a problem, however, no new products would ever be sold nor new brands launched. One of the most important uses of public relations in marketing support is in building awareness of a product or brand prior to its launch.

An example of a toy manufacturer using this approach is given in Case Study 9.4.

Case Study 9.4

Public relations for marketing support
Furby comes to Britain: Tiger Toys UK

Every toy manufacturer's dream is to have its product at the top of children's Christmas lists. Furby, a soft toy which would 'talk' to its owner, was launched for the UK market at Toy '98, a toy fair which aims to promote the top 20 toys for Christmas. One element common to crazes in toy buying is scarcity, and Tiger Toys wanted to tread the fine line between flooding the market and not being able to satisfy demand. Only 40 media samples of Furby were made available: seven were sent to the specialist consumer press four weeks before Toy '98 and the other 33 were sent out to the mainstream media two weeks before the toys were available from retailers. Over 400 press kits were given out at the event itself, where six Furbys were on show to be played with.

Media interest in Furby was rapid and sustained. Over the eight weeks following the launch over 300 calls a week were received from radio, television and the printed media resulting in over 3,500 press cuttings, 280 radio interviews and 85 television pieces. Furby was being talked about (and to – Furby's vocabulary made for good items on radio and television) everywhere.

Not all media interest in Furby was positive. Emma Carle, who was responsible for Furby's launch, had to deal with a number of issues such as private sale prices of Furby; stories of interference by Furby's electronics with hospital equipment, aeroplanes and televisions; issues of availability; and working conditions in Tiger Toys' factories.

Ongoing public relations activity in support of marketing Furby continued into 1999 with retailer roadshows; consumer and trade photo stunts and stories; new Furby product launches; product placement in television soap operas; competitions; joint promotional activity with licensees; a Furby fan club; and Furby day. All of these activities are intended to continue to stimulate media interest and thus provide editorial coverage in support of the marketing effort.

(*Source*: Emma Carle, PR Manager, Tiger Toys UK)

Re-positioning

When a product has ceased to be fashionable or is being overtaken by more modern competitors the company may cease to manufacture it, may modify it or may re-position it.

In the case of Swiss Army Brands, their public relations consultancy in New York used the centenary of the launch of the famous Swiss Army knife both to re-position the knife, and to launch some new products – watches and sunglasses – under the same brand name. Their media relations programme resulted in excellent coverage in national outlets such as the *Wall Street Journal*, *USA Today* and ABC-TV's news programmes. Swiss Army Brands' market-share in knives (there is one competitor) grew by 5 per cent with no increase in advertising. Sales of the Swiss Army Brand watches exceeded all expectations and, according to *Watch and Clock Review*, it is the most successful new watch line in the industry.

Overcoming negative perceptions

We have already seen the vital role played by public relations in crisis management. The messages in Chapter 6 are relevant to product recalls, whether these are a result of faulty manufacturing, poor quality control or tampering. However, the public may have a poor perception of a product for other reasons – because it is unfamiliar, or they have a vague idea that it is 'bad' for them. Two examples are given in Case Study 9.5.

Case Study 9.5

Overcoming negative perceptions
Olive oil and eggs

Consumption of olive oil, while high in the producer countries of southern Europe, was tiny in the UK, and the public perceived it as high in fat and thus unhealthy. The European Commission Department of Agriculture asked the Grayling Company in London to help increase sales of olive oil to safeguard the livelihoods of the farmers producing it. The programme targeted health professionals and consumers, and included presentations to the main olive oil importers and distributors. The Olive Oil Information Bureau was set up and managed by the public relations consultancy. An audit of health professionals at the end of the first year showed an improved understanding of the positive role of olive oil in a healthy diet, while independent research praised the work of the Bureau in increasing exposure for, and sales of, olive oil.

A similar campaign to encourage Americans to eat eggs was run by the America Egg Board. Research found that people liked eggs and associated them with families and nurturing atmospheres, but felt that their high-cholesterol content ruled them out as a healthy food. The 'Eggs are Back!' campaign, aimed at food purchasers and consumers, gave the message (endorsed by medical opinion) that it is OK to eat eggs in moderation. Celebrity spokespeople (a sportsman and a supermodel) were recruited to spread the message along with experts on nutrition and other scientists. A media relations campaign including video news releases and specially formulated press kits seemed to reach their target: a Gallup survey showed that 125 million Americans (65 per cent of the population) had heard in the previous six months that it was OK to eat eggs again.

(*Sources*: adapted from the Grayling Company and Hendrix 1998: 307–15)

Summary points

✔ This chapter brings together a number of specialist areas of public relations: media relations, central and local government public relations, international public relations, financial public relations, and public relations for marketing support.

✔ While most public relations officers list media relations as an activity they undertake, it is a specialised function which requires training and experience. Press officers issue information about their organisation, deal with inquiries from the media, and sometimes edit and produce house journals and newsletters. They need a good understanding of what makes news.

✔ Central and local government public relations officers increasingly act as consultants within their organisations. Although they tend to be providers of information rather than promoters, they do undertake campaigning activities. Market testing and compulsory competitive tendering are creating opportunities for new ways of working.

✔ Organisations may need to consider the global implications of their activities, whether or not they operate in the international context. Some of the issues which need to be considered in the international public relations context are the organisation of the public relations function, language and cultural differences, consistency of message and the logistics of operating in more than one country.

✔ All organisations which raise money from outside their own resources need to pay attention to investor relations. Day-to-day financial public relations may involve very closely targeted publics. Publicly quoted companies are required to present certain financial information in a prescribed format and have to produce an annual report and accounts. Special rules apply to the provision of information to investors at a time of take-over.

✔ Public relations is used in support of marketing, specifically to build and maintain product or brand awareness, in re-positioning, and in overcoming negative perceptions. Because of its greater credibility with audiences than paid-for advertising, public relations is sometimes chosen to lead the marketing of a new product or brand.

Discussion questions

1 As press officer for a pharmaceuticals company, how would you interest the media in the forthcoming opening of your new research laboratory?

2 The reorganisation of local government means that there may be up to 200 new chief executives appointed in the next few months. How can local government public relations officers use this opportunity to raise the profile of their work?

3 Consider the global issues which affect businesses today. What steps do companies need to take to ensure that their messages can be understood in an international context?

4 How could an investor relations programme improve a company's share price?

5 In what ways might an in-house public relations manager contribute to the marketing plan for a new family saloon car manufactured in Britain by a Japanese company?

Recommended further reading

Seitel (1995), Cutlip et al. (1994), Hendrix (1998), and Grunig and Hunt (1984) each has one chapter, while Caywood (1997) has several, on the subject of media relations and its practice in the USA. Nelson (1992) provides a critical view of the influence of public relations on the news in Canada. McNair (1996) looks at news and journalism in general in the UK, while Franklin and Murphy (1998) specialise in the local media, Yorke (1995) in television and Williams and Conroy (1994) in radio. Haywood in Hart (1995) is a straightforward 'how to' chapter on media relations practice in the UK.

Local government public relations in the UK is discussed by Fedorcio et al. (1991) and Walker (1996). Local and central government public relations in the USA is covered by Cutlip et al. (1994) in Chapter 15.

Black (1995) and Nally (1991) provide many examples of the practice of international public relations, while Culbertson and Ni Chen (1996) is a collection of essays analysing public relations as it is practised in a variety of countries.

Hanrahan (1997) in Kitchen covers investor relations and public relations for financial services. Chaper 17 in Seitel (1995) is a lively chapter on the subject. Sauerhaft (1997) in Caywood provides a useful view of the role of public relations in mergers and acquisitions.

Caywood (1997) is an advocate of the use of public relations for marketing support. His book has numerous examples contributed by practitioners and academics illustrating the value of integrated communications. Further useful texts in this area are Harris (1998) and Smith (1994).

Moloney (1997) in Kitchen is a good chapter on lobbying in the UK while Pertschuk (1986) gives a view of practice in the USA from the perspective of a former head of the Federal Trade Commission. Mack (1997) is a useful contribution from a practitioner, while Pedler and Van Schendelen (1994) provide a number of case studies on lobbying in the European Union.

References

Baker, B. (1997) 'Public Relations in Government', in C. Caywood, (ed.), *The Handbook of Strategic Public Relations and Integrated Communications*, New York: McGraw-Hill.

Black, S. (1995) *International Public Relations Case Studies*, 2nd edn., London: Kogan Page.

Bowman, P. and Bing, R. (1993) *Financial Public Relations*, Oxford: Butterworth-Heinemann.

Boynton, J. (1986) *Job at the Top: the Chief Executive in Local Government*, Harlow: Longman.

Caywood, C. (ed.) (1997) *The Handbook of Strategic Public Relations and Integrated Communications*, New York: McGraw-Hill.

Culbertson, H. and Ni Chen (eds) (1996) *International Public Relations: A Comparative Analysis*, Hillsdale, NJ: Erlbaum.

Cutlip, S., Center, A. and Broom, G. (1994) *Effective Public Relations*, 7th edn., Englewood Cliffs, NJ: Prentice Hall.

Fedorcio, R., Heaton, P. and Madden, K. (1991) *Public Relations for Local Government*, Harlow: Longman.

Franklin, B. and Murphy, D. (eds) (1998) *Making the Local News: Local Journalism in Context*, London: Routledge.

Grunig. J. and Hunt, T. (1984) *Managing Public Relations*, Orlando, FL: Holt, Rinehart and Winston.

Hanrahan, G. (1997) 'Financial and Investor Public Relations', in Kitchen. P. (ed.) *Public Relations: Principles and Practice*, London: International Thomson Business Press.

Harris, P. and Lock, A. (1996) 'Machiavellian Marketing: The Development of Corporate Lobbying in the UK', *Journal of Marketing Management*, 12 (4).

Harris, T. (1998) *Value Added Public Relations: The Secret Weapon of Integrated Marketing*, Lincolnwood, IL: NTC Publishing.

Hart, N. (1995) *Strategic Public Relations*, Basingstoke: Macmillan.

Haywood, R. (1995) 'Media Relations', in Hart, op. cit.

Hendrix, J. (1998) *Public Relations Cases*, 4th edn, Belmont, CA: Wadsworth.

IPR (1994) *The Registration of Professional Lobbyists*, London: IPR.

Mack, C. (1997) *Business, Politics and the Practice of Government Relations*, London: Quorum.

McNair, B. (1996) *News and Journalism in the UK*, 2nd edn., London: Routledge.

Miller, C. (1996) 'The Role of Professional Political Consultants – the Provider Perspective', paper presented at '*Lobbying: The Way Forward*', AIC conference, London, 7 March.

Moloney, K. (1994) *Lobbyists for Hire*, Aldershot: Dartmouth.

Moloney, K. (1997) 'Government and Lobbying Activities', in Kitchen, P. (ed.), *Public Relations Principles and Practice*, London: International Thomson Business Press.

Nally, M. (1991) *International Public Relations in Practice*, London: Kogan Page.

Nelson, J. (1992) *Sultans of Sleaze: Public Relations and the Media*, Monroe, ME: Common Courage Press.

New York Times (1999) 'What Bananas? Tariff fight baffles Europe', 5 March.

Pedler, R. and Van Schendelen, M. (eds) (1994) *Lobbying the European Union*, Aldershot: Dartmouth.

Pertschuk, M. (1986) *Giant Killers*, New York: W. W. Norton.

PR News (1996, 1997) Newsletter of the Institute of Public Relations Local Government Group.

Raine, J (1996) 'Proactivity beats reactivity', *PR News*, June.

Sauerhaft, S. (1997) 'The Role of Public Relations in Mergers and Acquisitions', in Caywood, op. cit.

Seitel, F. (1995) *The Practice of Public Relations*, 6th edn, Englewood Cliffs, NJ: Prentice Hall.

Smith, P. (1994) *Marketing Communications: An Integrated Approach*, London: Kogan Page.

Time Magazine (1999) 'Banana Wars', 135 (5).

Walker, D. (1996) *Public Relations in Local Government*, London: Pitman.

Williams, P. and Conroy, A. (1994) *The Radio Handbook*, London: Routledge.

Yorke, I. (1995) *Television News*, 3rd edn., Oxford: Focal Press.

Where do we go from here?

10

Key Issues

The aim of this chapter is to provide some pointers to the future of public relations practice. The key points covered are:

▶ the relationship between theory and practice in public relations;

▶ the two most important principles;

▶ careers in public relations;

▶ likely future developments.

In this final chapter we will look at the relationship between the theory and practice of public relations and see what lessons can be learned, we will define the two most important principles, we will see how recent entrants into the field of public relations are faring, and we will have a look at what the future holds.

Theory into practice

In Chapter 3 we looked at a number of theoretical models and their relation to public relations practice. Practitioners sometimes tell academics that theory is all very well, but they are doers and there is not much room in their doing-schedule for theory. Similarly public relations students working on placement commonly say that, in the real world of work, practices are very different from the ideals of the lecture room. So what is the relationship between theory and practice?

Let us look at practice, from the front-line operative's level to that of the board-room strategist. At the operating level, as we have already noted, a public relations practitioner who, when pressed, volunteers that 'I do it this way because I've tried it before and it works', is using a model of practice whether or not the person would recognise the expression.

The public relations officer who is responsible for planning and managing a public relations programme will almost certainly have produced the plan of campaign according to a formula or model of planning. Such models may be universal in their application.

Strategic thinkers must have a good understanding of the theoretical foundation of their discipline, whatever business they are in. Public relations strategists, looking into the future over a longer term, need to exercise their analytical skills rather than their practical know-how. An understanding of the theoretical underpinning is a pre-requisite in formulating strategy. Furthermore the discipline of studying, analysing and understanding whether or not to apply theoretical models in practice is extremely helpful in honing the intellectual skills needed to progress. This is one of the distinguishing features of a graduate in any field: the ability to think analytically and critically.

Public relations in the real world

How public relations people behave in the real world is, in fact, very much governed by theories which have been developed and tested to see if they work. This is the job both of academics and researchers, and of practitioners who can afford to spend time developing models. Public relations models enable practitioners to use a template for their programmes, without having to reinvent the wheel every time. While the use of theoretical models may not always be recognised or acknowledged, it is widespread.

However, the important point to be made is that theory acts as a foundation or a spring-board for practice. If a practice is theoretically sound, the practitioner can with confidence give vent to creativity.

Lessons learned

This is a useful point at which to look back and summarise the lessons learned in this introduction to public relations.

The business of public relations

Public relations is a strategic management tool which an organisation can use to establish and improve its reputation among key groups. The practice of public relations includes managing corporate affairs; identifying trends and spotting issues which will be of public interest; planning, managing and running information and awareness campaigns; crisis management; managing relationships with stakeholders such as employees, suppliers, customers, investors and the local community; and providing support for marketing activity. Public relations makes use of many different tools and activities including media relations; lobbying; printed, visual and multi-media materials; road-shows and exhibitions; conferences and speakers; research reports; and sponsorship.

Well-planned and executed public relations programmes can build a relationship of trust between an organisation and its publics, which helps the organisation to survive and prosper.

Public relations as a profession

Although public relations activities have been going on for centuries, it is only in the last 50 years that public relations has come of age. Public relations' roots in 'the public be fooled' school of publicity-generation have resulted in the negative image of 'stunts' as synonymous with public relations 'exercises'. Although professional institutes were formed in the late 1940s, public relations is not yet widely viewed as a profession. It is only very recently that membership of the UK institute has become contingent on the applicant's possessing academic qualifications as well as practical experience, and public relations officers can practice without the need to belong to the IPR. As they are not subject to the IPR's code of practice, nor to its disciplinary mechanisms, there are no sanctions against such practitioners if they behave in a non-professional way.

Public relations planning

Effective public relations is the result of careful planning. The process begins with analysis of the current situation and a consideration of how the objectives of a public relations plan fit in with the organisation's overall business plans. The planning model could be summed up as: why do we want to say what to whom, how shall we do it and how measure its effectiveness? The process is informed by research – at the start, to find out what the target audience's perceptions are, for example; during the public relations campaign, to track its progress; and at the end, to evaluate its effect.

Corporate public relations

This encompasses all the communications activities an organisation undertakes as a corporate entity. An organisation's corporate image – the perception which those who come into contact with it have of the organisation – is made up of four inter-connected elements: its personality, its reputation, its values and its corporate identity.

The corporate public relations process starts when senior managers consider the communication strategy required to fulfil the organisation's strategic objectives. They may start with a communications audit and subsequently develop a public relations plan. A corporate public relations programme could embrace staff communications, investor relations, sponsorship and community relations, together with corporate advertising and a corporate identity programme.

Crisis public relations

A crisis is always the subject of intense media interest. Successful issues management can often prevent an issue of public concern turning into a crisis. How organisations react and deal with crises affects their reputation with the public and their future relationships with stakeholders and with journalists. It is vital to be prepared for the unexpected, by brainstorming possible crisis scenarios, planning the public relations response and rehearsal. When a crisis comes, honesty is the best policy: secretiveness makes the organisation look untrustworthy. Openness, accuracy and sensitivity should be the watchwords of a crisis public relations team.

Internal communication

Good internal communication is vital to every organisation but it also acts as an underpinning to the success of the organisation's communication overall. Staff also receive external communication because they may be members of the local community, investors in the company, customers of the firm's products or services, they may read about the organisation in the papers or see it featured on television, or they may be local politicians or members of pressure groups. Good, open, two-way communication enables staff to feel part of the organisation, helps to motivate employees and improve their performance, and gives the management the benefits of feedback and suggestions from the experts at the sharp end.

Staff need to understand the purpose of internal communication programmes, which should be appropriate to the culture and management style of the organisation concerned. Otherwise such programmes may be greeted with incomprehension, disbelief, cynicism or hostility. Well-planned and appropriate programmes, on the other hand, can help to break bad news without lowering motivation and can assist the effective management of change.

Community relations and sponsorship

Good relations with the community are a pre-requisite for successful organisations. Every organisation needs to define its own community publics, but also to consider its role and responsibilities to society at large. Increasingly, the importance of public opinion and the value of reputation mean that organisations are operating 'under licence' from their communities. A company which fulfils its social responsibilities is not necessarily acting from altruism. It can benefit the company and give it a competitive edge.

When considering support for community activities, organisations need to ensure that their policy is clearly and consistently applied, and that it is in line with corporate objectives. Sponsorship is sometimes part of a community relations programme, but it is also used in support of marketing.

Specialist public relations

Most public relations practitioners are involved in relations with the media, whether in issuing information about their organisation or in answering inquiries from reporters. They need to understand what makes news, and many press officers have formerly worked as journalists.

There are other, more specialised types of public relations. These include lobbying; local and central government public relations, where former information officers are beginning to act as in-house consultants;

international public relations, and the global impact of companies; investor relations – an organisation's communication programmes with its financial stakeholders; and public relations as marketing support in launching or re-positioning brands, and in changing perceptions about products.

Two fundamental principles: clarity and integrity

Clarity of purpose

Throughout this book there has been great emphasis on the importance of analysis, planning, careful implementation and evaluation. It is easy to become tied up in the detail of a public relations programme, or to be carried away with excitement for the job in hand, and to lose track of the purpose of the activity. Clarity of purpose, from the planning stage and throughout, is vital.

Clarity of expression

Public relations practitioners need to be able to present messages in stimulating and memorable ways, whether in the form of written, visual or multi-media materials. Brilliant writers, great designers, creative thinkers with a flair for the unusual and the memorable all have an honoured place in the public relations world. So long as the flashes of brilliance are for illumination rather than display, the message will shine through. But the clarity of the message must not be obscured by the way in which it is presented. Remember David Bernstein's cautionary tale about the children's building bricks.

So my first fundamental principle is about clarity.

Clarity of purpose and clarity of the message are paramount.

Integrity

The second principle takes us back to another recurrent theme in this book: integrity.

Whether you are undertaking a programme of staff relations, or considering a community liaison plan, or working out how best to deal with an imminent announcement of bad news, you must have the integrity of your client, in-house or not, at the heart of what you do.

Integrity is not simply about truthfulness or accuracy, although both of these are necessary. It has to do with soundness, with wholeness, with completeness. There is nothing dodgy, no outward gloss masking a grubby interior. Rather, an organisation with integrity is transparent. It can afford to be open because it has nothing to hide. It can be trusted.

The public relations practitioner with integrity has an easy job. It is much simpler to make decisions, to formulate proposals and to carry out your job if you are comfortable with your own set of personal values and you always stick with them. On a more mundane level, it is much easier to work with facts than with stories that are constantly changing.

The second principle is:

Integrity generates trust.

Because reputations are founded on trust, integrity is fundamental to a good reputation.

Careers and public relations

This section of the book concentrates on the skills and knowledge required to get a job in public relations, with the possibility of a rewarding career in the field. That means having the ability to progress from the introductory level and to climb up the ladder to whatever level suits you. However, sometimes people study public relations and decide that they do not want to work in the field, so we will also look at how a degree or other qualification in public relations can be useful in getting a job and furthering a career outside public relations itself.

Case Study 10.1

Public relations graduate

Claudia McShane: Copeland Borough Council/Whitehaven Youth Trust

Claudia graduated from Leeds Metropolitan University in 1994 and went to work as Corporate Support Officer at Copeland Borough Council in north west England, acting in an administrative role, but with responsibility for an internal newsletter and a quarterly magazine. The council tended to want to avoid the press at all costs, but within 18 months Claudia had turned her job into that of Communications Officer, running all the council's internal and external public relations, including a fully functioning press office. She wrote and implemented the council's first communications strategy and has a high-profile position within the council's dominant coalition, reporting directly to the General Manager.

She feels her degree was very helpful in getting her a job – especially as the council was planning to do a communications audit and her final year group project was to do a communications audit. She started work in 1994 on a salary of £11,000 and is about to start a new job with the Whitehaven Youth Trust, setting up a Community Action Network, on a salary of £20,000.

Her peers tend to agree with her about the value of a degree in public relations. She says:

> We all used to mumble a bit when on the course (waste of time doing this) but when we all met up for the Graduation Ceremony in November, some of us already doing jobs in public relations, we all discussed how excellent the course was, all the skills and

theories we had learned that we were now able to put into practice – and to do that well.

(*Source*: email from Claudia McShane to author, 17 May 1999)

Careers in public relations

What skills and knowledge are required by employers? At entry level it is fairly clear that employers are looking for someone who can write a press release or feature article on arrival, and who will not need extra training in this skill. A survey of practitioners in Britain found that the overwhelming requirement was for writing skills, especially writing for the media, followed by interpersonal skills (Harrison and Yeomans 1999). This bears out the findings from a US survey (Bahls 1992: 22) which showed that when public relations practitioners are hiring graduates they look first for writing skills, then for other communicating skills, such as oral ability, good judgement and an understanding of media functions. This explains why graduates in journalism are often offered jobs in public relations, sometimes ahead of public relations graduates. As one employer put it:

> while I will not hire someone without a degree, neither would I hire someone out of college who hasn't worked for a college newspaper or public relations department. If you managed a baseball team, would you hire someone who had studied sports but who had never played?
>
> (ibid.)

Clearly, anyone who is looking for an entry-level job in public relations must be able to demonstrate skills and (preferably) at least some experience in writing. Public relations degree courses such as those at Leeds Metropolitan University (LMU) and Bournemouth University give students the oportunity to get that experience by spending a year on placement as an intern with a public relations consultancy or in-house team in the UK or, in the case of LMU's BA Public Relations with Languages, in another European country. LMU graduates also leave with a portfolio which they have put together during their three or four years at university and which helps prospective employers to see what kind of work they are capable of producing.

Public relations graduate

Adrian Leighton: Hertz Europe

Adrian was among the first wave of graduates from the University of Bournemouth in 1993 and secured his first job in early 1994 as an account executive at Paragon Golin/Harris. He moved on to the position of account manager at Edelman and now works as PR manager for Hertz Europe.

Case Study 10.2

He says:

> Although I would say you don't have to have a degree in PR to be
> good at the job, it is a good way into the industry as you are
> taught background skills such as writing a press release, which
> gives you an advantage when you start out.

He adds that the most useful part of the course has only recently come
to light: 'What I have found increasingly useful is the part of the course
which dealt with attitudes, persuasion and influence. These skills
become more relevant the higher you reach in the profession'.

(Source: PR Week 1999c)

Although there is an increasing number of public relations graduates
available for hire, there are plenty of opportunities for entry level posts.
Recruitment is buoyant among the 2,300 UK consultancies and 85 per cent
of *The Times* Top 1,000 companies have their own internal public relations
departments. In addition many public and voluntary sector organisations
such as government, the police, health services, charities, the armed forces
and pressure groups employ their own public relations staff (LMU 1998:
12–13).

In the USA the jobs market is also good, following a booming economy.
There is a particular shortage of public relations professionals who can
specialise in IT, ethical healthcare and the financial sector (*PR Week* 1999c:
23–4).

Case Study 10.3

Public relations graduate

Mark Button: Corporate Communications Manager, ClaraNET

Mark worked in retail management before taking a degree in public
relations, a subject he thought would bring together his skills and
interests in research, design, creative writing, presentation and
negotiation. He could also see that public relations 'had really begun
to establish itself within the boardroom and was starting to assume the
same importance that it enjoys in the States. It was also a massive
growth industry. Most of all, it was FUN'. He graduated in 1996 and
went straight to work with the Institute of Public Relations in London
as its PR Executive in charge of events management. He found this 'a
brilliant learning curve', with the opportunity to meet and learn from
the most influential figures in the industry, and a free hand to organise
the evening seminar programme. He went on from the IPR to work for
a consultancy, Vousden Levick Publicity, on account management,
writing proposals and pitching for business, and is now corporate
communications manager for ClaraNET, the largest Internet service
provider in the UK. He set up its public relations function and finds it 'a
brilliant job – interesting, fast moving and a very relaxed but
productive atmosphere. A great sector to be in at the moment'.

> Mark believes his degree showed that he was serious about being in public relations.
>
> > Going into this industry was one of the best moves I ever made. It takes a lot of hard work and is very rarely glamorous, but when you see a piece you've generated in the national press or your MD or client on TV it's a brilliant feeling. It's also quite a close community and there's always a million ways to progress your career relatively quickly if you apply yourself.
>
> > (*Source*: email from Mark Button to author, 17 May 1999)

Higher up the ladder a practitioner will be expected to have all the entry-level skills together with the ability to lead and manage other people, the ability to manage a budget, and the capability to commission, conduct and apply the results of research. Writing proposals and winning business through successful pitching may also be requirements. The further one progresses in a public relations career the more important are leadership qualities, the ability to problem-solve and think strategically, and to manage people effectively.

Careers outside public relations

The majority of public relations graduates get jobs in public relations. Bournemouth University (see Figure 10.1) found that 74 per cent of its graduates went to work in public relations, with most of the rest going into marketing. Similar statistics come from Leeds, where 80 per cent of its 1996 graduates went straight into full-time public relations posts, with many of the others going into marketing or retailing. Evidently the enthusiasm for public relations which the students showed on entry into the courses is not dimmed by their experience as undergraduates, and they generally choose to make public relations their first destination.

However, although an expanding profession can provide the entry level posts to soak up the talent leaving the universities, it may be a different story higher up the ladder. The IPR's 1999 membership survey (IPR 1999b) showed that about half of its members are now graduates (though most of these have degrees in subjects other than public relations). There may not be room for the relatively new graduates of public relations courses to progress to the top jobs in their field.

Fortunately for them public relations graduates have added value. As with all graduates they have the generic achievement of a number of transferable skills: managing tasks and solving problems, working with others, communication, and self-awareness being perhaps the most important. They share with graduates of other social sciences disciplines the attributes of social science graduates: the knowledge and skill to apply relevant theory and practice from business, media and mass

| **Figure 10.1** | *Results of a survey of graduates of Bournemouth University, conducted by Paul Noble* |

PUBLIC RELATIONS GRADUATES OF BOURNEMOUTH UNIVERSITY
SOME FACTS AND FIGURES

Just over 300 people graduated from Bournemouth University's degree in public relations in the six years from 1993 to 1998.

Where do they work?

The majority (74 per cent) work in public relations, with an even split between in-house and consultancy. Of these the majority are employed in consumer and business PR with about ten per cent employed in financial or celebrity PR. Marketing is the second major destination.

Would they recommend their degree to others?

Almost all (98 per cent) felt that the degree programme had helped them and 84 per cent would recommend it to others.

What were the most useful elements of the degree?

The 40-week placement for work experience was far and away (99 per cent) the most useful element of the degree with other useful elements including writing skills (96 per cent), presentation and research skills.

How much do they earn?

Of those who graduated in 1993, the majority of whom are in their late twenties, 70 per cent are earning more than £25,000, while one in twelve earns £35,000. This compares favourably with salaries for people of that age in the profession overall: account executive aged 25 – average salary £16,959; account manager aged 29 – average salary £24,396; PR officer aged 32 – average salary £20,645.

Source: PR Week 26 March 1999: 15–24

communication, politics, sociology and psychology; together with competence in data handling, mathematics, statistics and information technology. But in addition they have the 'field-specific' skills and knowledge which study for a public relations degree has brought them: the possession of a body of theoretical and historical knowledge of public relations and communication management, ethical understanding, and those specific practical skills (for example, in writing and in linguistic fields) which enable the graduate to communicate in an English-speaking and European context.

Some of the job histories of public relations graduates over the past ten years are given in Case studies 10.1, 10.2 and 10.3.

The future of public relations

What are the key issues for the future? Will public relations develop into a respected profession? How are current initiatives going to translate into the public relations business of tomorrow? Let us have a look at some of the factors which will affect public relations in the future.

Professionalisation

The prevailing view is that the public relations business is striving towards professional status, although some practitioners believe it is there already and a few think that public relations is a trade and always will be. Recent research undertaken at Leeds Metropolitan University sought the views of public relations practitioners.

> The continued efforts of the IPR to enforce professional standards both for new entrants and practitioners are bearing fruit within the industry.
>
> (In-house public relations manager)

> In recent years I believe the PR profession has gained a lot more respect. I see the profession developing very much hand in hand with marketing activities in general.
>
> (Public relations consultant)

> Perhaps in 10–15 years, as the current no-hopers retire or die, and the current crop of PR graduates reaches senior positions, then PR will become more respected.
>
> (Public relations consultant)

This view that public relations needs to be taken more seriously is echoed by others.

> Over the next five years the challenge will be to continue striving to raise standards of professional practice and selection procedures, while at the same time increasing awareness of the role and value of effective public relations within the business community and the public at large.
>
> (Freelance consultant)

> Public relations is winning its wings as a profession on the back of being able to demonstrate tangible benefits to the client. The more the profession evaluates the more it will be taken seriously as an integral and important part of the marketing mix.
>
> (MD, public relations consultancy)

The link with marketing communications is not always seen as helpful, though. As one respondent put it:

> 'Public relations as a profession is struggling to establish itself. It suffers from being too closely linked with marketing and organisations find it difficult to understand the difference between the two' (In-house press officer).

According to Quentin Bell, former chairman of the PRCA, it is a mistake to claim that the future lies with the merging of the marketing disciplines: marketing communications *must* be integrated, 'regardless of who owns the individual specialists'. His view is that the future will see the emergence of a divide between 'thinkers' and 'doers', with the thinkers taking the broad, strategic view of an organisation's communications needs. He believes that such thinkers are likely to come from the public relations profession because public relations practitioners alone 'take the widest of strategic overviews that don't just highlight customers as the prime audience' (Bell 1991: 195).

Public relations as a top management function

Public relations is increasing in importance for organisations. Their ability to explain their actions and policies to an ever more sophisticated and better educated public relies totally on good communication. A glance at the recruitment pages in the trade press confirms that appointments are increasing at the highest level in companies and in not-for-profit organisations.

This trend towards employing director-level public relations specialists is not the only manifestation of public relations' role in top management. In the public sector, where so many upheavals continue, the importance of the role of public relations in the management of change is being recognised. In the uncertain future facing local government, the NHS, the education sector and community services, communication strategies must be thought through and agreed by senior management. Their implementation by public relations specialists goes without saying.

The public relations practitioner has sometimes in the past been described as the keeper of the company's conscience, with a professional finger on the pulse of public opinion and a hot line to the policy makers in the board room. This is what the Royal Society of Arts, in its interim report on tomorrow's company, had to say of the future.

> Each company makes its own unique choice of purpose and values, and has its own model of critical business processes from which it derives its range of success measures. But tomorrow's company will understand and measure the value which it derives from all its key relationships, and thereby be able to make informed decisions when it has to balance and trade off the conflicting claims of customers, suppliers, employees, investors and the communities in which it operates.
>
> (RSA 1994: 1)

The role of public relations here is to identify publics – stakeholders, or key relationships – and to devise and deliver communication strategies for minimising conflicts.

Continuing Professional Development (CPD)

The IPR is currently considering how it should implement a CPD scheme for its members. While this is part of the continuing drive towards professionalism, it should also meet some very real needs.

For example, public relations practitioners need to develop their analytical skills, the better to take on for their clients issues of global significance, such as concern for the environment and unsustainable population growth. The presentation of public information is vital, as is the role of persuasion. The opportunity to take time out from doing, in order to think, as Quentin Bell might put it, is likely to lead to improved performance.

At a more practical level, CPD could include updating of skills; authorship of books, papers, articles and teaching materials; participation in seminars and workshops; and undertaking project work as part of formal academic studies.

Education, training and research

The Public Relations Education Trust (PRET) devised a training matrix for the IPR and PRCA. The matrix divides the public relations professional's career into five stages:

Stage 1: pre-entry

Stage 2: professional starter

Stages 3 and 4: developing and operating professional

Stage 5: experienced professional specialist and manager

The IPR's Diploma and university degrees cover all levels of the matrix, although it is expected that the skills and knowledge at levels 3 and above will be developed in the course of experience and over a period of time. The launch of the IPR's Diploma in 1998 provided a part-time alternative to study for those working in public relations. The syllabus covers strategic public relations and public relations planning, and requires candidates to undertake a project during three months of self-directed learning.

Looking at the subjects covered in undergraduate and postgraduate degrees, their syllabi are significantly wider than the material covered by the PRET matrix. Stirling University's MSc, for example, includes a module on business organisation and environment, while the MA at Manchester Metropolitan University links corporate and financial public relations to social responsibility. Undergraduates at Bournemouth study political and economic analysis, while their colleagues at Leeds Metropolitan University grapple with logic, epistemology and ethics on a module which brings together philosophy, politics and psychology.

Both undergraduate and postgraduate students at all those institutions mentioned are required to complete a dissertation reporting on an individual research project. As a result, a body of research and knowledge is gradually being built up. Dissertations have been practical (A Guide to Sponsorship); descriptive (The Role of PR in Re-cycling: a comparison between initiatives in Lille and Leeds); political (Conservative Party Political Broadcasts); company specific (BNFL and Local Community Relations); industry specific (Lobbying in the Scottish Fish Industry) and comparative (Internal Communications and the Management of Change at the National and Provincial Building Society and Rover Cars).

The future will see more research at a higher level and a greater volume of published material. The UK now supports two journals dedicated to publishing public relations research, and academic journals in other fields such as business and marketing are starting to publish papers reporting on public relations research.

The future of the public relations business, be it trade or profession, is in the hands of new practitioners, that is, of you, the reader. The most exciting and fulfilling aspect of many public relations academics' professional lives is the opportunity to interact with bright people who want to work in public relations, and some of our graduates are already doing us very proud indeed.

The public relations business needs to receive a continuing influx of people who bring with them honesty, clarity, accuracy, integrity, hard work and imaginative flair.

Summary points

✔ Theories are put into practice in the real world of public relations even though they are not always recognised as such. Strategic thinkers in the public relations world need a good grasp of the theoretical framework of their discipline, just as strategists do in any other field.

✔ This book has covered the business of public relations, public relations as a profession, public relations planning, corporate public relations, crisis public relations, internal communications, community relations and sponsorship and a number of specialist areas of public relations practice.

✔ There are two fundamental principles in public relations practice: clarity (both of purpose and expression) and integrity.

✔ The study of public relations qualifies the graduate to work not only in the field of public relations but also in other areas of business and management.

✔ In the future public relations is expected to become more professionalised. Public relations is being seen as a function of top management. Developments in education and training, continuing professional development, and academic research all point to a thriving future for the public relations business.

 ## Recommended further reading

There are plenty of opportunities for crystal-ball gazing – most texts on public relations conclude with a chapter or two on the future of the practice. These include Caywood (1997), Grunig and Hunt (1984), Seitel (1995) and Chapter 3 in Newsom et al. (1993).

Ehling (1992) in Grunig provides a thoughtful chapter on public relations education and professionalism in the USA. Chapter 4 of Grunig and Hunt (1984) also covers professionalism, while McElreath (1997) gives advice on career progression. He also provides as appendices the Code of Professional Standards for the Practice of Public Relations in the USA, the Code of the International Association of Business Communicators, and the Code of the International Public Relations Association.

Cardwell (1997) in Caywood looks at career opportunities in public relations. Chapter 2 in Cutlip et al. (1994) provides examples of the typical working day of a number of different types of practitioner, as well as discussing public relations education and professionalism. Hon et al. (1992) consider women in public relations.

References

Bahls, J. (1992) 'What credentials do you seek when you hire?', *Public Relations Journal* September, cited in Baskin, O., Aronoff, C. and Lattimore, D. (1997) *Public Relations the Profession and the Practice*, 4th edn., Chicago, IL: Brown and Benchmark.

Bell, Q. (1991) *The PR Business*, London: Kogan Page.

Caywood, C. (ed.) (1997) *The Handbook of Strategic Public Relations and Integrated Communications*, New York: McGraw-Hill.

Cutlip, S., Center, A. and Broom, G. (1994) *Effective Public Relations*, 7th edn., Englewood Cliffs, NJ: Prentice Hall.

Ehling, W. (1992) 'Public Relations Education and Professionalism', in Grunig, J. (ed.), *Excellence in Public Relations and Communication Management*, Hillsdale, NJ: Lawrence Erlbaum Associates.

Grunig. J. and Hunt, T. (1984) *Managing Public Relations*, Orlando, FL: Holt, Rinehart and Winston.

Harrison, S. and Yeomans, L. (1999) 'Public Relations Education in the UK: A Review of Its Relevance to Public Relations Practice', presented to PRSA Educators Academy Research Conference (18–20 June), University of Maryland.

Hon, L., Grunig, L. and Dozier, D. (1992) 'Women in Public Relations: Problems and Opportunities', in Grunig, J. (ed.), *Excellence in Public Relations and Communication Management*, Hillsdale, NJ: Lawrence Erlbaum.

IPR (1999b) *1998 Membership Survey*, London: Institute of Public Relations.

LMU (1998) *BA (Hons) Public Relations Course Handbook 1998–99*, Leeds: Leeds Metropolitan University.

McElreath, M. (1997) *Managing Systematic and Ethical Public Relations Campaigns*, Chicago, IL: Brown and Benchmark.

Newsom, D., Scott, A. and Turk, J. (1993) *This is PR: The Realities of Public Relations*, 5th edn, New York: Wadsworth.

PR Week (1999c) 'Beware the lure of the US dollar', 26 March.

RSA (1994) *Tomorrow's Company: Interim Report*, London: RSA.

Seitel, F. (1995) *The Practice of Public Relations*, 6th edn, Englewood Cliffs, NJ: Prentice Hall.

Bibliography

Allinson, R. (1993) *Global Disasters: Inquiries into Management Ethics*, New York: Simon and Schuster.

Bahls, J. (1992) 'What credentials do you seek when you hire?', *Public Relations Journal* September, cited in Baskin et al. (1997).

Baker, B. (1997) 'Public Relations in Government', in C. Caywood (ed.), *The Handbook of Strategic Public Relations and Integrated Communications*, New York: McGraw-Hill.

Barton, L. (1993) *Crisis in Organizations: Managing and Communicating in the Heat of Chaos*, Cincinatti, OH: South Western Publishing.

Baskin, O., Aronoff, C. and Lattimore, D. (1997) *Public Relations the Profession and the Practice*, 4th edn., Chicago, IL: Brown and Benchmark.

Beder, S. (1998) 'Manipulating Public Knowledge', *Metascience* 7 (1): 132–9.

Bell, Q. (1991) *The PR Business*, London: Kogan Page.

Bernays, E. (1928) *Propaganda*, New York: Liveright.

Bernays, E. (1952) *Public Relations*, Norman: University of Oklahoma Press.

Bernays papers, Letter from Dr. George F. Buchan, Box 85, Library of Congress, cited in Tye (1998).

Berge, D. T. (1988) *The First 24 Hours: A Comprehensive Guide to Successful Crisis Communications*, Oxford: Blackwell.

Bernstein, D. (1986) *Company Image and Reality*, London: Cassell.

Black, S. (1989) *Introduction to Public Relations*, London: Modino.

Black, S. (1993) *The Essentials of Public Relations*, London: Kogan Page.

Black, S. (1995) *International Public Relations Case Studies*, 2nd edn, London: Kogan Page.

Bland, M. and Jackson, P. (1992) *Effective Employee Communications*, London: Kogan Page.

Boorstin, D. (1962) *The Image, or What Happened to the American Dream*, New York: Atheneum.

Booth, A. (1988) *The Communications Audit: a Guide for Managers*, Aldershot: Gower.

Boston College (1995) *1995 Profile of the Community Relations Profession*, Chestnut Hill, MA: Center for Corporate Community Relations at Boston College.

Botan, C. and Hazelton, V. (1994) *Public Relations Theory*, Hillsdale, NJ: Lawrence Erlbaum Associates.

Bowman, P. and Bing, R. (1993) *Financial Public Relations*, Oxford: Butterworth-Heinemann.

Boynton, J. (1986) *Job at the Top: the Chief Executive in Local Government*, Harlow: Longman.

Bradford Council (1986) *Out of the Valley: Bradford MDC's response to the Bradford City Fire Disaster 1985–86*, Bradford: Policy Unit.

Bunta, R. (1992) 'Employee Volunteerism: A Complement to Corporate Philanthropy', *Journal of Corporate Public Relations* 3.

Burson, H. (1974) 'The Public Relations Function in the Socially Responsible Corporation', in M. Anshen (ed.), *Managing the Socially Responsible Corporation*, New York: Macmillan.

Caywood, C. (ed.) (1997) *The Handbook of Strategic Public Relations and Integrated Communications*, New York: McGraw-Hill.

204

Center, A. and Jackson, P. (1995) *Public Relations Practices: Managerial Case Studies and Problems*, Englewood Cliffs, NJ: Prentice Hall.

Clampitt, P. (1991) *Communicating for Managerial Effectiveness*, Newbury Park, CA: Sage.

Clutterbuck, D., Dearlove, D. and Snow, D. (1992) *Actions Speak Louder: A Management Guide to Corporate Social Responsibility*, London: Kogan Page/Kingfisher.

Corley, P. (1994) Letter to the Editor, *Guardian* 20 April.

Culbertson, H. and Ni Chen (eds) (1996) *International Public Relations: A Comparative Analysis*, Hillsdale, NJ: Lawrence Erlbaum Associates.

Culf, A. (1993) 'Press toughens rules to avert statutory curbs', *Guardian* 5 May.

Cutlip, S. (1994) *The Unseen Power: Public Relations, a History*, Hillside, NJ: Lawrence Erlbaum Associates.

Cutlip, S. (1995) *Public Relations History from the Seventeenth to the Twentieth Century*, Hillsdale, NJ: Lawrence Erlbaum Associates.

Cutlip, S. and Center, A. (1978) *Effective Public Relations*, 5th edn, Englewood Cliffs, NJ: Prentice Hall.

Cutlip, S., Center, A. and Broom, G. (1994) *Effective Public Relations*, 7th edn., Englewood Cliffs, NJ: Prentice Hall.

D'Aprix, R. (1996) *Communicating for Change: Connecting the Workplace to the Marketplace*, San Francisco, CA: Jossey Bass.

Deppa, J. (1993) *The Media and Disasters: Pan Am 103*, London: David Fulton.

Diamond, J. (1993) 'Have pen, will travel . . . and get paid for it', *Guardian* 7 June.

Dozier, D. (1981) 'The Diffusion of Evaluation Methods Among Public Relations Practitioners', East Lansing MI: Public Relations Division of the Association for Education in Journalism Annual Conference.

Ehling, W. (1992) 'Public Relations Education and Professionalism', in Grunig, J. (ed.), *Excellence in Public Relations and Communication Management*, Hillsdale, NJ: Lawrence Erlbaum Associates.

Ewen, S. (1996) *PR! A Social History of Spin*, New York: Basic Books.

Ewing, R. (1997) 'Issues Management: Managing Trends through the Issues Life Cycle', in Caywood, C., op. cit.

Fahri, P. (1992) 'Time Out from Our Commercial for a Word from Our Sponsor', *Washington Post* national weekly edition March 2–8.

Fedorcio, R., Heaton, P. and Madden, K. (1991) *Public Relations for Local Government*, Harlow: Longman.

Ferguson, C. (1999) 'Television News', in Harrison, S. (ed.), *Disasters and the Media: Managing Crisis Communications*, Basingstoke: Macmillan.

Fischer, R. (1997) 'A Theoretical Basis for Public Relations', in Baskin et al., op. cit.

Fombrun, C. (1995) *Reputation: Realising Value from the Corporate Image*, Boston, MA: Harvard Business School.

Franklin, B. and Murphy, D. (eds) (1998) *Making the Local News: Local Journalism in Context*, London: Routledge.

Garbett, T. (1981) *Corporate Advertising: the What, the Why and the How*, New York: McGraw-Hill.

Gibson, J., Ivancevich, J. and Donnelly, J. (1985) *Organizations*, Plano, TX: Business Publications.

Goldman, E. (1948) *Two-way Street: the Emergence of the Public Relations Counsel*, Boston, MA: Bellman.

Granatt, M. (1999) 'A Central Government Perspective', in Harrison, S. (ed.), op. cit.

Granatt, M. and Dowle, D. (1993) 'Managing the Media Needs at Major Incidents', *Metropolitan Police Journal* (issue unknown) 23–7.

Gronstedt, A. (1997) 'The Role of Research in Public Relations Strategy and Planning', in Caywood, C., op. cit.

Grunig, J. (1992) 'Symmetrical Systems of Internal Communication', in Grunig, J. (ed.), *Excellence in Public Relations and Communication Management*, Hillsdale, NJ: Lawrence Erlbaum Associates.

Grunig, J. and Hunt, T. (1984) *Managing Public Relations*, Orlando, FL: Holt, Rinehart and Winston.

Grunig, L. (1997) 'Excellence in Public Relations', in Caywood, C., op. cit.

Hamilton, S. (1987) *A Communication Audit Handbook: Helping Organisations to Communicate*, Harlow: Longman.

Harlow, R. (1976) 'Building a Public Relations Definition', *Public Relations Review 2* (Winter): 36.

Harris, P. and Lock, A. (1996) 'Machiavellian Marketing: The Development of Corporate Lobbying in the UK', *Journal of Marketing Management* 12 (4).

Harris, T. (1998) *Value Added Public Relations: The Secret Weapon of Integrated Marketing*, Lincolnwood, IL: NTC Publishing.

Harrison, S (1994) 'Codes of practice and ethics in the UK communications industry', *Business Ethics: a European Review* 3 (2).

Harrison, S. (1997) 'Corporate Social Responsibility: Linking Behaviour with Reputation', in Kitchen, P. (ed.), op. cit.

Harrison, S. (ed.) (1999) *Disasters and the Media: Managing Crisis Communications*, Basingstoke: Macmillan.

Harrison, S. and Yeomans, L. (1999) 'Public Relations Education in the UK: A Review of Its Relevance to Public Relations Practice', presented to PRSA Educators Academy Research Conference (18–20 June): University of Maryland.

Hart, N. (1995) *Strategic Public Relations*, Basingstoke: Macmillan.

Haywood, R. (1991) *All About Public Relations: How to Build Business Success on Good Communications*, 2nd edn, Maidenhead: McGraw-Hill.

Haywood, R. (1994) *Managing Your Reputation: How to Plan and Run Communications Programmes that Win Friends and Build Business*, London: McGraw-Hill.

Haywood, R. (1995) 'Media Relations', in Hart, op. cit.

Hendrix, J. (1998) *Public Relations Cases*, 4th edn, Belmont, CA: Wadsworth.

Hess, A. (1948) 'Our Aims and Objects', *Public Relations* 1 (1).

Hewlett Packard (1993) *Standards of Business Conduct*, Palo Alto, CA: Hewlett Packard Company.

Hiebert, R. (1966) *Courtier to the Crowd: The Story of Ivy L. Lee and the Development of Public Relations*, Ames: Iowa State University Press.

Hill, J. (1963) *The Making of a Public Relations Man*, New York: David McKay.

Hon, L., Grunig, L. and Dozier, D. (1992) 'Women in Public Relations: Problems and Opportunities', in Grunig, J. (ed.), op. cit.

IPR (1991) *Public Relations As a Career*, London: Institute of Public Relations.

IPR (1992) 'News Item', *Public Relations: Journal of the IPR*, London, May.

IPR (1993a) 'More research findings', *Public Relations: Journal of the IPR* 11 (3).

IPR (1993b) *Sword of Excellence Awards 1993*, London: Institute of Public Relations.

IPR (1994) *The Registration of Professional Lobbyists*, London: Institute of Public Relations.

IPR (1999a) *Handbook*, London: Institute of Public Relations.

IPR (1999b) *1998 Membership Survey*, London: Institute of Public Relations.

Irvine, R. (1987) *When You Are the Headline: Managing a Major News Story*, Homewood, IL: Dow Jones Irwin.

Jefkins, F. (1988) *Public Relations Techniques*, Oxford: Butterworth-Heinemann.

Jefkins, F. (1992) *Public Relations*, 4th edn, London: Pitman.

Kitchen, P. (ed.) (1997) *Public Relations Principles and Practice*, London: International Thomson Business Press.

Koten, J. (1997) 'The Strategic Uses of Corporate Philanthropy', in Caywood, C., op. cit.

Kotler, P. (1984) *Marketing Management*, Englewood Cliffs, NJ: Prentice Hall.

Lasswell, H. (1948) *Power and Personality*, New York: Norton.

L'Etang, J. (1998a) 'The development of British Public Relations in the Twentieth Century', Glasgow: IAMCR Conference.

L'Etang, J. (1998b) 'State Propaganda and Bureaucratic Intelligence: the Creation of Public Relations in Twentieth Century Britain', *Public Relations Review* 24 (4).

Lionberger, H. (1960) *Adoption of New Ideas and Practices*, Ames: Iowa State University Press.

LMU (1994) 'Communications Audit' (final year PR degree project), Leeds Metropolitan University, Leeds.

LMU (1998) *BA (Hons) Public Relations Course Handbook 1998–99*, Leeds: Leeds Metropolitan University.

Mack, C. (1997) *Business, Politics and the Practice of Government Relations*, London: Quorum.

Marley, P. (1999) 'A Tale of Two Cities: Liverpool', in Harrison, S. (ed.), op. cit.

Marston, J. (1979) *Modern Public Relations*, New York: McGraw-Hill.

McDonald, J. (1990) 'Accidents do happen: an emergency response plan for Unocal', in Moss, D. (ed.), *Public Relations in Practice – A Casebook*, London: Routledge.

McElreath, M. (1997) *Managing Systematic and Ethical Public Relations Campaigns*, Chicago IL: Brown and Benchmark.

McNair, B. (1996) *News and Journalism in the UK*, 2nd edn, London: Routledge.

McQuail, D. (1994) *Mass Communication Theory*, London: Sage.

Miller, C. (1996) 'The Role of Professional Political Consultants – the Provider Perspective', paper presented at 'Lobbying: the way forward' AIC conference, London, 7 March.

Mitroff, I and Pauchant, T. (1990) *We're So Big and Powerful Nothing Bad Can Happen to Us*, New York: Carol.

Moloney, K. (1994) *Lobbyists for Hire*, Aldershot: Dartmouth.

Moloney, K. (1997) 'Government and Lobbying Activities', in Kitchen, P. (ed.), op. cit.

Moloney, K. (1998) '"It's a PR job": A question of reputation and its consequences for teaching, researching and doing PR', *Working Papers in Public Relations Research No. 2*, Bournemouth: School of Media Arts and Communication, Bournemouth University.

Murphy, R. (1989) 'Game Theory as a Paradigm for the Public Relations Process', in Botan and Hazelton, op. cit.

Nally, M. (1991) *International Public Relations in Practice*, London: Kogan Page.

Nelson, J. (1992) *Sultans of Sleaze: Public Relations and the Media*, Monroe, ME: Common Courage Press.

Newsom, D., Scott, A. and Turk, J. (1993) *This is PR: the Realities of Public Relations*, 5th edn., New York: Wadsworth.

New York Times (1999) 'What Bananas? Tariff fight baffles Europe', 5 March.

Olasky, M. (1987) *Corporate Public Relations: A New Historical Perspective*, Hillsdale, NJ: Lawrence Erlbaum Associates.

Olins, W. (1989) *Corporate Identity*, London: Thames and Hudson.

Peach, L. (1987) 'Corporate Responsibility', in Hart, N. (ed.), op. cit.

Pearson, R. (1992) 'Perspectives on Public Relations History', in Toth, E. and Heath, R., *Rhetorical and Critical Approaches to Public Relations*, Hillsdale, NJ: Lawrence Erlbaum Associates.

Pedler, R. and Van Schendelen, M. (eds) (1994) *Lobbying the European Union*, Aldershot: Dartmouth.

Pertschuk, M. (1986) *Giant Killers*, New York: Norton.

Pinsdorf, M. (1987) *Communicating When Your Company is Under Siege*, Lexington, MA: Lexington Books.

Portway, S. (1995) 'Corporate Social Responsibility: the case for active stakeholder management', in Hart, N. (ed.), op. cit.

Potts, J. (1976) *Public Relations Practice in Australia*, Sydney: McGraw Hill.

PR News (1996, 1997) Newsletter of the Institute of Public Relations Local Government Group.

PR Week (1993a) 'The Westminster Experiment', 13 May.

PR Week (1993b) 'Letters from the Grass Roots', 13 May.

PR Week (1998) *PR Week* Public Relations Awards.

PR Week (1999a) 'Campaigns' and Business Television', 19 February.

PR Week (1999b) 'Analysis', 19 March.

PR Week (1999c) 'Beware the lure of the US dollar', 26 March.

PR Week (1999d) 'Campaigns', 30 April.

Puchan, H., Pieczka, M. and L'Etang, J. (1997) 'The Internal Communications Context', in Kitchen, P. (ed.), op. cit.

Quirke, W. (1996) *Communicating Corporate Change*, London: McGraw-Hill.

Raine, J. (1996) 'Proactivity beats reactivity', *PR News*, June.

RSA (1994) *Tomorrow's Company: Interim Report*, London: RSA.

Saffir, L. (1993) *Power Public Relations*, Lincolnwood, IL: NTC Business Books.

Sauerhaft, S. (1997) 'The Role of Public Relations in Mergers and Acquisitions', in Caywood, C., op. cit.

Schramm, W. (1953) 'How Communication Works', in Schramm, W. (ed.), *The Process and Effects of Mass Communication*, Urbana, IL: University of Illinois Press.

Seib, P. and Fitzpatrick, K. (1997) *Public Relations Ethics*, Fort Worth, TX: Harcourt Brace Jovanovich.

Seitel, F. (1995) *The Practice of Public Relations*, 6th edn, Englewood Cliffs, NJ: Prentice Hall.

Shannon, C. and Weaver, W. (1948) *The Mathematical Theory of Communications*, Urbana, IL: University of Illinois Press.

Sleight, S. (1989) *Sponsorship: What It Is and How to Use It*, London: McGraw-Hill.

Smith, A. (1991) *Innovative Employee Communication*, Englewood Cliffs, NJ: Prentice Hall.

Smith, P. (1994) *Marketing Communications: An Integrated Approach*, London: Kogan Page.

Smythe Dorward Lambert (1990) *Your Employees – Your Edge in the 1990s*, London: Smythe Dorward Lambert.

Smythe, J., Dorward, C. and Reback, J. (1992) *Corporate Reputation: Managing the New Strategic Asset*, London: Century Business.

SOED (1993) *The New Shorter Oxford English Dictionary*, Oxford: OUP.

Stauber, J. and Rampton, S. (1995) *Toxic Sludge is Good For You! Lies, Damn Lies and the Public Relations Industry*, Monroe, ME: Common Courage Press.

Tench, R. and Yeomans, L. (1997) 'Corporate Advertising: the Generic Image', in Kitchen, P. (ed.), op. cit.

Time Magazine (1999) 'Banana Wars' 135 (5).

Toft, B. and Reynolds, S. (1994) *Learning From Disasters: A Management Approach*, Oxford: Butterworth Heinemann.

Tye, L. (1998) *The Father of Spin*, New York: Crown Publishers.

Van Riel, C. (1995) *Principles of Corporate Communication*, London: Prentice Hall.

Varey, R. (1997) 'External Public Relations Activities', in Kitchen, P. (ed.), op. cit.

Walker, D. (1996) *Public Relations in Local Government*, London: Pitman.

Wallace, I. (1959) *The Fabulous Showman: The Life and Times of P.T. Barnum*, New York: Alfred Knopf.

Washingtonian, The (1995) 'Hit the Road, Mick', January.

Watson, T. (1997) 'Measuring the Success Rate', in Kitchen, P. (ed.), op. cit.

White, J. (1991) *How to Understand and Manage Public Relations*, London: Business Books.

Williams, P. and Conroy, A. (1994) *The Radio Handbook*, London: Routledge.

Windahl, S., Signitzer, B. and Olson, J. (1992) *Using Communication Theory*, London: Sage.

Worcester, R. (1983) 'Measuring the Impact of Corporate Advertising', *Admap*, September.

Wragg, D. (1994) *The Effective Use of Sponsorship*, London: Kogan Page.

Yorke, I. (1995) *Television News*, 3rd edn., Oxford: Focal Press.

Index